Trash Culture

Trash Culture

Essays in Popular Criticism

David LaGuardia

To order additional copies of this book, contact:
Xlibris Corporation
1-888-795-4274
www.Xlibris.com
Orders@Xlibris.com
50609

Contents

For Juana, with love and admiration.

Acknowledgments

I wish to thank my colleagues at Dartmouth College who, after reading an early draft of this manuscript, expressed their enthusiasm for it and encouraged me to keep working on it. I am especially grateful to John Rassias, who has never stopped bugging me to get this book out, and whose friendship and support have been vital to me over the last fifteen years. I also want to thank Tom Conley and George Hoffmann, who have often expressed their appreciation of this text to me over the last few years.

Preface

This book is a practical introduction to critical theory through the analysis of concrete examples. The problem of my choice of objects, which I examined over the course of more than a decade, between 1996 and 2008, is that popular culture is involved in a phenomenon of acceleration that makes it difficult for the critic to discuss television shows, celebrities, movies, styles, sports teams, fashions, cars, even foods that will be recognizable to the reader by the time the text gets into print. When the following essays are finally published, the likes of the Spice Girls, Britney Spears, Pamela Anderson, and Eminem may not even be known as footnotes on the page of fleeting fame. Like boxes of cereal or bottles of aspirin, notes on popular culture should always have expiration dates of some kind, since beyond a certain time their interest becomes incomprehensible and loses its effect: a quick glance at the *Beach Blanket Bingo* or *Muscle Beach Party* movies made by Annette Funicello and Frankie Avalon in the 1960's will confirm the truth of this statement. To give you another example, in the early and mid 1990's, music videos were seen as a hip and interesting "genre" that had to be examined by academic discourse. Ten years later, the music video is as dead as Boris Karloff in *The Mummy*, which means of course that it can always come back to life and become "un-dead," which is one of my favorite concepts. One day in the not-too-distant future, archaeologists will open up the enormous and perfectly preserved landfills that we stuffed with usable material goods during the course of the disastrous 20th Century, and they will probably be baffled by at least two things: 1) how we could have "thrown away" so many things that could have been re-used and recycled; 2) what purpose could have possibly been served by many of the things preserved there, such as the countless exercise machines meant to sculpt particular body parts that people bought enthusiastically, used for a week or a month, left lying around the house for a few years, and inevitably threw away. This text is an attempt to examine a rather random sampling of trash cultural artifacts before the passage of time renders them strange and unrecognizable.

11

By the time this book gets into print, the "texts" and objects that I discuss in the following pages will probably already be in the symbolic landfill to which all trash culture is doomed from its very conception. As such, my work here is a kind of future-perfect archaeology that digs through the trash heap of history in its continuous progress toward the obliteration of manufactured things and their meanings. In the age of trash culture, every object sold as a commodity—a television program, a fashionable dress, a pair of sunglasses, a hot new car—is already a relic of itself practically from the moment of its production. The essays in this book are comments on objects that exist only in an increasingly tenuous present, hence the essays themselves will shortly be something like illegible notes about forgotten and buried commodities, whose use values (if they ever had any) have been completely lost and remain ineffable to the critic who tries to understand them. In essence, then, this book is a flippant and somewhat comic elegy on the fragile and ephemeral material world that surrounds us, and which invests or even generates our being in the present as it runs away from us continuously, remaining always just beyond our grasp.

Introduction

Trash culture consists in part of a set of practices in which large or even massive groups of people participate, following implicit rules that are tacitly or even overtly understood and demonstrated by each participant in the group. By enacting this understanding, the individual generates or performs his or her identity momentarily by becoming absorbed in the activity at hand, which often manifests the collective will of the spectators who are also essential to the display of the cultural act. The players, actors, technicians, musicians, designers, and so on who actually perform the activity are merely surrogates who act out a collective desire for what is perceived as domination, perfection, happiness, coolness, youthfulness, sexiness, etc. Trash culture is thus the enactment of fundamental processes of collective knowledge, or better yet their "re-enactment," to use a term from (bad) television shows of the 1970's. An explication of its most salient features reveals modes of being and awareness that are among the definitive characteristics of our age. Some definitions and clarifications are necessary to this task.

I will use the word "trash" throughout this text in reference to a rather large and diverse category of social phenomena. Beyond the essential definition of "trash" as literal refuse, usually domestic in nature (industrial waste, for example, cannot be considered trash—corporations do not "take out the trash" in the same way that John Doe does), there are numerous metaphorical meanings of the term that are frequently used and understood in American English. "You're nothin' but trash, Johnny, and you always will be"—one can imagine Joan Crawford saying this to Broderick Crawford in a *film noir* from the 1940's, meaning that the latter has no intrinsic or social value, that he is plebeian, that he has been unable to assume an acceptable social role. In this somewhat archaic sense, the term "trash" signifies "low class" or "riff-raff" (to keep with the forties theme), as in the unpalatable expression "white trash," which conjures up images of mythical endogamous families living in shacks and trailer parks in the Appalachian or Smoky Mountains. In the popular imagination, white trash—which, interestingly, can be either singular or plural—are perhaps at the lowest possible point of the social scale, since they are thought to be genetically defective, anti-social, murderous, rapacious, suspicious of strangers, abnormal, even subhuman. The film *Deliverance* is the most chilling vision of this phantasmal and paradoxically racist stereotype. People who may actually belong to the white trash category—judgments such as these are dangerous and almost impossible to make—seem to prefer the term "redneck," which was co-opted and even stylized by country singers such as Gretchen Wilson, a self-proclaimed "redneck woman," who sang the title song from her CD bearing the same name on the broadcast of the Grammy awards in 2005: "Well I ain't never/ Been the barbie doll type/ No I can't swig that sweet champagne/ I'd rather drink beer all night/ In a tavern or in a honky tonk/ Or on a four wheel drive tailgate . . ." Looking at her in her tight jeans, cowboy boots, and rhinestone-studded vest, the first words that come to mind are "Texas suburban SUV-drivin', mall-shoppin' woman," rather than "redneck woman." Fortuitously, one of the verses of the song reads as follows: "You might think I'm trashy/ A little too hard core/ But get in my neck of the woods/ I'm just the girl next door."

For the first time in history, perhaps, cultural elites that are often willfully divorced from the realm of popular culture refuse to recognize its value and function for the vast majority of people living in the United States and, to some extent, in the other Western countries. In contrast, the literate class that produced the religious culture of the European Middle Ages and the Renaissance, with its rituals and festivals, shared many of the same values as the majority of the people living throughout these periods in diverse cultural contexts. For example, the work of François Rabelais, especially as it is explained by Mikhail Bakhtin, documents the complexities of a late-medieval, public, festive, and religious culture that was beginning to come to its end when *Gargantua* and *Pantagruel* were published in the 1530's. Rabelais combines the best of Humanist, Evangelical, Renaissance "high" culture with the most obscene language and gestures imaginable, which were part and parcel of popular, "carnivalesque" culture at the time. During the Renaissance, there was no such thing as "trash" culture, since the prophets of high culture enjoyed low cultural jokes and events just as much as anybody else, and often provided their own in their books. If you don't believe me, see the poems devoted to the pleasures of shitting in chapter 13 of Rabelais's *Gargantua*.

Such a combination of "high" and "low" art forms is virtually impossible in our day, since almost anyone who considers him or herself an expert in high art cannot extol the virtues of, say, mud wrestling, "girls gone wild," and tabloids. The cultural phenomena, activities, and events that structure the everyday lives of most Americans (e.g., Spring Break) constitute a conceptual land fill for the highest members of a social hierarchy who continue to base their ideas of life and art on conceptual categories (beauty, symmetry, balance, logical development, depth) that are linked to archaic modes of artistic production, as Walter Benjamin remarked in his seminal article, "The Work of Art in the Age of its Mechanical Reproduction." Trash culture is inevitably (post)industrial, mechanical, electronic, digital, and, increasingly, virtual. It is the by-product, or perhaps even the waste product of a capitalist nation-state that previously functioned on the basis of mass production, but which now has "outsourced" the stench, suffering, and pollution of all that to poorer countries, while it itself remains in control of the super-structural elements that organize that production. The participation in trash cultural activities, which occupy a large but quite restricted region of this superstructure (the exercise of political power, for example, by those who occupy this domain would be an anomaly), involves hyperbolic consumerism: there have to be more and more teams, more digital channels to cover them, more types of sports shoes, more compact discs to buy and mp3s to download, more and more complex special effects, more explosions and murders and bullets, more showgirls, more macro hotels that are simulacra of entire cities, more pictures of naked bodies, more and bigger bodies being thrown out of the wrestling ring, more and more different kinds of breakfast cereal, ever more machines to shape, sculpt, trim, and tuck peoples' bodies. I could extend this catalogue indefinitely.

The public's insatiable need for a temporal, ritualistic structure within the context of post-industrial capitalism (action movies in the Summer, introspective movies in the Fall, family movies during the Holidays, love stories in the Spring) to replace the ritual structure of agricultural Christianity produces an enormous amount of material that *must* be consumed and *must* be rejected and thrown away if ever new cultural products are to take their place. (The anxiety produced by this consumerism is perhaps what gives the Bible such a special status in the USA as the *one* book that contains the *one* truth that cannot be thrown away. Ironically, it's the best-selling book of all time.) Trash culture is, therefore, based upon the manufacture of literal and figurative "objects" that have to be obsolete from the moment of their conception, since capitalism requires the continuous consumption and disposal of older merchandise in favor of newer merchandise in order to keep "the economy" going and growing. "It's the economy, stupid," as a famous political slogan once proclaimed. The cult of the beautiful object that was typical of manual production, and which generated the aesthetic apparatus that is still at work in our universities, art museums, and symphony halls, simply has no place in the realm of trash culture, unless one counts such things as Lladró statues, Thomas Kincaid paintings, and Tiffany lamps, available in massive quantities in virtually any mall in the US, as beautiful works of art, rather than as grotesque parodies.

But what is culture? It would be impossible for me to formulate an all-inclusive and exhaustive definition of this term. I will limit myself to a simple working definition, based on Louis Althusser's work on interpellation, the material process through which ideologies "call" individuals into being as subjects. My examples will make this definition clearer. Culture is, first of all, collective. It requires modes of understanding and their corresponding sets of practices that are embraced and shared by large groups of people, whether consciously or unconsciously. Three individuals who engage in some kind of collective activity do not constitute a culture; in contrast, a hundred thousand people who dress according to a certain code, who listen to a certain kind of music, who ingest certain kinds of food, and who speak in a certain way *do* constitute this set of activities as a sub-culture. Think of the "grunge" phenomenon, which was somewhat unique to Seattle before MTV marketed the look and the sound to the entire world briefly in the 1990's, to such an extent that so-called "super models" wearing thousand-dollar plaid shirts by Armani and hand-sewn Italian leather combat boots could be seen on the runways of Paris and Milan at that time. Or think of the multiple sub-cultural groups that occupy the "trendy" places of any big town or city from Albuquerque, to Boston, to Columbia, SC: punks, skateboarders, rappers, "emo guys and girls" (see emo-corner.com), metrosexuals, bikers, surfers, pimps, preppy kids, Goths, jocks, etc. All of these sub-groups are defined by clothes, music, books, posters, cars, hair, shoes, colors, modes of speech, and so on, which, by functioning together, constitute conceptual nexuses or "constellations" within which the identities of the members of each group negotiate their individual significance and being. These groups of objects call individuals into being as subjects who express their identity within material practices; simultaneously, these sets of behaviors and their corresponding things develop as consequences of individuals who display their identities as members of a group, defined by the material manifestations of the ideas that make them recognizable as such.

Secondly, the collective nature of culture means that an individual participates in that culture if he or she obeys certain rules while breaking others, and engages in certain practices while rejecting others. Your average white Eminem fan from the suburbs cannot happily wear a three-piece suit and Sebago shoes, in the same way that he cannot actually like and listen to the music of Perry Como, for instance, unless, of course, he transfigures the suit and the music to such an extent that they obey the explicit rules and codes of crossover hip-hop. Back in what now seems like ancient history from the point of view of accelerated trash cultural time, when grunge was still fashionable, the Nirvana video for "In Bloom" played with this notion of rules by dressing the members of the band in 1950's suits, and having them appear on a mock version of the Ed Sullivan show, the set of which they destroyed when they returned to their own clothes and hairdos. Outkast did the same thing a dozen years later with "Hey Ya," mocking white racial stereotypes by dressing black performers in tweeds and riding caps and having them appear on a British television variety show in front of an all-black audience. Subcultures constitute and unflinchingly obey sets of rules that determine who is within that culture, and who must be excluded from it if the culture is to exist as such. The clash between the owners of the NBA franchises and the players regarding the proper dress code for press conferences in 2005 was an eloquent demonstration of this: a true "believer" in hip-hop culture, such as Allen Iverson, simply could not find anything to wear when he was obliged to put on a "shirt with a collar," according to the new rules. On a much more sinister note, members of gangs in Los Angeles can literally be shot if they're caught wearing the wrong color on the wrong side of the street.

Thirdly, then, culture is inherently moral, and every culture or subculture functions or exists by virtue of value judgments that are typical of moral codes. People who belong to cultures and subcultures believe that it is *better* to think, act, eat, dress, smell, seduce, scream, walk, spit, etc. in one way than in another. In many cases, a culture has to define its enemies and its evils so that it can define itself. The punks, for example, used to say that Pink Floyd was the enemy. Back when I was doing bong hits and playing the upright jazz bass in my friend Jim's basement in the late '70's (unlike President Clinton, we inhaled too much), we used to think that disco fever was the enemy, though now I look back on the Tony Manero/Bee Gees/K.C. and the Sunshine Band/Kool and the Gang phenomenon with a nostalgia that has been successfully packaged and sold to men and women my age for the last twenty years by the trash culture industry. Young people who invest their identities in their love of Eminem, Limp Bizkit, Prodigy, Death Cab for Cutie, the Killers, Panic at the Disco, and even the venerable U2 cannot possibly like Britney Spears, 'N Sync, Justin Timberlake, Kelly Clarkson, or whoever else has taken their place. This is essentially for moral reasons: people who listen to that "other" kind of music are less intelligent than we are; their music has less artistic value than ours; the messages of their songs are less profound than ours, etc. In essence, there is no difference between these judgments of value and those by which the bourgeoisie of the 19th and early 20th centuries distinguished itself from the working class and the colonies, those "others" who didn't like the same music, food, clothes, books, fashions, buildings, gods, and manners as they themselves.

Fourthly, culture is brought into being by groups of people; it also brings groups of people into being. Culture involves the collective generation both of the group as an entity and of the individual identities within it, by means of codes, rules, morals, objects—in short, by means of sets or collections of knowledge that are implicitly and explicitly understood by the group, which sometimes are not recognized or discussed analytically as such, but which are embodied in constellations or clusters of commodified things. If culture calls groups into being, it also calls each individual into being as a certain kind of person. Who are you? "I'm a biker," you might answer, showing me your tattoos and your Harley. From an abstract point of view, there is no difference between this response to my ontological question, and the following one: "I'm a stock broker," you might respond, wearing a gray suit and tasseled loafers, as you put your golf bag into the back of your Mercedes. Identities that are type cast in this way are defined by the objects that operate as accessories to them. As we'll see a bit further on, in some extreme cases identity itself becomes a kind of accessory that is constantly renewed and redefined by an increasing number of things. Moreover, in our age, the most radical examples of "accessorized" identity formation—poor Britney Spears comes to mind—are extremely fragile in their dependence on material commodities, and can break down at any moment, requiring extensive "rehab." (A Grammy-winning popular song of 2007, sung by Amy Winehouse, proclaimed proudly and repeatedly: "[They] tried to make me go to rehab, but I said no, no, no.")

This book describes the implicit bodies of knowledge that define distinct groups as sub-cultures, especially as they interact with mass-produced commodities and products, and especially to the extent that this interaction generates individuals as subjects who act out their identities as members of these groups, all of this according to their own sense of conscience and free will. In the case of academic or aesthetic criticism, one conducts this kind of critique in the context of an implicit understanding that obtains between its writer and its readers. A music critic writing plot summaries and analyses of operas assumes, as does his or her reader, that opera is an art form that has an intrinsic and unquestionable aesthetic value, despite the fact that from a more demanding point of view, opera itself was a kind of trash culture for the masses: Beethoven thought of Rossini as a Philistine pop composer, for example. In this book, I would like to suspend this kind of value judgment, though my biases and prejudices, some of them undoubtedly unjust, will be visible throughout it. Here, in contrast, I will examine the (possible) conceptual constellations that emerge in relation to wrestling, tractor pulls, exercise fads, rock groups, sports, movies, discos, comics, Elvis worship, shopping, etc., without pronouncing any overt judgments on their artistic value from the rather limited perspective that has defined academic criticism since its inception. More specifically, I will describe the procedures by which individuals within these groups seem to structure their own identities and subjectivities in relation to the codes and object/commodity clusters that define subcultures.

To summarize, then, the cultural artifacts that I will examine are "trash" because they are produced as commodities that must be bought, consumed, and thrown away in order for the hierarchical, economic systems that produce them to continue functioning. They also belong to the category of trash because they are consumed by a segment of the population (the vast majority of the people) which is perceived to be on the bottom end of the social and intellectual hierarchy. Thirdly, trash cultures have been, and continue to be denied any aesthetic value by elitist cultural critics who concentrate on art objects that belong to archaic modes of manual production, characterized by technical mastery, hand craftsmanship, and uniqueness. In contrast, the objects that drive trash culture are meant to be mass-produced and infinitely repeatable, and require merely a kind of inspiration, luck, financial support, marketing, and perhaps an intuition of what a given public wants to see or hear in order to be economically successful or "good." A piece of trash culture is hence an object/product that embodies a collective body of knowledge which itself engenders a group of individuals as subjects, in the most general sense of this latter term: a subject is a person who acts in accordance with sets of rules and bodies of knowledge that he or she internalizes from social contexts, freely and willfully recognizing the values represented in that knowledge as the bases of his or her own identity.

Moreover, here I will examine the different kinds of ideological "software" that our capitalist means of production are continually "installing" in the hardware of our brains, just as viruses piggy-back their way into our hard drives in unopened spam e-mails and begin eating away at our files, or just as spy-ware continuously contaminates our computers without our knowledge of it happening. It should perhaps be noted here that when I began writing the following essays in 1996, most of the objects relating to e-mail and the internet that I named in the preceding sentence had barely been conceived (who could have imagined spam and spy-ware at the end of the first Clinton administration?). These processes serve as metaphors for what has happened to subjectivity late in the postmodern game, or on the threshold of what was already called the post-postmodern age in the mid '90's by architectural theorists. The irony of this fundamental mode of self-identification through semi-unconscious cultural assimilation is that individuals adopt, of their own free will, and according to their own notion of conscience, moral superiority, necessity, or even duty, sets of commodified behaviors with which they have been "infected" simply by living within a certain mode of production. As I will argue in the conclusion of this book, here at the end of a long period of intense capitalist domination (and what is the current position of China in the global economy but the apotheosis of capitalism?), subjectivity has become a kind of vanishing point, black hole, landfill, or overcrowded hard drive into which the global market is continuously dumping materials that have rather peculiar characteristics: initially recognized as indispensable to the very being of the individual who buys them, they quickly become obsolete, old, or "out of fashion," and are stored somewhere in the subdirectories of one's mind, never to be found again, unless they are reactivated by enforced nostalgia.

For example, halter tops, tube tops, and ponchos, those staples of women's wardrobes back in the '70's, became obligatory fashion items again in 2005. The final item on this list became a must for women across the United States when the hostess of a popular television program, *Martha Stewart's Living*, wore a poncho, knitted for her by a fellow inmate, when she left prison in the Spring of that year after serving a sentence for securities fraud, I believe. The enforced nostalgic reactivation of objects from the past does not mean that one can simply look through the attic in order to find the clothes that one wore twenty or thirty or even forty years ago. On the contrary, an object that has the actual aura of time and wear is incompatible with reactivated nostalgia, since the look of "oldness" and wear somehow has to signify "newness" and "fashionableness" at the same time if it is to be bought. A company by the name of Smeg is now producing refrigerators and toasters that look like appliances from the 1950's, just as the current Japanese owners of the Triumph motorcycle brand are producing replicas of the legendary 650 Bonneville of the '50's and '60's, the sight of which sends a flutter through the chests of men like me who rode the original bike when we were teenagers back in the '70's. The purists who insist on having the original motorcycle or refrigerator from those periods are a breed apart (to which, by the way, any number of television programs and magazines have been dedicated), since today one prefers the fully-functional copy of a machine to its cranky and aging original (see, for example, the replica VW Beetles and Ford Mustangs now being mass produced and sold). Similarly, if one were to pull an old pair of moth-eaten jeans, with oil stains and frayed ends, out of the closet, and to wear them as a fashion item, they somehow would not look the same as the "anti-form" Levi jeans that are sold for exorbitant prices throughout the Western world. Enforced nostalgia products require an oxymoronic "new oldness" so that they can be displayed by their owners as signifiers of this fashion trend. This example is but one of dozens of modes by which individuals consciously structure their outer appearances as manifestations of their (temporary) identities, which, at least in their external aspects, are continuously shifting with the times, even if this shift concerns only the smallest possible item of one's clothing. One might perform a similar analysis of people's opinions, politics, books, music, food, gardening, entertaining at home, vacationing, tourism, home decoration, cars, and so on. Within the process of consuming, personal identity and subjectivity are found at a continuously shifting, and perhaps even increasingly vanishing point at which diverse activities intersect.

What is the role, then, of the cultural critic educated in the realm of high culture who is fascinated by popular culture? Should it be to proclaim the intrinsic aesthetic value of, say, wrestling, monster truck rallies, and Las Vegas gambling tournaments? Or should it be to wring one's hands and beat one's breast at the demise of high culture, which has currently assumed the status of the (anti-)protagonists of zombie and vampire movies: as Dr. Van Helsing says of Count Dracula, "High culture is un-dead, *nosferatu*"? It seems to me that neither of these possibilities is appropriate to the study of the things that I will examine here. One accomplishes nothing simply by substituting the objects one wishes to affirm as necessary in the institutionalized place of existing value structures: reconfiguring homosexuality, for example, into tidy and manageable married couples with health care benefits and suburban lawns merely continues the same kind of bourgeois orthodoxy that was affixed to heterosexual marriage at the end of the 18th century, as Foucault remarked thirty years ago. A critique that would attempt to enthrone the unquestionable aesthetic values of popular artifacts would do roughly the same thing. On the contrary, one might claim that one likes trash culture precisely because it is ugly, garish, campy, tacky, kitsch, etc, and because it has no need whatsoever of aesthetics, even if the adepts of certain of its manifestations may qualify some of its aspects as "beautiful." Think of your basic, carnivalesque American football game: fat, drunk men wearing dog or pig masks, reeking of beer and Cheez Whiz; 300 pound monsters bleeding in the mud; cheerleaders in skimpy skirts dancing badly to terrible music. Such a concentration of ugliness, such a display of a very problematic and historically-contingent kind of masculinity is simply fascinating and might even be proclaimed "beautiful" in a kind of "antipodal" way, to paraphrase Nietzsche.

To give you another example, I was once at a playoff game between the Philadelphia 76ers and the Boston Celtics, when at a certain point in the game, at which an aging Derrick Coleman tipped in the winning basket, a black man beside me hugged me as we were jumping up and down, and proclaimed, "it's beautiful! It's beautiful! It's beautiful!" The critic of trash culture should be interested in the formal processes and structures that make this kind of proclamation possible, and that compel grown men to transcend the rather formidable racial boundaries that separate them (the same man had complained bitterly to me earlier that there weren't enough black women (2 out of 20) on the Sixers' dance team, a statement with which I heartily agreed) in order to hug one another with joy at their shared appreciation of a certain kind of ideologically saturated spectacle. Who are these two men, black and white, who embrace at this moment? What is the basis of their being that motivates their acts? How can a public event in which they participate allow them to transcend a fundamental category, that of race, which otherwise obliges them to move in separate and segregated spheres? Why doesn't the interpellation of these men as fans and supporters of their city's team who are momentarily indifferent to race carry over into the city beyond the doors of the arena? These are the kinds of questions that interest me here.

As for trash culture's respectable and wealthy cousin, high culture, let it lurk in the shadows of these pages. Like Dracula, high culture may be un-dead, but since it is and always has been a super-structural effect of material substructures, no amount of hand-wringing and breast-beating will ever restore it to our fantasy version of what it may have been in any number of mythical pasts, since the material bases of the society in which we live will never again be what they were in former times. The cultural critic's job is to analyze the systems of values, the modes of interpellation, and the kinds of subjectivity that are embodied in specific types of objects that might be included in the category of trash as I've defined it here. The following pages will undertake analyses of this kind, suspending as much as possible the aesthetic prejudices that have, for centuries, constituted cultural analysis itself. Through accumulation and sampling, the following analyses are intended not to proclaim the death of culture, but rather to examine its transfiguration into a wide range of objects in the age of global capitalism. Moreover, the goal of these essays is to delineate the rather peculiar and unprecedented kind of subjectivity that defines us at this particular moment of our collective history. As many thinkers have proclaimed, the goal of philosophy is to define and describe who we are in the present. The following pages attempt to grasp and to hold on to this fragile moment of identity before it dissolves into another one that will develop in a dialectical relation to the unforeseeable cultural commodities of the future, whose existence will condition and transform our own to such an extent that we will no longer be able to understand what we were at this present moment that is, paradoxically, already the past.

Batman Forever

I was in a charter flight from New York to Madrid, in a Boeing 757, watching *Batman Forever* after a decent meal, if such a thing is possible in "coach" class in an airplane. In this type of plane, there are about ten television screens that hang from the ceiling above the central aisle (this was before the introduction of Airbuses and 777s that have individual screens and menus in every seat on trans-Atlantic flights). I could see the scenes of the movie reproduced in different sizes and at different distances from my seat, and I thought to myself that this absolutely artificial environment, thirty-three thousand feet above the Atlantic Ocean, was saturated with a kind of cultural information and knowledge that was, inevitably, inundating my mind with images and stories intended to call me into being as a certain kind of subject (to wit, a consumer). In a standard jetliner, especially one that belongs to a Western company (I was in an Air Europa charter, which belongs to Iberia airlines), everything is a product: the plane itself is a product that had to be sold to an airline; the stewardesses are products meant to sell a certain image of the airline (I recall here that the first stewardesses on commercial airlines had to be of a certain height and weight, meaning that the first (male) clients of the airlines could be lured into the body of the plane by the delicious expectation of coming into contact with a desirable form of the female body—in other words, the female body as object of desire was a kind of prop meant to sell a certain kind of merchandise, as it has been throughout this century.); the duty-free goods are, of course, products that the consumer/passenger has the good fortune to buy at inflated prices that are said to be tax-free (what a bargain!); the flight itself is a product that is advertised regularly on television, in the newspapers, and on-line (those of us who live in northern climates know that the airline companies are going to bombard us with images of blue Caribbean waters in January and February). The French sociologist Marc Augé characterized airports, subways, highways, and so on as "non-places," since these particularly modern spaces belong to anyone, are home to no one, and everyone is essentially the same in them. I would argue that the "non-place" of the jetliner is a space that is saturated by the forces of market capitalism, which continuously call into being individuals as consumers of all kinds of products.

Since everything around me in that flight was saturated by the idea of commerce and consumption, what role did the story told by *Batman Forever* play in constituting my fellow passengers and myself as consumers? Could it be that the typical American comic book hero is nothing more than a representative of the super consumer, elevated to the n-th power, with a buying power that is super-human? More importantly, if *Batman Forever* is a medium through which a capitalist production machine interpellates its viewers as specific kinds of subjects, what kind of critique could one make of the aesthetic values and techniques that the film represents? Does the aesthetic of the film play any role whatsoever in the process by which the viewer becomes a consumer?

An artifact such as *Batman Forever* is a prime example of trash culture since it has little or no aesthetic value from the point of view of the academic establishment and the Boards of Trustees that tell them what they can and cannot teach, while it undoubtedly participates in a procedure that disseminates ideology into the being of individuals, who spontaneously and willingly act as they must act if such a created object is to fulfill the purpose of its existence. In simpler terms, *Batman Forever* is crap next to *A Midsummer Night's Dream*, but it performs a fundamental function in our society that must be analyzed from the bottom up, as well as from the top down. What happens to the spectator when he or she watches the film? Critics such as Walter Benjamin have always known that a film has to produce masses of spectators who are willing to buy a ticket in order to see it. At the end of the cinema's first century, when *Batman Forever* was made, this essential need for a mass audience was exacerbated, and the film as commodity had to be surrounded by satellite products. Now a big budget film not only draws millions of spectators who feel that they *have* to see it, but they also later go online or, less and less frequently, to the store to buy the soundtrack and the book that was based on the screenplay, or the novel on which the screenplay was based, and the video or DVD for their collection. If a film does not sell itself to a mass audience, it literally dies. But if a film is a success, its impact on large segments of the population is enormous, and it effects everything from the way people dress, to the way they sing, talk, walk, dance, and, most importantly, the ways in which they think about themselves. That this mass effect should be transmitted to the population via an essentially artistic and aesthetic medium should not be ignored by the cultural establishment of the universities, in which one tends to focus on films that fulfill the aesthetic requirements imposed by a tradition of scholarship that has nothing to do with the media and the methods of production that are characteristic of our age.

Batman Forever provides a vivid illustration of one side of this intersubjective equation. A rich man, the CEO of an electronic company, overcomes the traumatic and violent loss of his parents that haunts him by using his knowledge of technology to become a super-human champion of justice. Batman is *cool*, not only because his gadgets and his costume are black and sleek, but also because his technological persona derives from a dark and mysterious past. Batman is beyond the law in a city that is a labyrinth of crime and criminals. In this context, the only way to combat crime is to go beyond the Machiavellian limits of the law, to be more radical, more daring, more willing to use sophisticated equipment than the inept representatives of civic order. The law that this super-hero represents is a paradoxically individualistic one, since Batman's solitude requires an enormous amount of capital, and an army of mechanics and technicians (never seen in the films) to maintain all of the gadgets that surround and fortify his physical being. One need only look at the Batcave, the Batmobile, the Batboat, the Batplane, etc., to realize that this material support of Batman's crepuscular activities costs a lot of money and requires a lot of labor. Moreover, there is the sinister implication in the new versions that Bruce Wayne has the means to become Batman because he is somehow responsible for the violent death of his parents. In other words, the birth of the cyber-techno-hero in his sleek black car and his impenetrable Batgear is Oedipal, and Batman is a neurotic who is trapped at the pre-adolescent stage at which the child wants to kill his father in order to become his own kind of mutant parent.

As a mutant father, then, Batman gives birth. The films of the '90's and '00's thus figure an uncanny procreative procedure whereby Batman engenders the villains that he must kill at the end. In the first *Batman* film, Jack Nicholson becomes the Joker after being pushed into a horrendous chemical pit by Batman. In *Batman Forever*, Tommy Lee Jones becomes Two Face when one of the criminals he is prosecuting throws acid at him, and disfigures half of his face—of course, the criminals were brought to trial by Batman, the implication being that the super-hero's attempts to follow the normal methods of justice can only result in its mutation. Similarly, Jim Carrey is an employee in Bruce Wayne's factory whose brilliant projects are spurned by the millionaire executive. As a result, Batman has another mutant criminal/child to fight in the form of the Riddler. In the Batman films, Freud's repetition compulsion goes amuck, and the same cycle of birth, confrontation, and death (or madness) is destined to be repeated *ad infinitum*, just as Bruce Wayne is destined to relive and rediscover the primal scene in which his parents were killed. In *Batman Forever*, the introduction of Robin repeats the same primal scene, when Chris O'Donnell's character loses his parents in another violent attack by Batman's mutant children.

The Batman films are thus about an entire complex of social phenomena. First is what Freud calls "the family romance," in which the future neurosis of the young Bruce Wayne is assured by the murder of his parents. Second is the projection of this neurosis into an entire social landscape, since Gotham City is nothing other than a projection of Bruce Wayne's/Batman's phantasms—otherwise, why would the entire city be completely dominated by Batman's mutant children? In *Batman*, Jack Nicholson's Joker proclaims: "This town needs an enema!" Indeed, what Gotham city needs is to be purged, but not necessarily of its criminals. It needs to be delivered from the source of its evils, which is Batman, after all. The movement of these stories is thus always in two contradictory directions: one toward the Batcave, which the innumerable Oedipal monsters are bent upon destroying; the other toward constructing *alternative* Batcaves (the Joker's palace, the Riddler's empire, Mr. Freeze's frozen lair, Poison Ivy's greenhouse, etc.) that are likewise devoted to the destruction of the entirety of Gotham city.

In short, everything that one sees in the Batman films is about the subjectivity of the main character, which contaminates the rest of the visual space. The overriding emotions that pervade these films are *guilt* and the desire for *vengeance*, on the part of both Batman and those whom he engenders by his actions. They are thus parables that describe the emotions of each one of us who identify ourselves as members of technological societies. If Batman's famous forerunner, Dracula, was a manifestation of modern British guilt about the colonization of its Empire (the Count, a foreigner, comes to London to suck the blood of the most succulent of English virgins, Lucy Westin, whose name coincidentally includes the word "West"—this is an inversion of what happened in actuality), then Batman is a manifestation of postmodern American neurotic guilt about our faith in the individual and in technology. Cars, boats, airplanes, electronics factories, and our own version of the Batcave (the Pentagon, perhaps?) have made us what we are today, that is, a country that believes that high technology is the supreme good at the basis of our so-called "standard of living," and that every individual American has the right to life, liberty, and the pursuit of happiness, meaning the right to buy a digital satellite dish, a microwave oven, a cell phone with internet access, a home theater, a notebook computer, several video game consoles, a Blackberry, etc. The irony in all this is that this country that prides itself on its technical prowess has routinely and deliberately suppressed the development of some technologies, such as fuel efficient engines, electric propulsion, clean renewable energy sources, and so on, for the sake of individual greed and corporate profits.

The supremely American happiness of infinite ownership rests upon a fundamental traumatic secret, which is that our country has become what it is—the only Superpower in George Bush Sr.'s "New World Order," or the defender of world democracy against George Junior's "axis of evil"—at the expense of killing its own Founding Fathers. Two hundred and thirty odd years ago, one of them wrote in Philadelphia, my home town, the following words: "We hold these truths to be self-evident: that all men are created equal . . ." Every time that an American picks up his or her cell phone, he or she unconsciously has to know that there are billions of people on this planet who are going to bed hungry, who don't know if RAM and ROM are animals or Egyptian gods, and who have probably seen some kind of warfare that was financed or supplied with weapons by some Western power. For every Hubble telescope, space shuttle, super computer, or fabulous commercial airliner that our nation brings into being, there is also a mutant child being born somewhere, a Noriega, a Marcos, a Shah Pahleva of Iran (in a sense the Ayatollah Khomeini was our mutant child also), a Pinochet, a Bautista, a Franco, an Idi Amin, a Baby Doc, an Osama Bin-Laden—the list could probably go on indefinitely. Hell, we needn't go that far to find the evidence of our own neurosis—for every point of the Dow Jones Industrial Average, there are five murders in the United States every year. Any one of our cities contains its own violent and glamorous version of the so-called "Third World" (I say glamorous because Hollywood never tires of making films about fantasy versions of our inner cities). All of us are Batman, in other words. I'm willing to bet, however, that most of the people who go to see the Batman movies see only how cool they are, how cool Batman's car is ("Chicks always dig the car," Batman says in *Batman Forever*), how cool his gadgets and fights are, what a cool mansion he has with his collection of classic motorcycles and classier cars. I'm willing to bet also, however, that Gotham City leaves one feeling uneasy because it's so *familiar*. It could easily be "inner city" Philadelphia, or Baltimore, or Detroit, or Cleveland, or Atlanta, or Los Angeles, or New York. The French often say, "Descartes, c'est nous." In the United States, we say, "Batman, c'est moi."

Speaking of chicks, Batman always manages to become involved with an amazing blond woman who is fascinated by his persona. She is always a kind of consecrated yuppie, she lives in her own impressive apartment (without the electronic foundations, stalactites, and stalagmites of the Batcave, which is itself a combination of male and female, vagina and phallus, womb and madman's workshop), she is competent and slim and sleek, yet somewhat naive in her fascination with bats. Because of her relationship with Batman, she is in danger of being killed or mutilated, or even worse, in the second film, she becomes a mutant herself (Michelle Pfeiffer—long forgotten is the more voluptuous and comic Julie Newmar—becomes Catwoman). Batman's sex life is motivated by phantasmic and fantastic women who come to him, seeking to solve the mystery of his identity, which must remain forever hidden. She is a reporter who is obsessed by the story of the man who is a bat (Kim Basinger), or a psychologist enthralled by multiple personalities (Nicole Kidman), or a woman who has her own obsessions with the children of the night (cats and bats are coupled for more than phonetic reasons—Michelle Pfeiffer). In other words, if the Oedipus complex establishes Batman's identity as essentially neurotic, his sex life is inevitably frozen at the Oedipal stage, which must be overcome if one's identity is to become "normal." He joins only with women who, like him, are transfixed by this question, or who reproduce his own problematic relationship to his past.

In allegorical terms, this means, perhaps, that women as objects of masculine desire in our society have to obey a certain masculinist narcissistic necessity. Her body has to be altered by technology; it must become more and more like Barbie's, less and less like Rita Hayworth's or Marilyn Monroe's—Pamela Anderson, of whom I will speak in a later section, was the poster child of this phenomenon in the 1990's. In short, Batman's neurotic desire assumes that woman exists as an unconscious support of a wounded masculine sexuality. The material existence of American women is increasingly obliterated and negated in a society that is obsessed with a "technologized" image of the female body, pumped with silicone, bathed in rejuvenating creams, strained by excessive exercise, drained by anorexia, smoothed out by botox, while American men are increasingly slaves to an altered image of the female body that rarely can exist in everyday life. The effect of the film, whether it is anyone's intention or not, is to produce subjects who affirm in their own flesh the technological, capitalistic functioning of existence. It obeys an aesthetic that is technical, collective, and logistic, rather than being artistic, individual, manual, and masterly. As a consequence, it has an eerie kind of beauty that effects those of us whose nervous systems matured in a context of machines and electronics in a visceral way. For, there can be no doubt about it, the Batman films have a rather complex and troubling kind of beauty, if one can take them seriously and get beyond the feeling that they are incredibly stupid (I'm thinking especially of *Batman and Robin*).

Each of us, as individual beings brought to consciousness in late 20th—early 21st-century America, is Batman. This means that the series of films about this superhero, each of which was a box office smash, calls each of us into being as a certain kind of subject. We suffer from the guilt feelings of having been responsible for the death of our parents (the Founding Fathers?). We claim the right to hide within the neurosis of our own individuality, which gives birth to a world of scary monsters (the subculture of militia members, armed to the teeth, and convinced that there is a conspiracy to take over the U.S., is the most radical manifestation of this general tendency; Rush Limbaugh and the endless "liberal" conspiracies that he invents, imagines, or describes are milder manifestations). The absolute right to a fierce individualism is accompanied by an absolute faith in technology in America, which results in a kind of "technicization" of the body that wants to make it more and more predictable, symmetrical, efficient, machine-like. Watch a fitness competition on ESPN (the "other" Disney network) sometime, and you'll see what I mean. The price of technological individualism is an urban/suburban structure in which pockets of absolute (ethnic) poverty and violence are surrounded by sprawling (white) suburbs, with hundreds of malls and beltways, and millions of cul-de-sacs with houses full of gadgets: Nintendo, Sega, Wii, X-Box and Playstation, 500-channel digital stereo television sets and home theaters, Stairmasters, Nordictracks, and

Soloflex muscle machines, Multimedia PCs and Macs with high speed Wi-Fi connections, CD players and DVD's, and garages full of woodworking tools for potential home renovators. In other words, the suburbs are full of Batcaves to which the Bruce Waynes and Vicky Vales of the world can retire after their daily dosages of violence in the inner Gotham cities, which for white suburbanites have been transferred to endless highways and beltways, saturated by meaningless road rage, and interrupted by occasional police chases, like the famous one in 1995 in which O.J. Simpson fled from the police in his white Ford Bronco along various interstates in southern California. This new kind of primal scene was recorded from helicopters and transmitted live via satellite to millions of homes across the US.

The Late Elvis

One of my favorite memories is of what was perhaps the first television broadcast via satellite (at least the first one that I remember). It must have been about 1973 or 1974, and the program was *Elvis: Aloha from Hawaii*, which, thanks to the miracle of YouTube, the new Holy of Holies of popular culture, one can watch in bits and pieces whenever one wants. By this time, two years or so before his death, the icon that was Elvis had been transformed from the young rockabilly hero with his swiveling hips and his pompadour haircut to the fat, middle-aged black belt karate champion (supposedly) with gigantic sideburns and white sequined jumpsuits. I vaguely remember being disappointed by Elvis's performance at the ripe old age of nine, a feeling that has been confirmed by watching the show again more than three decades later. By that time he was drugged and dazed, he sang in a slurred voice, and his show consisted of posing with his (unplugged) guitar and flicking a seemingly endless supply of sweaty scarves from his shoulder into the audience, where they would be caught by breathless and ecstatic fans. Let's be honest, this later version of Elvis was quite mediocre. He was so heavy that he could barely move; "Suspicious Minds" and the like were boring and redundant, though nostalgia has made them sound better now than they did then; the white jumpsuits, the huge dark glasses, and the mutton chop sideburns created an ensemble that is interesting only from an anthropological point of view, like some kind of relic from an almost incomprehensible bygone age. I always preferred the young Elvis, slim and dreamy, too hot to show on television from the waist down, Lieber and Stoller's Elvis, the dancing inmate of "Jailhouse Rock," the horn toad of "Heartbreak Hotel," the black and white image on the Ed Sullivan show. Curiously, however, the image of The King that continues to captivate the American imagination, more than thirty years after his death, is that of the constipated post-Las Vegas Elvis. In 1995, the *New York Times Magazine* even went so far as to report that, apart from the various sightings, pilgrimages to Graceland, massive birthday celebrations, and so on, Elvis was becoming a kind of saint, who had healing powers for those who "believed" in him, whatever that means. I myself once witnessed a kind of Elvis sighting: in the early '90's, I was walking in a very small town in the South of Spain (La Ronda), when there he was in front of me, a very skinny version of Elvis (sideburns, haircut, and big sunglasses included) carrying a gigantic boom box that was blasting "Viva Las Vegas." I imagine that these kinds of sightings take place pretty much everywhere in the Western world. The question is, why do these phenomena focus on the image of the late Elvis, instead of on the early one?

We have to go back to the mid-'50's when Elvis first became famous to understand the appeal of the image he adopted just before his death. The Althusserian hypothesis that I will be using throughout these essays is that trash culture calls individuals into being as certain kinds of subjects. This is certainly true of the young Elvis, who achieved a kind of fame that was unprecedented for a performer of popular music. Before Elvis, Frank Sinatra was certainly the most popular singer of the '40's and early '50's, but his fame was insignificant compared to that of Elvis for technical reasons. A big band singer made it into the hearts and homes of Americans via the radio, which has an effect that is quite different from that of television. Despite the fact that women swooned at Sinatra's concerts, the visual element that might have propelled Sinatra into the domain of hallucinatory pop super-stardom such as Elvis and the Beatles knew it was lacking, since most people never got to *see* Sinatra perform, and since television did not yet exist on a global scale when he was at the height of his early career. Elvis was perhaps the first performer to embody a pop music *sound* that was supported by a *look*, which included everything from his haircut, to his shoes, to the jackets he wore, to the way he curled his lip or swayed his hips. The association of a look with a sound has been a commonplace ever since Elvis (perhaps unwittingly) introduced this kind of musical marketing concept in the 1950's, and now every new generation of singers has to develop its own looks and sounds: consider the progression from the Beatles, to the Doors, to Jimi Hendrix, to K.C. and the Sunshine Band, to the Sex Pistols, to New Wave, to Springsteen, Michael Jackson, Prince, and Madonna, to Nirvana, Pearl Jam, Guns 'n Roses, U2, the Smashing Pumpkins, Kid Rock and Matchbox Twenty, Third Eye Blind, Sugar Ray, Eminem, Limp Bizkit, Alanis Morrissette, Radio Head, Avril Lavigne, Gwen Stefani, Shakira (her hips don't lie), Pink, Kelly Clarkson, and so on indefinitely into the future, as long as music constitutes a "business" that sells products by whatever means, whether in stores or online.

While Sinatra had his own rather conservative look—how deceiving looks can be—and a distinctive sound that revolutionized music all over the Western world, he simply didn't have the material means to become as popular as The King. In order for his band to be heard in the days of bad P.A. systems, it had to contain ten saxophones, four trumpets, three trombones, and a drummer, bassist, and pianist working away, unheard, in the background. Elvis and those who followed him took advantage of the invention of electric guitars, better microphones, and especially of television to sell their style all over the world. In other words, pop music since Elvis has been permeated or saturated by technological developments, and it continues to be so to this day. The use of digital sampling and computer animation to make music videos is nothing more than an extremely "technified" version of what Elvis did first back in 1956 or so: the numerous technicians it takes to produce a good video are all devoted to giving a specific look to the specific sound that another group of technicians has already developed. With the boy and girl bands that dominated the airwaves in the early years of the twenty-first century—'N Sync, Backstreet Boys, Cristina Aguilera, Britney Spears—this marketing of a sound reached its logical apogee, or perhaps its logical dead end: there was no substance to these singers, merely shimmering surface, pop-driven sounds, banal vocals about teen love (which is far from being a new subject of pop songs). As for the hip-hop and the so-called R&B now days—Lil' Kim, Sysgo, Usher, etc. (Sam Cook, Jackie Wilson, Otis Redding, and Marvin Gaye are spinning in their graves, I hope)—that has crossed over to a white suburban audience, the people who sell it seem to be concerned only with conspicuous visual displays of wealth and commodified female bodies. In Sysgo's "Thong Song," for example, the singer in his leather pants and gold chains drives a Bentley convertible across the bridges of South Florida toward beaches where oiled women in skimpy bikinis gyrate on white sand. Other hip-hop videos feature speed boats and helicopters, super hot motorcycles and Ferraris, and extra-large limos in which portable bars overflow with Crystal Champagne. We're a long way from Elvis's forbidden pelvis.

The second reason that Elvis became so popular in the '50's has already been commented upon by everyone who has thought a bit about his career: Elvis played the race card, as Johnny Cochrane might have said in the context of the O.J. Simpson Trial. Elvis sang the music that had been developed first by black Americans, and which had formerly been restricted to speakeasies and juke joints. The race card is complicated by the fact that many of these songs were written by two prolific and brilliant songwriters from New York City, Lieber and Stoller. Of course, there is no reason why two educated Jewish boys from Manhattan couldn't write African-American songs: Big Mama's version of their "Hound Dog," which preceded Elvis's, seems to me to be the essence of the soulful and gorgeous black American music that accompanied me through childhood, most of which has probably been lost to history (consider the series of fortunate accidents that left us with the masterpieces of the great blues singer Robert Johnson, about whom we know nothing). The verb *seems* is important in the last sentence: at the risk of sounding essentialist and racist, Elvis was not black, and the men who wrote his songs were not black, so he could not possibly have been singing authentic African-American music. The music that made Elvis famous was a kind of collective hallucination. The people who screamed as they listened to it believed, perhaps, that they were listening to a white boy who dared to sing what they imagined to be black music, when in fact Elvis sang as he *imagined* black folks would sing, and he sang songs that were written by white men who wrote in what they *imagined* to be a black musical language (one need only listen to the James Brown recordings from the period to appreciate what an "authentic" black musical language was; Chuck Berry, a black man writing in what we can suppose to be an authentic African-American musical language, never had near the success of Elvis). In essence, then, Elvis first introduced a new kind of marketing that transformed music into a product and a "business"; second, Elvis as icon signified a collective and somewhat aleatory and even surrealistic thinking about rather difficult problems of race, which would come to a head shortly thereafter in the Civil Rights Movement of the 1960's. This is not to say that Elvis was consciously thinking about the racism that dominated the South and that still divides our country (think of the Simpson Trial and Barack Obama's campaign for the presidency); rather, Elvis gave a public and commodified form to contradictions and unconscious desires that were bubbling under the surface of American society, and which would find such eloquent representatives in Martin Luther King, Jr. and Malcolm X, whose voices would soon be silenced by violent means.

Elvis as a product, icon, and image of social complexity called masses of individuals into being as subjects, and continues to do so to this day. I should say that it's difficult to know, at this stage, whether Elvis's explosion on the public stage called an entire class of individuals into being, or whether there was an entire class of individuals waiting for Elvis to give them a look, a sound, a style, and an attitude, or whether this same look, sound, style, and attitude were always there in a certain segment of the American working class (we have to remember that Elvis was a truck driver before he became famous), waiting to be packaged and sold to a mass of "consumers" eager to have themselves personified as rock 'n roll heroes. Like almost everything else in the realm of the human, the phenomena of trash culture are like the chicken and the egg, which means that we will never be able to know whether the infrastructure produced the superstructure or vice versa. Whatever the case may be, when Elvis first appeared on the Ed Sullivan show some fifty years ago, millions of individuals all over the world seemed to realize suddenly that they, too, wanted to be *cool* like Elvis, and more importantly, that they wanted to *buy* a little piece of that cool etched in vinyl. The scene in Jim Jarmusch's *Mystery Train*, in which a Japanese tourist with a perfect pompadour haircut argues with his girlfriend while walking the semi-abandoned streets of Memphis about who is better, Carl Perkins or Elvis, demonstrates that the process is still going on today. This was perhaps the first time in history that literally millions of people all over the globe proclaimed that their own identity was predicated on the way they cut their hair, walked, talked, moved, dressed, spoke, on the music they liked, on the cars they drove, etc. In other words, with the appearance of Elvis, individual identity on a mass scale began to be mediated by industrially produced and sold commodities, spawning Elvis clones and imitators all over the world, some of whom are still performing, like Johnny Hallyday and Neal Diamond.

There is an important difference between the Elvis phenomenon and, for example, the more strict codes of dress and behavior that identified individuals as members of the *haute bourgeoisie* of the type described (or mocked) in the novels of Marcel Proust. While ladies and gentlemen at that time certainly had to dress in a certain way, maintain certain opinions, and be surrounded by an equipage (houses, carriages, servants) that defined them as such, their code of comportment was in no way linked to a cult of personality that developed from a kind of devotion to a single person. The followers of Elvis got their hair cut and sneered in a certain way because Elvis did so first, and not simply to show that they belonged to an exclusive class (it is true, however, that the entire Elvis phenomenon had a great deal to do with a confrontation of classes), in the same way that the punks got their nipples pierced or wore mohawks because Johnny Rotten or Sid Vicious did it first. In short, this was the first time, at least in American history, in which mass media provoked a massive and collective conception of individual identity based upon a series of fetishes or tokens: hair, pants, cars, music, golden suit jackets, or, for the women who were under Elvis's spell, a certain hysterical attitude of devotion.

The Nazis were perhaps the first to enforce a mass and collective definition of individuals by means of a technified film and propaganda apparatus that consciously and intentionally created a cult of the Führer. In essence, there is no difference between this kind of propaganda and the marketing that continues to impose identities and identifications upon us today—in some Romance languages, such as Spanish, for instance, the constant advertisements that are stuffed into one's mailbox are called simply "propaganda." This frightening creation of a fictitious personality that serves as a model for the standardized identity of each individual in the mass is much closer to the Elvis phenomenon than any possible literary antecedents. The hundreds of *literati* in Europe who wore yellow vests and contemplated suicide after reading Goethe's *The Sorrows of Young Werther*, or the hundreds of (would-be) adulteresses who emulated the protagonist of Flaubert's *Madame Bovary* may have been influenced to identify themselves with these fictional beings. In the case of Elvis, in contrast, a flesh and blood being was somehow forced to assume a fictional identity that itself was produced by an intersection or collision of technological and historical factors: the development of electric guitars, better amplifiers, and television intersected with the "crossing-over" of African-American music to a white audience. Elvis, a poor boy from Mississippi, became "The King," a character who became an icon for the phantasmic identity of millions of people. It is clear that this imposed, fictional identity was much too powerful for Elvis himself, who eventually lost his life and being to it.

We're still left with the enigma of the late Elvis as icon, who is in the process of becoming a kind of pagan saint. Nowadays, whenever there is a convention of Elvis impersonators, they almost invariably dress in the white-sequined-jumpsuit-huge-sunglasses-gigantic-sideburns outfit that I remember from the *Elvis: Aloha from Hawaii* broadcast. An important exception to the rule that the image of the late Elvis is the one that endures must be mentioned here. When the U.S. Postal Service was finally convinced to issue a stamp honoring Elvis, consumers were given a choice between two very different images of the early Elvis and the late Elvis, and I believe that by a majority vote of stamp-buyers from around the country, the image of the early Elvis eventually became the largest-selling stamp in the history of the Post Office (which was probably the only profit-making postal service in the world in 1995, largely due to sales of the Elvis stamp, I would like to believe). The reason for this selection of the "sacred" image is quite simple: in the same way that the image of the Sacred Heart of Christ that circulates on Mass cards is an idealized one (a light-haired or even blond and blue-eyed Jesus with an enormous heart glowing in his chest, surrounded by a halo, and thorns that couldn't possibly be dangerous), so the image of Elvis that constitutes his official canonization in a mercantile economy must be an idealized sort of cartoon figure of a young Elvis, his greased hair bobbing over his forehead, grasping an old-fashioned microphone. In this regard, one should note that when the aforementioned Robert Johnson was put on a postage stamp, the famous image of him staring at the camera holding his guitar was used, with one crucial edit: the cigarette dangling from his lips was cut out.

What really dominates the mass imagination, however, is the image of the other Elvis, which is much more akin to the *true* images of Christ and the Saints that captivated the collective mind of Medieval Europe, evident from a brief look at altar paintings from the eleventh to the sixteenth centuries (the Prado museum in Madrid has a particularly good collection): Jesus on the Cross, his legs broken, his face covered in the blood dripping from the thorns jammed into his brain, blood spurting from the wound in his side, and streaming from the nails in his hands and feet, just like the images of Saint Sebastian pierced with dozens of arrows and beaten to death, or of a decapitated Saint Dennis carrying his head in his hands, the blood spurting from his neck. The image of the late Elvis that fascinates us, and which supposedly has healing powers for his devotees, is inscribed in this same kind of sacred iconography that was the foundation of Western religion for millennia: that is, Jesus and the Saints appeared consistently as figures of human suffering, since perhaps the most important concept of Western Christendom is the idea that Jesus took upon himself the suffering of the human race, which was caused by Original Sin.

The depictions of this suffering during the Middle Ages were hyperbolic, since individual existence at this time was full of hardships brought on by incessant wars, the constant threat of famine, frequent epidemics, etc. The constant contemplation of the image of a suffering Christ undoubtedly made their difficult lives more bearable for our Medieval European ancestors.

Similarly, the late Elvis bears a kind of suffering for millions of ordinary Americans. He took the burden of having a fictional, technically-generated, mercantile identity forced upon him, and like the images of the Medieval Saints, the icon that he became tended toward the hyperbolic. While it was obvious that he was gaining more and more weight, and becoming more and more immobile, the rumor circulated that he was a karate champion, and he even tried out some karate moves on stage, with comic effects. His sideburns became bigger and bigger, to the point that they almost obscured the sides of his face. His jumpsuits became more and more elaborate, with ever more sequins and rhinestones, ever more scarves to throw in the audience. His sunglasses assumed proportions that obscured his eyes, eyebrows, and half of his cheeks. The late Elvis is an excessive being who becomes increasingly identified with the cathedral of Graceland and the city on steroids that is Las Vegas. In this progression toward the icon of the late Elvis, we see the fetishes of his fictional identity gradually obscuring the existence of his body, to the point that his biological being could no longer bear the weight of the abstract identity that was forced upon him. In a sense, Elvis died for the essential "sin" of a market economy whose continual demand for new products continually imposes new fetishes of identity on individuals. At the end of his life, Elvis was nothing more than a dying body enveloped in layer upon layer of objects that had been generated by his public image, and by his status as a privileged product that had to be continually renewed and resold. As such, the image of the late Elvis is an appropriate icon for the existence that each of us has to bear in our current historical context, in which the "market forces" and "the economy" that our politicians are always wringing their hands about are all important. His is, perhaps, a kind of postmodern saintly image that makes the suffering of millions of individuals bearable, and hence it potentially has a healing effect for all of us. No wonder Graceland has become a modern pilgrimage site, not unlike Santiago de Compostela or Lourdes.

The Abdominal Obsession Phenomenon

One of the principal attributes of trash culture is that it is a mechanism of power that influences the subjective identities of men and women literally by imprinting itself on their bodies. Perhaps there is no more eloquent and concise image of this process than the "washboard" stomach that all of us (myself included) want to have these days in the United States. In almost any K-Mart or Wal-Mart across this country, there is a separate aisle devoted to Ab-Blasters, EZ-Crunches, 8-minute Ab videos, Ab-Flexes, Ab-Curls, Ab-Rollers, etc., etc., etc. Let's face it, a washboard stomach is possibly the most unnatural feature to grace the human anatomy since the invention of the pierced nose at the dawn of human civilization. This does not necessarily mean that a muscular abdomen is a bad thing (in Pilates, they call this part of the body one's "core.") All cultural artifacts and phenomena are intrinsically un-natural, no matter how gushy Romantic critics might be about the "organic" quality of Beethoven's Symphonies or Monet's "instinct" for color and shadow. Acculturation is essentially an imposition of discipline on the body until impossible movements of the limbs are perceived by the individual as "natural" or "instinctive." Anyone who has developed a decent technique on the piano, as a ballet dancer, or as a painter will attest to the truth of this statement. People will not naturally learn Chopin's *Études* or chiaroscuro without the imposition of a ferocious regimen of practice, practice, practice, which is the bane of children the world over. Similarly, very few men or women will naturally develop washboard abs without intensive exercise. Think of Buster Crab, Johnny Weismuller, Burt Lancaster in *From Here to Eternity*, and all of the other pre-exercise-craze hunks who lacked muscle definition and who pulled their bathing suits almost up to their armpits not only because it was fashionable to do so, but also to hide their sort of smooth, bulging bellies, which are what "normal" bellies look like on men who are wading deep into middle age. I'm thinking, for example, of John Travolta's decidedly non-washboard abs when he is being sprayed with a hose by Harvey Keitel in *Pulp Fiction*. Somehow, somewhere, in some way, the mysterious powers that rule over us all (even those of us who are supposedly in positions of power) have decided that washboard abs are desirable, and now people will have ribs removed, will be lipo-suctioned to the point of agony (and in a few rare cases even to the point of death), and will endure endless "Torso fitness" classes, Pilates classes, and Ab-rolling sessions in order to get a stomach that looks like the thing my great-great-grandmother used to wash her clothes on.

The sad fact of the matter is that no matter how many reps you do on your EZ-Crunch on your couch, while watching reruns of *Roseanne* and eating donuts, you will *never* have abs like those fortunate few in Hollywood (Demi Moore, for example) who work out for an hour and a half *every day*, and who eat nothing but soy protein, tempeh, grilled Tilapia, and organic mezclun. In a sense, the ab craze is a kind of modern foot binding, which was a manifestation of patriarchal power in not-so-ancient China, or the waist-binding of Victorian cultures of European descent (America included), or the elongated necks imposed on some members of some African tribes, or the flattened foreheads imposed on others, or the salad plates that some Africans carry in their lips, or the messages that some South American tribesmen can carry in their extended earlobes, and so on, and so on. Human beings abandoned nature when they decided to stand erect. My aching back and your aching back are testimony to the fact that nature did not want us to support all of our weight on two legs with our lower back muscles serving as a crucial pivot. Once we left nature, there was no turning back, which means that in culture, and especially in *trash* culture, anything and everything is possible within the rather vague physical limits of the human body. In other words, the general mechanism by which power and its dissemination inscribe themselves on the body of the individual can develop in any direction whatsoever. For instance, as I write these lines, it is fashionable for some people of all ages to get tattoos and to pierce whatever parts of their bodies they wish (like the character played by Roseanne Arquette in the aforementioned *Pulp Fiction*, who has eighteen body piercings). Piercing at one point was viewed as something extreme, radical, and marginal, at least in the West (more on this in a moment). When such a practice is co-opted into the cultural mainstream—the middle-aged waitress at the sleepy diner I went to in rural New Hampshire one day had a "tribal" tattoo around her biceps—then it becomes necessary to repeat the process in order to make it extreme again, at which point one gets eighteen body piercings or eighteen tattoos. As Foucault taught us, however, the nature of power is that it will always find new ways of penetrating and dominating the body, while it will always seem to those who open themselves to power's infiltration that they are expressing their "individuality" in this way, at least in our culture (the case of the tribesman elongating his neck or flattening his forehead as a sign of his belonging to the tribe is somewhat different—in that case, he *erases* his individuality and submits his identity completely to that of the group). If the development of trash culture continues in the same direction, I can imagine a not-too-distant future in which it will be cool to have a finger or even a limb amputated (as in the Japanese mafia ritual of loyalty), or to shoot oneself, or to walk around with a knife or an arrow sticking out of one's chest, or to submit to torture and humiliation, much in the way that people already are hanging themselves, sometimes with fatal consequences, in so-called "auto-erotic acts" that involve near-death experiences which, sometimes, are simply death experiences.

In comparison with these more radical departures from what may be perceived as a "normal" state of affairs, the abdominal obsession phenomenon is rather banal and domestic. For this reason, it is perhaps the most insidious of power's eruptions in our daily lives, along with the anorexia, waif, or heroin-addict look that was fashionable for a time on catwalks in the '90's, and which continues to impose a ridiculously low body-mass-index on fashion models. Anyone can be hooked by the ab-session: grandmothers, grandfathers, moms and dads, kids just home from school, visiting cousins, and so on. When he was finishing high school, a nephew of mine was getting ready to go to Cancun for "Senior Week," that session of debauchery that most graduating high school students treat themselves to after what they perceive as four years of indoctrination and discipline. Partly as a joke, or partly as a manifestation of some kind of ab-anxiety, he asked my sister to buy him an Ab-Blaster thing-a-majig for Christmas, so that he could chisel his abs for the trip he would be taking in June. The endless info-mercials about ab machines project a glow of health and happiness that should be associated with the discipline of sculpting the mid-section in only eight minutes a day, which is as easy as flossing or brushing your teeth. Every member of the family could buy his or her own ab machine, only to realize that there simply is no way to change one's musculature without the intensive daily workouts and radical diet changes that our Hollywood stars and starlets impose upon themselves. Perhaps this is the beauty of the unwritten ab strategy (like all strategies of power, it cannot be made explicit, otherwise people may not allow themselves to be subjected to it): it functions by means of a fundamental lie that makes the individual feel as though he or she is to blame if his or her mid section does not resemble those of the fitness trainers on TV after the eight minute a day, twelve week program that they always recommend on the info-mercials. In this case, if the Ab-Blaster doesn't work, the victim will buy an EZ-Crunch, and if that doesn't work, he'll move on to the Nordic Track or Bowflex system, or even to one of those devices that shocks the ab muscles into activity while the individual who bought the device sits in front of the television. At this point, power has a hold of him, and produces him as a subject who desires a *potential* body that exists as a reality only for a very limited percentage of the population. From here on out, power, wherever and with whomever it may reside, will continue to multiply the potential bodies that we all want to have: the body that receives a massage twice a week; the body that does yoga; the body that has the proverbial D-cup breasts or ten-inch penis; the body that can run ten kilometers in under forty minutes; the body that can dance until dawn at the age of fifty; or, in my earlier examples, the body that cuts, pierces, tattoos, tortures, hangs, and dismembers itself as a mark of coolness. Just as systems of mass production and mass destruction are limitless, so the possibilities of trash culture's imprint on the body of the individual, or on the individual's desire for his or her own body, will never reach their end. This thought crosses my mind as I do my crunches and bench presses every other day, as I have for the last fifteen years or so, in a gym where lately people have been doing all sorts of extravagant movements with gigantic, air-filled, multi-colored balls, in order to achieve an optimum physique. But that's the subject of another chapter.

Junk Food

I'd be the first to admit that sometimes you just have to have a Big Mac, a large fries, and a Coke. If you eat these kinds of things often, however, you will soon be as big as a house and an assiduous client of the local coronary unit. Despite the lack of nutritive value of junk food such as burgers and fries (though the high protein content of your average burger is quite nutritious), I'd be willing to bet that there are few Americans born after World War II who haven't experienced an almost insatiable craving at one time or another for potato chips, Dunkin' Donuts, Pepperidge Farm cookies, Fritos, Doritos, Cheetos, nachos, tacos, hot dogs (chili dogs, cheese dogs, etc.), cheese fries, fried chicken, pizzas, and my own particular favorite, the Philly Cheesesteak with fried onions (the street corner where the cheesesteak was invented, 9th and Passyunk in Philadelphia, has a kind of mystical significance for me). The United States has been a hyper-industrialized machine nation for more than a hundred years, which means that we produce an incredible amount of goods (a quarter or so of the world's products were made in the USA near the end of the 20th century; by the time you read this, China will certainly have surpassed that mark). Food is an integral part of the massive market economy in which we live, and the American companies that dedicate their activity to producing food as a commodity are some of the largest and most well-known in the world, as any American who has traveled extensively abroad knows. The trademarks of Coca-Cola and McDonald's, as well as those of Kellogg's, Nabisco, Pepsi, Kentucky Fried Chicken, Pizza Hut, etc. are virtually universal symbols, recognized from Singapore, to San Francisco, to Sydney, to Shanghai, to Seville, to Stansted Airport. You can go to almost any large city in the world and know that there is a McDonald's nearby; the number of "MacDo's" in Paris, for example, is becoming truly alarming, and has led to demonstrations decrying the threat that they pose to traditional French cuisine, and has provoked an alternative, "slow food" movement. My brothers have often told me the story of their trip to the Philippine islands, which they "survived" (they tend to dramatize) thanks to the seemingly limitless supply of ice-cold Pepsis that appeared out of the most improbable and ramshackle houses. I once went to a typical late-Winter feast (known as a *calçotada*) in the countryside near Reus, in Catalonia, with two dozen Catalans and a few Americans. Our meeting point was the McDonald's in Reus.

Our mode of production and our faith in a market economy have generated a process that has transformed food and drink into global commodities. In other words, our tendency to value goods on the basis of their brand names (Levi's or Guess or Diesel jeans are cooler than Wrangler's and Lee's, Pantene Pro V shampoo is better than the CVS brand), which is an effect of incessant marketing, also applies to food. This means that our tastes and appetites are determined as much by the marketing attributes of the foods we eat as they are by their taste and smell. Everyone knows that a charbroiled half-pound hamburger from their local steakhouse or barbecue, which in some places are becoming harder and harder to find, especially with the franchising of the Outback and Longhorn steakhouses and their like, is about a hundred times better than a Quarter-Pounder from McDonald's, a Whopper from Burger King, or a Wendy's burger. What we like about the commodity-burgers is the way they look, the way they're packaged, the atmosphere of the restaurants, and the taste that is associated with the entire apparatus that manages to sell us a 10-cent hamburger for two bucks. What matters in a Big Mac is not its taste, otherwise everyone would choose hamburgers from their local barbecue, steakhouse, etc; what really matters is the abstract yet palpable set of attributes that envelopes, penetrates, engulfs, and in effect constitutes the Big Mac as an entity. For foreigners, McDonald's undoubtedly once had an appeal because it signified America and the American way of life that has saturated the collective imaginary of the West in films and television for the last forty or fifty years. Every time a Muscovite eats a Big Mac, he is also eating a little piece of America; the next time you are abroad, go into a McDonald's and savor for a few minutes the uncanny and even uncomfortable feeling of being back home as you sit in those familiar plastic chairs and smell the familiar, processed odors of "pasteurized processed cheese food" and near plastic fries. The food is merely a material basis of the true product that these companies sell, which is a kind of subjective experience, an identification of oneself with a certain kind of desire, attitude, and look.

There are two kinds of junk food that participate in this process of subjectivization. All junk food is more or less portable, but one kind is always identified with a certain kind of place. Every city has its places that are associated with specific foods: Geno's, Pat's, and, my own favorite, Steve's, in Philadelphia are renowned for their cheese steaks, at least among the local population. A cheese steak only tastes right when it is eaten outside Pat's, in the cold, on a Saturday night, with all of the neon lights illuminated, with someone selling Christmas trees across 9th Street, in front of the Capitolo playground, and with the Vietnamese, Cambodian, Chinese, Hispanic, African-American, Irish, and Italian kids of the neighborhood dressed to party, promenading up and down the streets, and with dozens of fat guys returning home from a Sixers game. The experience of that place seems to penetrate the spongy roll, the greasy onions, and the melted Cheez Whiz, and one remembers Sly Stallone jogging by in the first Rocky film, and one says to oneself, unconsciously, "this is me, I'm here, and I'm cool, I'm experiencing something authentic." When I was in Kansas City, my uncle was gracious enough to take me to Arthur Bryant's barbecue, which had been frequented by numerous former presidents, among them Jimmy Carter and Harry Truman (of course). Along with the Gargantuan number of calories one ingests in this fantastic place (the baked beans and ribs are truly extraordinary), the experience is what counts. You stand there chewing on bones and fat, looking at the pictures on the wall, and the huge bellies, covered with white aprons stained with barbecue sauce, of the guys who serve you the ribs, and you look out of the window to see the eerie kind of silence of a decaying American urban environment, and you feel somehow content to find yourself in that place at that time. In the 1990's, Bruce Willis, Sylvester Stallone, Arnold Schwarzenegger, et. al. took this concept and decided that it could be implanted in any city in the world. I once had lunch in their *Planet Hollywood* in Barcelona, now happily defunct, where one could dine surrounded by a veritable barrage of clips showing the owners in their fictional roles. Whether the food in this kind of place is good or not is irrelevant; in such a place, they could serve Army rations, and a certain kind of person—the kind that eats at the Hard Rock Café in every city he visits—would leave happy, since what matters in such a restaurant is the unconscious sense of having experienced something, of having lived some kind of packaged adventure, simply by going out to lunch. For children, this sense of adventure is certainly the important element of going to dinner at McDonald's, where kids have their own special category of food, the brilliantly-named "Happy Meal." Junk food concentrates the idea of being in an exciting place, and the individual's experience of this excitement as a minuscule moment in the temporal development of his or her identity, which is typical of the junk food that is identified with particular places. Lately, this idea has been abstracted and rarefied to such an extent that it can be implanted almost anywhere (in contrast, when Pat's Steaks tried to franchise its product, the result was a marketing disaster).

The second type of junk food is extracted from the identification of food with a place, which is its normal condition (one has to make a veritable pilgrimage to the finest restaurants, such as those of Paul Bocuse outside of Lyon and Ferran Adriá north of Barcelona), and is virtually intended to be eaten on the move. This means that the appeal of this type of portable junk food to individuals is even more abstract and universal. As a consequence, Americans are almost always eating something, in situations that are unthinkable for the majority of mildly sophisticated Europeans of a certain age (while their younger counterparts are adopting more and more American habits—I've seen scores of college and high school students eating sandwiches and sipping their Starbucks coffee on the Boulevard de Montparnasse at lunchtime in Paris). We eat potato chips, tortilla chips, Cheetos, Doritos, donuts, hamburgers, slices of pizza, cheese fries, hot dogs, etc. while driving, walking down the street, waiting in line, watching movies (serious cinemas in Europe, such as the one in Lyon where I saw *Pulp Fiction* for the first time, don't even sell *popcorn*), during concerts, riding bikes, etc. This tendency to eat all the time sometimes reaches extremes that are intolerable even for some Americans: once during a concert of the Philadelphia Orchestra at the Academy of Music, the folks sitting next to me up in the cheap seats (at that time, two bucks on a Saturday night) were eating Chips Ahoy chocolate chip cookies and drinking Hershey's chocolate milk throughout the *Adagietto* of Mahler's 5th symphony, with their feet up on the seats in front of them, of course. While this chocolate orgy is perhaps inappropriate in a classical context—*perhaps* inappropriate, because for most people, going to see an orchestra is no different than going to the movies—American tradition dictates that spectacles require food, and this tradition invades the usually anal-retentive context of classical music in the Summer, when the smart set leaves behind its furs and diamonds to picnic under the stars in Tanglewood, Fairmount Park, and Saratoga Springs, accompanied by the incidental music of the Boston Symphony Orchestra and the Philadelphia Orchestra going on somewhere far away under a protective hood.

Whether it is appropriate or inappropriate, the portability of junk food provides a certain thrill and even sense of adventure for the person who eats it on the run. Back when I was working as a bicycle messenger in Philly, one of the few thrills of my day came at five o'clock, when I would buy two soft pretzels with mustard from a vendor and begin my ten-mile trip home on my bike, trying to eat and avoid being killed in rush-hour traffic at the same time. How many Americans eat Big Macs and Dunkin' Donuts in their cars on the way to work, or on the way home from work? How many of us go through the drive-thru in order to sit in the parking lot in our cars and scarf down a hamburger or a piece of fried chicken? One might argue that the stereotypical image of the American as someone who has no time to sit down to a meal because he or she works all the time is the true source of junk food's portability. Whatever its origin may be, the truth is that we *like* eating and drinking on the run now, and that any kind of trip in an automobile, for example, is incomplete without a large coffee, an order of fries, or a bag of chips. It's difficult for us to imagine that 400 million Europeans drive cars that are not even equipped with *cupholders*, for Christ's sake, while even the ever-resourceful Japanese have neglected to recognize the importance of food and drink for the American driver: the cupholder in my Honda Civic was unable to hold a 16 oz. Snapple, for example. It would be stretching it a bit to claim that portable junk food calls the individual into being as a certain kind of subject, and determines his or her identity to an extent. Nevertheless, there is no doubt that the general and officially-recognized habit (and adventure) of eating in the car is a fundamental part of our identities as Americans.

Another aspect of portable junk food concerns its relationship to the act of being a spectator, as I have already mentioned. What would a movie be without popcorn? There is a certain kind of satisfaction involved in sitting on the couch, sipping a Pepsi and eating a bag of Doritos, while watching a bad movie at two o'clock in the morning. What is the source of this satisfaction? What does it say about my own conception of my identity? If we were to explain to Benjamin Franklin what it means to be watching the *Invasion of the Body Snatchers* on a Saturday night, waiting for the pizza and Cokes to be delivered, how would we do it? The pleasure of having a long night ahead of you, with two pizzas on the way, a B-movie coming on with some wacky hosts, preferably in costume, and a warm bed waiting for you at 2 a.m. is like few others, for a number of reasons that are more or less evident to us, but which would be absolutely opaque to Mr. Franklin, who nonetheless would have been delighted to see how far his discovery had been developed. The first and most obvious of these is the pleasure, comfort, freedom, and leisure of ending the work week, and of knowing that, at such a late hour, there is nothing that has to be done, no phone calls have to be made, no errands have to be run, nothing has to be bought or picked up or delivered, etc. If you are one of those people who feels as though you *have* to go dancing in night clubs on Friday and Saturday nights, you are an unfortunate and unconscious victim of the market economy's irresistible or even "sublime" force (as Fredric Jameson might say). The typical kid or post-kid who "goes clubbing," as we used to say when I was an adolescent, has to have the right kind of shoes, jeans, dress, shirt, hair, perfume, car, boyfriend or girlfriend; he or she has to go to the right clubs, drink the right drinks (or take the right drugs, as in the transition from acid to pot to speed to meth to coke to crack to ecstasy to heroin between 1970 and 2000), dance to the right music. All of these are products that the night-clubber feels compelled to buy during the weekend, unlike my imaginary friend waiting for Little Caesar's or Domino's to deliver (those of us fortunate enough to live in cities where local pizzerias flourish always choose these over the national chains I have just named). In part, his pleasure derives from the fact that he feels the exhilarating freedom of being allowed to waste his time, without having to respond to a boss's orders or to the demands of the time clock for a brief and thus precious moment.

Nevertheless, the junk food junky (this was the title of a song in the '70's) sitting on his couch in his underwear with a family-sized bag of Cheetos and a two-liter bottle of Pepsi is, evidently, a consumer of a different sort. In any relatively large community (and these days, even in trailer parks in the middle of the boondocks, thanks to UPS and the internet), there is an enormous demand for prepared food and other goods that can be delivered to the home. The basic thrust of developments in "information technology," formerly known as "computer science," is to transform the television into an interactive device that allows the individual sitting at home to buy and sell almost any kind of merchandise, from stocks and bonds to plane tickets to shoes and undershirts. Once the television finally becomes an internet device that can be turned on and operated by flipping a switch and scrolling through menus with a remote, the world as we know it is going to explode, or implode, or simply plode in every direction at once. (This is already starting to happen, in fact, with internet-ready cell phones and Blackberries.) Those of us who have been sitting alone for years in front of our television sets late at night know that the perverse pleasure involved in this activity is one of consumption. Your eyes strain toward the set. They can't seem to see enough. Even though there are fifty-seven channels and nothing's on, as Springsteen once sang in a forgotten song, you have to watch at least three movies at once and two sporting events, skipping parts of all of them and all of the ads (except the ads for phoney dating services, or phone sex lines). You stuff your face down to the last cold piece of pizza or the last Cheezit, and you drain the dregs of a pathetic regional basketball quarterfinals (if you're a man) or a dismal sentimental tear-jerker involving broken marriages, lost children, crippling diseases, etc. (if you're a woman), and you finally go off to bed, vanquished only by the need for sleep, but not by the satiety of your appetites, which know no limits.

In other words, anything and everything that is in front of you has to be consumed, and the portable junk food I have mentioned is merely the material side of an abstract procedure that must arrive at its logical conclusion: the products for which our market economy has created a need must be disposed of (i.e., ingested and expelled) by the consumer, so that new products can be produced and consumed. The commodification of food goes hand and hand with the commodification of images, and both of them create individuals as insatiable subjects in both of these domains. Since the United States is the capital of junk food, it is also the land of the overweight. Nowhere do you find as many fat people as you do in our gracious country. You will rarely see a genuinely obese person in France or Spain, for example, where fatty substances such as cheese, cured sausages, and olive oil are the bases of the local diets. While the citizens of the Slavic nations with their robust appetites may eat much more than we do (go to a Polish Christmas Eve celebration, if you don't believe me), they are stocky rather than being obese. In contrast, you would undoubtedly be able to find five or ten astoundingly overweight people on any trip to your local K-Mart or Wal-Mart or shopping mall, waiting in line to buy super pretzels or cheese fries. The mass production of food and the marketing that produces a need for it have created a nation of more or less obese people who are always hungry, who are always on the lookout for a snack bar or a bathroom, and half of whom soon will be diabetic or pre-diabetic. Similarly, the commodification of images on television and in the movies has created a nation of individuals (and increasingly, a world of individuals, as the incredible success of *Bay Watch* over the course of a decade proved) who continually need to consume certain kinds of stories, just as we always have to have a bag of chips and a soda in hand.

Thus we could tell Benjamin Franklin that the pleasure we feel on a Saturday night, with the pizzas on the way and *The Attack of the Fifty-Foot Woman* or *Plan 9 From Outer Space* playing on cable, is essentially the pleasure that a dog feels when he performs tricks for his master. The society in which we live has bred us to be animals who have insatiable concrete and abstract appetites, while the health or illness of our "economy" depends upon the maintenance of these appetites, whether anyone intended things to be that way or not. Junk food is an integral part of this whole.

Greenwich Village, Las Ramblas, Covent Garden, Les Halles

Here's a chapter for travelers of the Western world. There's a certain aesthetic that dominates the young (under 35?) part of the population in the world-class cities mentioned in my title. You all know the look, which is probably a toned-down version of what punks and gay men were doing to their bodies more than thirty years ago already (alas!): hair dyed various bright colors (orange, yellow, blue, white) and shaved in various places; pierced ears, noses, eyebrows, lips, tongues, belly buttons; torn, dirty clothes and army boots; tattoos in strategic places, etc. My first encounter with this kind of look was back in the second half of the 1970's. I was washing dishes in a posh French restaurant in downtown Philadelphia, La Panetière, which was transformed into a not-so-posh Cajun restaurant after the owner, Peter von Starck, one of the dons of the local restaurant scene, died an untimely death brought on by too much of his favorite drink, vodka with grapefruit juice, despite all of that vitamin C. Most of La Panetière's waiters were gay. One of them was on the punky side—he had moderately spiked hair (the patrons from Grace Kelly's Main Line would have been unable to bear an authentic multi-colored Mohawk), a constant snarl on his lips, and, most shocking of all for a boy such as myself from working class, racist, homophobic Northeast Philly, he had both of his nipples pierced, as he proudly demonstrated to all of us in the changing room at the end of the night. As far as I know, in 1978-1979, pierced nipples were indeed something extremely strange, and were seen only in the most marginal of populations that were trying to establish their identities as different from the mass of bourgeois wanna-bes (the real bourgeoisie in America has been invisible to most of us since they moved out to their enormous houses on Long Island and in Connecticut nearly sixty years ago. Think of Humphrey Bogart's commuting character in the original *Sabrina*). Punks really were outsiders at the time, and the only alternatives for them were violent death (Sid Vicious) or a transformation into more "normal" members of society (Johnny Rotten, or, the ultimate case, that pseudo-punk Sting, who has become a pseudo country gentleman, living in his castle in the English countryside, making pseudo-literary references to Chaucer in his CD titles, and dreaming about desert roses in advertisements for Jaguar automobiles). The punks distanced themselves from the rest of us by using their bodies as signifiers of difference, as my friends in academics would say. They pierced every body part that was pierceable, changed their hair color every week (like one of my room-mate's lovers in college), poured Coke into it to make it stand up straight and look dirty, ripped their clothes and wore heavy, ass-kicking army boots, got tattoos and abused their bodies with drugs until they were as waifish as apprentice vampires. They wounded each other in clubs by "slash dancing," if I remember correctly. The punk "movement" or phenomenon was a feverish attempt on the part of the disenfranchised members of a Western industrial society whose material base was on the verge of collapsing to establish a cultural value and an identity for themselves via the inscription of a system of markers on their own bodies, since they were the only things in their possession. While it reached us here in the States much later than its inception in Britain, its first few years were exciting indeed for those of us who were sick of Barry White, Donna Summer, and the Bee Gees.

Lo and behold, by the beginning of the new millennium, Barry White and Donna Summer were hot again, and the punk body code had been co-opted or "colonized" by the apparatus of power (as Foucault would have said). In other words, nowadays you can almost get a tattoo and have your belly button pierced in Macy's or Nieman-Marcus, and the sort of funky, cosmopolitan, international sections of the West's large cities have become virtual theme parks of "alternativity," where masses of youths on foreign exchange programs congregate to spread around their parents' cash. It should be added that numerous other components have been added to the punk aesthetic, while others have been eliminated. A full-fledged punk with a purple Mohawk is more a rarity these days than he or she would have been back in the '70's, while kids with multi-colored, somewhat shaved hair, nose rings, and tattoos are more common now perhaps than at any other time in history (we have to remember that Shakespeare himself had long hair, earrings, and probably a tattoo or two). In early 2008, I went to a concert of the Philadelphia Chamber Orchestra, which played Berg's *Lyric Suite* and Bartok's *Divertimento for Strings*; the concertmistress, who was an extraordinarily disciplined and accomplished musician, had a nose ring, a pierced lip, a spike through her ear, and an emo haircut. Similarly, back in the '90's, the kind of disco fashion that my friends and I loathed back in the '70's made a strong comeback, from the streets of Queens to the runways of Paris and Milan. At one point in the last decade, while strolling Las Ramblas in Barcelona, or the Boulevard de Strasbourg in Paris, or Houston Street in the Village, or the sort of Mall at Covent Garden in London, you could see swarms of teenagers in tight black bellbottoms, hipsters, platform shoes, and form-fitting polyester shirts with bright prints (I had a Filipino friend who used to steal these shirts from Sears back in the '70's, which meant that all of my friends and I wore them, with brown leather jackets that looked like plastic, just like the one that Travolta wears in the opening scene of *Saturday Night Fever*). Today, nearing the end of the new century's first decade, if you look around you casually at any of these places, you will see people dressed according to vestimentary codes that *signified* something at a given period of time, but which no longer mean anything other than the desire of the person who dresses that way to be fashionable. In any crowd in London, New York, Paris, Barcelona, Amsterdam, or Berlin there are bound to be "rockabillies", "hippies," "punks," "disco kids," "ravers," "head bangers," "heavies," and so on. All of these terms are in quotation marks because the dress codes that mark the inclusion of individuals within these groups no longer necessarily imply the mode of life that these codes were meant to embody or to inscribe on the body when they were developed.

When Brando donned his cap, his jeans, his boots, and his leather jacket in *The Wild Ones* back in the '50's, he was wearing the uniform of the former soldier who rebelled for no particular reason against the banal world of prosperity that he found upon his return from Hitler's war. Now if someone wears a Perfecto jacket that he/she bought in the Village or at the flea market at Clignancourt on the north side of Paris, he/she doesn't necessarily have to be a hell-raising, whisky-drinking biker who is probably suffering from PTSD. He/she can just as easily be a clerk in a 7-11. The important point of the jacket is the opportunity that it provides its wearer to say that he/she bought it in the Village, or in Paris (the Frenchman would rather say that he bought his in New York, and vice-versa). In other words, one kind of narrativity that saturates the object is substituted for another as these vestimentary codes are unearthed and parodied by later generations. At first, the story that clothing as signifying object told concerned the identity of its wearer, determined by a set of attitudes, actions, and opinions that he or she held with respect to the historical situation at hand. When the code is resurrected and "colonized" or "cannibalized" by a later configuration of power, it signifies merely the subjugation of the individual who feels compelled to adhere to it, and the extent to which his/her body is saturated by power. What matters in the latter instance is *not* the expression of a rebellious identity that is derived from adherence to a group; rather, the wearer wants to adhere as closely as possible to a dress code that was cannibalized by the clothing industry and disseminated through fashion magazines and television commercials. Perhaps the most noteworthy characteristic of post-modernity in the West is that it continues to produce sub-cultures (i.e., sets of products that may be sold to emerging market groups) by cannibalizing its past. In other words, we are living in a market-driven version of Nietzsche's eternal recurrence, with all of the spiritual and redemptive dimensions of this eternal repetition sucked out and thrown in the dumpster.

A quick glance at recent history demonstrates that this was not always the case. In fact, the United States has been particularly fertile in producing original sub-cultures, often linked to technological and technical developments, throughout the 20th century. This enormous factory nation has generated everything from comic books to cartoons, from basketball to tractor pulls, from jazz to tap dancing to blues to psychedelia to disco to hip-hop. During the '70's, however, this process began to be interrupted by *nostalgia* for the past, the first stage in its cannibalization. Perhaps economic and historical factors combined to suspend the impressive fecundity of American culture: Nixon took the country off the gold standard, and abandoned a foolish, brutal, and impossible post-colonial war (as I revise these notes in 2008, it is clear that American Presidents have not learned from the familiar, banal dictum claiming that one is doomed to repeat the errors of history if one is ignorant of them); the oil crisis seemed to signal the end of the limitless expansion and prosperity with which a "Manifest Destiny" had seemingly blessed this country, to use the frightening and brutal rhetoric of right-wing politicians. At this point, the improvement in international communications meant that culture began to go partially global, and the two cultural strands that I have been describing developed simultaneously on both sides of the Atlantic, perhaps as a reaction to the economic and political crises of the moment. On the American side, the reaction was a descent into frivolity and denial in the disco movement, in the desperate search for pleasure that barely concealed the violence that pervades our culture, as is more than evident from the most powerful representation of the disco age, *Saturday Night Fever*. On the other side was a violent protest against power that ultimately destroyed itself, as in the death of Sid Vicious. Both of these developments were mere surface phenomena, like the symptoms of hysteria that Freud discerned as the flotsam and jetsam of unconscious traumas bubbling up to the surface. Power quickly absorbed them, transformed them into products, and threw them back at restless populations like bones thrown to hungry dogs. These days, power doesn't wait for people to recognize the difficulties of their situations: by continually cannibalizing the past, it throws palliatives and soporifics to the public of consumers who, in this age of relative peace and prosperity, happily eat them up and reproduce them within and upon their own bodies. Today, the primary means of sedating the population is by convincing them that the most banal details of their everyday lives are important enough to appear on television, and to make them famous for the proverbial fifteen minutes that Andy Warhol foresaw so long ago.

As a means of understanding a different mode of cultural production in the United States, consider the hippy movements of the 1960's. The music of that period was authentically about a new American revolution, one that took place in public demonstrations of a kind that we rarely see in the United States anymore (in France, on the other hand, demonstrations are virtually the national pastime, and have been incorporated into everyday life, including riot police and clean-up crews that escort and follow *les manifs* down the streets of Paris once or twice a week). In the '60's, a large number of important but largely unwritten social institutions were at least partially reformed. The institutional racism that has always dominated this country and that continues to dominate it was at least made illegal by the Civil Rights Act of 1964. Feminism granted women new freedoms, though the movement was stopped short of an Equal Rights Amendment to guarantee them. A new openness with regard to sex and marriage became commonplace, resulting in an unprecedented promiscuity in this country that came to an end only with the disaster of the AIDS epidemic. Music and fashion participated in all of these developments, calling for an end to the Vietnam war, to racism, to sex and age discrimination (at least against the young), to the insane pressure to marry and have kids, and so on. The hippy dress code had never been seen before in the West, and the music that incarnated the ideology of the hippies had never been heard before, based as it was on technological developments (new amplifiers, distortion techniques, new electronic instruments such as Ray Manzarak's organ), new drug experiences (LSD, mainly), and a new contact with Eastern music. Perhaps the somewhat invisible apparatus of power that rules the Western world realized that revolutionary developments of this type could no longer be allowed to surface all by themselves, and after punk, disco, and New Wave, which were all relatively harmless, it began generating mere revisions, rewritings, or cannibalizations of past fashions, sounds, and looks. Nowadays a masterful pop song like Britney Spears's "Toxic" is a postmodern mixture of styles and sounds, all of them colonized and cannibalized: Arab string orchestras, spaghetti Western soundtracks, James Bond soundtracks, Bollywood musicals, and electronic drum tracks.

Of course, the problem of *intentionality* is inevitable when it comes to analyses of power as it manifests itself in the domain of trash culture. *Who* decided that the '70's were going to be fashionable again in the '90's? *How* did they implement and disseminate this fashion, if it was done by any group of individuals? The *why* of this process has already been sketched above: after the 1960's, movements that effected masses of people could no longer be left to chance after the events of the decade that pushed the country to the verge of a revolution. Postmodern techniques of power are unavoidably conservative, which is perhaps the key to understanding them. Power today is not an individual or a group of persons in a room deciding what they are going to do, and how they are going to do it; rather, it is a system or set of relations that is a global effect of millions of individual decisions. The most important element in the set of relations that constitutes power is undoubtedly the *visual* one. Generations after the introduction of television into almost every American household, when the ruling class itself is composed of people who could not imagine life without this most crucial of media (Laura Bush's evocation of how she watched *Desperate Housewives* while her husband, "Mr. Excitement," fell asleep beside her, was particularly eloquent), the sets of images that constitute the fashions I have been describing have become historical artifacts that are engraved in the minds of those of us who grew up in the '60's, and that television is continually reactivating in the minds of younger viewers in order to sell itself and the products that keep it alive. Given the weight of its history (the cinema itself is now more than 100 years old, while its little brother the television is half that), this medium is now continuously looping back upon itself, and parody is becoming one of its normal modes. *No one* controls the point at which completely new genres begin to be affected by their own history. In this sense, the fact that fashion and music have been cannibalizing the past since the beginning of the '90's was decided simply by the development of the system itself, rather than by anyone's intention. The interplay of power and pop culture has reached a state of equilibrium out of which only new technological developments will be able to shake it. Thus the four places in my title will continue to be saturated by pastiche, parody, nostalgia, and impossible postmodern mixtures of styles as generators of fashion modes that are essentially cannibalistic, in which the present consistently thrives by eating, digesting, and expelling the waste products of the past.

Football

While basketball may be more aesthetically pleasing, and while baseball
may be the so-called "national pastime," football is the quintessential American
sport. The reader should bear in mind that my remarks here will be colored by
the fact that I am, have been, and will always be a fanatical fan of the gridiron
and of almost everything that has something to do with the game itself, while
I detest and deplore a whole series of things that have to do with fan violence,
public financing of privately-owned stadiums, the sexism of cheerleading, the
economics of the game, and so on. For example, the Super Bowl alone generates
five billion dollars in bets every year, which means that this one game produces
more economic activity in two weeks than the profits of most of the large
multinational corporations in a very good year (the spectacular profits of the large
oil companies in the last decade are an exception). Recently, American cities
such as Cleveland, Baltimore, Chicago, Gary, St. Louis, Los Angeles, Houston,
and Seattle have been cutting each other's throats to see which gets to steal an
NFL franchise from which. City governments across the nation go into virtual
bankruptcy to build new stadiums that will attract teams, while banks, airlines,
telephone companies, and other corporations drop enormous sums of money
in order to affix their names to these buildings. In other words, like the other
major sports, football is what we might call capital intensive, and its presence
in major metropolitan areas moves quantities of goods and services that inject
new blood into moribund urban economies (for example, if ARA catering is
a major force in the economy of Philadelphia, with its own skyscraper on the
eastern side of Market Street, it is because it handles the concessions at the
Wachovia Center (home of the Flyers and Sixers), Citizens Bank Park (home
of the Phillies) and Lincoln Financial Field (home of the Eagles)). Moreover,
the advertising revenues that football generates for the networks that broadcast
the sport are, undoubtedly, an important part of their bottom line at the end
of each fiscal year (everyone knows that the advertising time bought during
the Super Bowl is the most expensive in existence). If football is America's

sport, it is because it moves the most money, both in the colleges and in the pros, while it could be that the intensity of football's market activity may be in the process of threatening the diversity of the sport itself, for instance in the copyright and salary cap conflicts that have emerged between the owner of the Cowboys, Jerry Jones, and the NFL. It is quickly becoming clear that the best and most aggressive business organizations always win the Super Bowl: the Cowboys, Steelers, Forty-Niners, Redskins, Patriots, Giants, Packers, Broncos, Bears, Raiders, Rams, Ravens, and Colts are the only teams to have won the championship in the last twenty years, with more than half of these going to the first four teams on my list.

Aside from the economic aspects of the game, which are threatening to consume it entirely, football is perhaps the purest manifestation of the American spirit, as Hegel might have said if he had known about the NFL. What is the secret of its pleasure for those of us who are devoted to the sport, and how does it come to enthrall such an important part of our identities? The first response to these questions should underline the fact that football, like most sports, is decidedly a male-dominated activity, and those of us who dedicate a significant part of our time to thinking about football are men. If I may be allowed to sound like a sexist pig for a moment, the sports industry for men is what cosmetics, clothing, and shoes are for women, perhaps, though there is no real equivalent in the realm of women to the sheer *waste* of material and time constituted by sports in the masculine domain: after all, one has to dress, wear shoes, and take care of one's skin, while sports serve no personal utility whatsoever, the collective and political utility of sport being another matter. After recognizing the futility of sport and the stupidity of its domination of the male psyche, to which I myself am subject, I can move on to an analysis of the effects of men's subjection to football. In any large city that has an NFL franchise, there is also a talk radio station (WIP, 610am in Philadelphia, WFAN, 660am in New York) that is devoted mainly to a public discussion of the local teams, which is dominated by talk of football during the NFL's season. Absurdity of absurdities: literally thousands of men, and an occasional woman, call in to talk about strategies, players (everything from their private lives to the kinds of shoes they wear on the field), coaching decisions, trades, upcoming games, exhilarating victories and crushing defeats, heroes and goats, fantasy leagues, etc. Why are there so many men in so many cities who think that it is important for them to give their opinions publicly about such matters, in such bad English, and in such preposterous accents (I'm particularly fond of the thick Philly accents one hears on WIP)? What does it say about their conceptions of themselves as individual subjects, and how does football, among other sports, manage to produce this kind of subjectivity?

Let's look at the fan at the moment of his "capture" (as Lacan might have said) on a Sunday afternoon, sitting on the edge of his sofa in front of a bowl of Buffalo wings and a six pack of beer. Watching football is not a solitary activity. The typical fan would rather be in a bar in his home city, with a raucous partisan crowd, cheering and yelling the triumphs or tragedies of his beloved team, than in the silence of his own living room. Thus one of the primary elements of watching football is the social (male) bonding that it brings about. This is not to say that male or female bonding is necessarily a bad thing. While the term "male bonding" is inescapably pejorative, it remains true that the kind of companionship that men find in sports performs a vital social role: I, for one, would rather see this seemingly fundamental urge satisfied on the gridiron and in sports bars than in boot camp and on the battlefield, where men acted out this urge for millennia before the invention of the major team sports in the 19th century, and their mass dissemination after World War II. That singularly competitive people, the ancient Greeks, clearly saw the relationship between war and sports (see Plato's description of the education of the ideal state's guardians in *The Republic*), as did the fascist, national socialist, and communist dictators who did their best to ruin the 20th century. Like the member of a fascist youth group, or even of the United States Marines, the football spectator experiences a momentary *suspension* of his will in the collective will of thousands of fans, roaring with one massive voice after the home team scores a touchdown. People, especially if they are male, seem to need this kind of submission of their will to the greater desire of the group. In the late 1990's, the phenomenon that appeared in stadiums across the United States of fans who rooted for the Dallas Cowboys even against their own home team was, perhaps, a manifestation of this same process on an even more collective level. The Cowboys were called "America's team," which meant that the will or the desire of each individual for victory and for mastery was subsumed into a whole that transcended local boundaries to reach national proportions. In other words, the legions of fans who waved their silver and blue (the colors of the Cowboys) at home games in Jack Kent Cook Stadium (Redskins), The Meadowlands (Giants), and even Veterans Stadium (Eagles) were participating in a kind of fascistic unification of an imaginary collective will that is represented iconographically in the team's colors and uniforms. My heart of hearts, which bleeds Philadelphia Eagle Green, finds this kind of sportive fascism repulsive and downright insulting.

The second aspect of the football fan's capture by the game is perhaps more obvious—his self-identification with the impressive prowess and skill of the players, who become ideal versions of himself, of the physique, the speed, the strength, and the quickness that he would like to have, and that are indeed far-removed from where he sits on his couch, with his beer gut, his six pack of Bud, his bag of Cheez Doodles, and his extra-large pizza (see "Junk Food" above). Does this kind of identification call the individual football fan into being as a certain kind of subject? An affirmative answer to this question would be stretching it quite a bit; nevertheless, there is a sense in which the watching of football makes your run-of-the-mill fan feel as though he is, momentarily, fleetingly, in his own virtual reality in which he himself somehow participates in the phenomenal exploits of his athletic heroes. Your average football fan whines constantly about his team, is lazy, overweight, and even brutish at times (please understand me, guys—I'm just projecting all of my own worst characteristics onto my imaginary fan). Yet, in that moment when the wide receiver on his team runs a fade pattern against the fastest, loudest, most trash talking d-back in the league (remember Deon Sanders in his heyday?), and catches a touchdown over the d-back's outstretched fingers, and the fan butts heads, or high-fives, or bangs bellies with the guy on the couch next to him, you better believe that he is transported from his usual mundane existence of working 9 to 5, and suddenly, he becomes, for an instant, a tele-participant in the freak chance occurrence that often occurs in football, when intense practice and bodily discipline interact with good luck to become what is perhaps the ultimate American spectacle. The last, breathtaking Super Bowl before this book went to print, won in a dramatic fashion by the New York Giants in February of 2008 after several players made spectacular plays on the final drive, is a classic example of this phenomenon.

Then of course there is the strange sexual undercurrent to football that haunts the collective consciousness of these United States. Every high school kid in this country consciously or unconsciously dreams of being the star quarterback on the football team, which means that he ultimately dreams of being the desirable young hunk who fills the nascent fantasies of the cheerleaders doing jumps and flips over on the sideline while he is getting his ass kicked by bloodthirsty blitzing linebackers. In American popular iconography from the '40's and '50's, the head cheerleader and the star quarterback were the ideals of the young couple destined to be fruitful and multiply in this land of amber waves of grain—imagine Jimmy Stewart in a leather helmet and Donna Reed in her best wholesome poodle skirt, barely revealing a sexy ankle in its white sock. In general, that was the sense of this image, wholesomeness, the two models of youth and happiness joined together in a kind of proto-nationalist (if not proto-fascist) spirit that was supposed to be whipped into a frenzy at high school pep-rallies. You can imagine them a few years later, in their white house with its picket fence, their two babies, the football uniform and the cheerleading costume starched and stored in the attic, Jimmy going off to work at an insurance company, Donna making pie or jam. The undercurrent that has always haunted this image, however, and which was its real meaning, was the idea of hot sex under the bleachers, a kind of primal sexual energy that was being molded and channeled by sport and bodily discipline toward its proper end, i.e., the reproduction of the perfect, fecund American family. Think of the scene in *Animal House*, in which a fraternity brother seduces the head cheerleader, leading her to discover that there is more to sex than just giving her quarterback boyfriend a hand job with rubber gloves on in the back seat of their car. Or think of one of the crucial early scenes of *American Beauty*, in which Lester Burnham comes out of the sexual "coma" he has been in for a decade when he sees his daughter's friend, Angela Hayes, perform her cheerleading routine in the high school gymnasium. The ambiguity of the cheerleader-quarterback duo (wholesomeness combined with rampant sexuality) remains a constant of American culture to this day in the big football schools, from Ohio State to Penn State, from Florida to USC. I'll leave the interpretation of the muscular male cheerleaders who cavort and gavotte on the sidelines with the rather normal-looking girls in conventional uniforms who for some reason embody the sexual fantasies of millions of boys growing up in this country (except, perhaps, the boys who accompany them on the sidelines?). In the pros, however, the image completely loses its striking ambivalence, and what may be an interesting homosexual undertone that I've just encapsulated in my last sentence. The cheerleaders of the NFL are either too inept, ditsy, and clumsy, or too "sexy" (they're too buxom, their teeth are too white, they have too much hair, their legs are too long, etc.), and are choreographed into pathetic and unsynchronized perfection. These cheerleaders are like the fashion and exercise magazines they sell at convenience stores—dull, glossy representations of impossible bodies that are vaguely desirable, in a world of cellophane-wrapped toaster pastries and powdered donuts, in which all you care about is getting a hot cup of coffee before going to work. Unlike the cheerleaders in college, who embody a fundamental dimension of America's perception of itself, the pro league's cheerleaders are mild distractions from the real business on the field and in the stands, which lies beyond the drama of reproduction that plays itself out on America's campuses every Autumn, allegorized by college cheerleaders.

Camille Paglia, the controversial author of *Sexual Personae*, said once in a televised interview that football was controlled violence. While no doubt millions of football fans would agree with this claim at first glance, upon further reflection I'm sure that most of them would agree that football's essential fascination is more abstract and more *tactical*. For, football is the tactical game *par excellence*. What really matters to any football fanatic is to be mentally involved in the guessing game that goes on between the two coaches calling the offensive and defensive plays, and the greatest pleasure that the game affords is the astonishment of seeing the stroke of inspiration that is known as a "great call," which simply wins or loses a game. Let me give you an example, of which some of the details may be inaccurate. Philadelphia, Veterans Stadium, December, 1996 or so. The annual meeting of the Eagles and Cowboys on Philly's home turf. It's ten degrees out, but the wind chill factor is ten below. The Eagles have been pounding away at Troy Aikman, Dallas's fair weather quarterback, all day long. Nevertheless, because they are champions, the Cowboys are still winning the game by two points. They have the ball almost at mid field. It's fourth and a foot. They have the wind at their backs. Barry Switzer, the Cowboys' coach, decides to go for it. He calls a "load left." Emmitt Smith takes a handoff and heads left, into the desperate charge of the Eagles defense. He comes up short! The Eagles take over on downs! But wait a minute, something strange has happened. The ball was snapped before the ready signal was given. The Cowboys have another chance. What will the Cowboys do? Will they punt? Will they go for it again? If they go for it again, what will they do, fake the run and go for a short pass? Fake the run and go for a bomb to Michael Irvin? What defense will the Eagles play? The players come up to the line and . . . Emmitt Smith takes a handoff to the left side of the line and . . . he comes up short! The defensive coordinator on the Eagles had outguessed Barry Switzer by calling a run blitz to the left side of the Dallas line! He knew that Switzer was going to call the same play! The Eagles take over on downs, drive twenty yards down the field, and score the game winning field goal into the wind. The Cowboys, America's team, are crucified in the ensuing week in the press.

What matters to the true football fan is being there at that moment (even via the miracle of television), on the field, ten below zero, the game and the season depending on one play call, after all of the momentum has shifted back and forth from team to team, in the midst of a rivalry that has been going on for decades. Sportscasters like to speak of "history," and this is precisely what the fan wants, to be part of the unfolding of sports history towards its ultimately meaningless destiny. Nietzsche once wrote that man would rather have the void as his purpose than be void of purpose. Substitute "fan" for "man" in this sentence, and you get the idea of what pro football is all about. Any true fan knows the dread of the void that fills him while the Vince Lombardi trophy is being awarded after the Super Bowl. This means that he will have to live for seven months without football (which is perhaps why the NFL draft, in the month of April, has become such a huge media event, right in the middle of those seven months of enforced gridiron abstinence). This means that his Monday nights will be empty, that his Sundays will have to be devoted to more mundane tasks, like cutting the lawn or wallpapering the basement. This means that there are no more football pools and conversations about trades and draft choices. This means that he doesn't have the playoffs to look forward to for another year. While the season lasts, he is an active participant in the inevitable dialectical movement of his team's micro history toward its logical end, as Hegel might have said. During the rest of the year, he is just a normal guy who tries to get psyched about baseball and housework. If religion was the opium of the people for Karl Marx, since it blinded them to social injustices by making them believe that they were involved in a more ideal destiny than the mundane one of paychecks, overtime, and workman's comp., then football has become the heroin of the average working male in the

United States. At least religion offers you the prospect of paradise, one version of which for true football fans like me would be an eternal Monday night at the beginning of the season in September, with a steak on the grill and a cold beer in the fridge, with the Eagles and the Cowboys coming on at nine o'clock live from the Linc in South Philly.

Prince, Madonna, Springsteen, and Michael Jackson

Here's a bit of pop-music history: as I first wrote these lines, on the threshold of 1997, the four giants of the music industry of the 1980's whose names appear above had seemingly been completely eclipsed by younger stars. The pseudo doo-wop music of Boyz-II-men replaced the post-disco party-time music of the almighty Michael Jackson, whose monumental *History* collection languished in record stores, while the four boyz from Philly had a string of syrupy number one hits. Madonna's sort of sexy dance music was overshadowed by the trills and thrills of Mariah Carey, or by anorexic, post-Sinead Irish girls like the singer of the Cranberries, or by the ubiquitous grunge chic, yodeling, or downright screaming of Alanis Morrissette, or, surprise surprise, by the pseudo Joni Mitchell of the late '90's, Jewel. [Here's a micro update for the intervening ten years. In 2000-2001, Cristina Aguilera, Britney Spears, the Backstreet Boys, 'N Sync, and a bunch of other boy and girl bands blew everyone else out of the water. In 2007-2008, the music video is literally dead; music stores like Tower Records have closed their doors; songs are sold mostly in MP3 formats over the internet via I-Tunes; and the only famous singers these days are survivors of and participants on the *American Idol* television program, or stars of teen programs on the Disney Channel like *Hannah Montana*.] He who was formerly known as Prince, the inventor and king of Minneapolis funk, has not really been replaced, since funk seems to be, at least for the moment, a dying language as far as the public is concerned, unless we count Britain's Jamiroquai, who was able to reactivate and cannibalize funk for a while. While rap stars like Coolio and Snoop Dogg seemed at that moment to be the heirs of (the now late) James Brown, their music never attained the levels of mass-hysterical popularity that was associated with the four artists in the title of this chapter. Finally, the Boss seemed to be dead, despite his gorgeous "Streets of Philadelphia," which won him an Oscar, and which the Honorable Edward G. Rendell, the former mayor of Philadelphia, should have bought from Springsteen in order to promote my home town. The genre of the sort of working class dude from Jersey who plays the guitar despite the disdain of his girlfriend's parents ("I know your mom don't like me, 'cause I'm playing in a rock n' roll band . . .") is dead and buried, after the angst of Kurt Cobain and Pearl Jam and the endless string of other bands from Seattle. One of the most interesting phenomena of trash culture for those of us who lived through one of its culminating moments in the 1980's is the sudden demise of its gods, who have now become mere historical artifacts, instead of forces to be observed on MTV and VH1, two channels that have not shown music videos for years. I don't mean to say that Springsteen, Madonna, Prince, and MJ aren't popular any more, especially Madonna, after her Ray-of-Light stage, her Geisha/Indeterminate Arabian woman phase, and her Kabbala-inspired, mother of two children in British boarding schools, kids-book writing phase (on a "Famous Friends" program on the "E!" network, viewers were informed that Madonna "did fun Kabbala things" with her friend Gwyneth Paltrow; for the life of me, I can't imagine what a "fun Kabbala thing" might be); rather, I mean that the time when anything they did sold multiple millions of records and filled stadiums all over the world has long since passed, and can be understood only as an historical curiosity. The hysteria that they generated during the Reagan years is now looked upon with nostalgia, it is no longer lived and felt by mass populations, much in the same way that the hysteria for Fabian and Franky Avalon in the '50's became incomprehensible with the arrival of the Beatles and Jim Morrison. For kids weaned on Nirvana, Public Enemy, the Beastie Boys, Rage Against the Machine, Eminem, Limp Bizkit, the Strokes, and the Killers, Michael Jackson and the Boss make no sense. Once a phenomenon of trash culture loses its hold on the masses, it becomes a mere footnote to the footnotes of a history that no one will ever read or write. Already, rewriting and revising this bit of pop music history in 2007-2008, ten years after I began it, seems like an attempt to write a history of incomprehensible events from a foreign culture, which look like those endless fundraising programs that they now show on PBS, on which very old, overweight, overly-dyed singers from the 1950's and 1960's are stuffed into tight gold suits and propped up in front of microphones, where they sing before geriatric audiences struggling to dance in Las Vegas, Branson, or at the New Jersey State Fair.

In general, the "historicization" of trash culture—there was once a "History of Disco" documentary aired on VH1, which also regularly showed "classic" episodes of American Bandstand, not to mention the immediate historicization of pop culture in programs such as "I love the '80's" or "I love the '90's"—is a trend that the mass media are imposing on the youth of our nation. In the case of "reality television," the present is already looked at as if it were in the past, since every moment is narrativized from the point of view of a second, parallel present that is actually the future in relation to the given moment that is being presented. A phenomenon of trash culture that becomes an historical monument can potentially live a second life in the minds of the masses, as in the spectacular comeback of one of the ultimate '70's icons, John Travolta, or the '50's nostalgia (*Happy Days, American Graffiti, Laverne and Shirley, Grease*) that ruled television in the '70's themselves. The VH1 histories of the '70's would have one believe that absolutely everyone alive at the time was enthralled by the image of Tony Manero lighting up the dance floor, and by the idea of waiting in line to get into Studio 54, which is far from the truth. For every disco-dancing fool at the time, there were eight or nine rockers who were nostalgic for the Beatles, Three Dog Night, Creedence Clearwater Revival, and the Doors, and who believed that disco was the absolute proof that American culture had finally fallen into a bottomless pit of shit from which it could never be extracted. Those who weren't nostalgic were completely immersed in bands like Kiss, Black Sabbath, Ted Nugent, Lynyrd Skynyrd, Blue Oyster Cult, and the inevitable Led Zep. In the mind of the nostalgic citizen of the '90's and early '00's, however, none of this diversity existed in the '70's. Everyone spent hours in front of the mirror, adjusting gold chains and blow drying mounds of fluffy hair, getting ready to go to the disco. The truth of the matter was, however, that the most popular discos of the time, such as the Ripley Dance Hall on South Street in Philly (replaced by a Tower Records store in the late 1980's, which closed in 2007—the pace of pop music's evolution seems to be accelerating), were essentially nostalgia places where people went to party to '50's and '60's dance tunes, mostly from Motown. But then again, nostalgia might be defined as a manifestation of people's longing for social unity, which they imagine to have existed in the past, but which is absolutely lost in the present. The '70's were a horrific time to live in America's big cities, full of racism and poverty, and with downtowns that emptied out after the end of the business day. But nostalgia doesn't understand anything about *real* history, and the person who is nostalgic for the '70's somehow sees only the dance scenes in *Saturday Night Fever*, without remembering the grim violence and despair portrayed throughout the film.

So now Springsteen, Michael Jackson, Madonna, and Prince are in the process of becoming living historical artifacts, instead of the pop-culture phenomena they once were. Looking at their videos from the '80's, it is hard for us to imagine how they could have provoked so much excitement among millions of spectators. In the not too distant future, very few people will know who Prince, Michael Jackson, Springsteen, and Madonna were, let alone how they influenced the ways in which we listen to music. In order for cultural phenomena of this type to be experienced as such, they have to be studied, whereas the importance of a real historical event like the Battle of Hastings in 1066 is lived by every single speaker of English on the planet in a direct and visceral way. In contrast, people born in the 21st century will have to study their music history carefully in order to understand why Elvis caused fainting and heart palpitations, and why Madonna was hailed even by serious scholars as a revolutionary figure in the efflorescence of a certain kind of "feminist" values.

The impact of these four giants of pop culture lies then in the fact that their early productions were witnessed by an enormous public as pseudo-historical *events*, after which pop music could never be the same again. In the realm of trash culture, this need to live something that can be qualified as "historic" is a common characteristic: whole cities, like Las Vegas, have been built so that "tourists" and "consumers" can have simulated historical experiences that are repeated continuously, which perhaps explains why there are so many impersonators of all kinds in "entertainment capitals" of this type. I remember quite well the moment when Michael Jackson became the pop icon, during the live broadcast of Motown's 25th anniversary concert, in 1983, shortly after the release of *Thriller*. Nothing prepared the audience of that Motown special for what was going to happen. Suddenly, the shy young man and erstwhile kids' cartoon character was transformed into the aggressive, crotch-grabbing dancing machine who would dominate the radio waves of the 1980's. After having sung his hits from his days as the lead singer of the Jackson Five, MJ grabbed the microphone, and said to the audience: "Yeah, those were the old songs, and you know, I like the old songs. But what I really like are the new songs." While he was speaking these words, the opening drum track of "Billie Jean" kicked in exactly on cue, and MJ began thrusting his hips and spinning and tapping his heel in his characteristic manner. When he moon walked backwards across the stage near the end of the song, the house erupted, and the TV viewer had the impression that the lines between the old and the new eras of pop music had been clearly demarcated, since no one had ever seen or heard anything like what MJ had just performed with such ease (watch the dance scenes from *Saturday Night Fever* on YouTube, or reruns of *American Bandstand* from the late '70's if you want to see what pop dancing was like before Michael became a mega star). Viewers had the feeling that they had just lived through a moment of history that would be remembered for years, and so millions of them bought *Thriller* as soon as they could, as a kind of memorial to the mediated (in the philosophical sense) version of history through which they had just lived. MJ himself seems to have been aware of his own status as the personification of an historical event when, in 1997, his compilation of greatest hits was entitled *History*, on the cover of which he appeared in the shape of a kind of Stalinesque statue.

Grasping the effect that Madonna had on the public consciousness is much more difficult and risky. Of her first hits, "Like a Virgin" was the song, accompanied by the images of the video, that engraved her in the world's consciousness. It was undoubtedly a shock that a young white woman could sing openly about the fact that she was "sexually active." Black women had already been doing so for decades, most notably the Queen of disco, Donna Summer, but then in the racist popular consciousness of white America, blackness already signified a kind of dangerous sex: thus when a poor little white boy from Mississippi started singing more or less black sounding songs—a quick listen to Big Mama's version of "Hound Dog" will give you an idea of the difference between the real thing and Elvis's version of it—he signaled the existence of a literal Dark Continent of eroticism for a white public stifled by Eisenhower, McCarthy, *Father Knows Best*, and *The Donna Reed Show*. Remember that Elvis's dangerously swiveling hips, the signifiers of his eroticism, were never shown even in black and white on *The Ed Sullivan Show*. Madonna was not simply following this same path, since her music never was written or sung in an African-American idiom. She never had the voice to sing black music in the way that Mariah Carey and Cristina Aguilera do. Madonna barely has any range at all, and has never been much of a singer. Instead, at the start of her career, she was about projecting a certain kind of image that is best expressed in "Like a Virgin," that of a strong, independent young woman who knows what sex is, who has a certain character and experience of the world, and yet who knows how to return to that state of innocent enjoyment of the first time she made love. The song places its male listeners in a flattering position to which they are particularly susceptible: its female voice says, "you, my lover, make me feel as though sex is something completely new and wonderful." The overriding implication of the song, however, is what Madonna's voice perhaps communicated to its female listeners: "but we all know that I've had sex lots of times before, and I can feel this way whenever I want to." "You make me feel shiny and new," as the song says, implies that "I'm not shiny and new at all." The song thus beguiled its listeners into believing that they were hearing exactly what they wanted to hear: male listeners were told that they would always be the ones who gave women their first ecstatic experience of sex; female listeners were told that they would always be like virgins, no matter how much sex they had.

Unlike Michael Jackson, who was a surprisingly asexual being (no matter how much he tugged at his crotch), Madonna always consciously and deliberately tried to project the image of a sensual and desirable woman, which she continues to do on the verge of reaching the age of fifty. Her remarkable talent for remaking herself for different periods goes far beyond anything the other three singers on my list have been able to imagine. Madonna now sells her music only via the internet; her songs are written and produced by young, trendy musicians and DJs, as they have always been. Of the four musicians in my title, she is the one who has most consciously been able to follow the unfolding of popular music as an historical phenomenon, and to package herself as a kind of experience of historical change that is a commodity for sale. As an artist who self-consciously projects herself as a product that exists only within polymorphous media images, she is simply unsurpassed (watch her video for "Jump," seemingly inspired by Wong Kar Wai, on her website, and you'll see what I mean). Unlike the late

Elvis, who was completely engulfed and obliterated by the identity he was forced to inhabit, Madonna has somehow managed simply to *be* the multiplicity of images she has projected into the public domain over the course of the last thirty years, which is no small feat, and which has enabled her to become an extremely wealthy woman who now lives in England, in a castle somewhere, from which she sends her children to proper boarding schools. In her latest incarnation in 2008, Madonna's last CD, "Hard Candy," was for sale in the checkout line of the Whole Foods supermarket chain, as well as on her quite impressive website.

Undoubtedly the most enigmatic of these four is (once "the artist formerly known as") Prince. His case is probably the clearest illustration of the general principle that what sells in commercial pop music is not so much the music itself, as it is the idea that the music represents. Since the inception of music videos in the '80's, this idea has become increasingly linked to images. At the height of his career, Prince was perhaps the most masterful manipulator of this complex of image, sound, and "concept," shall we say, for lack of a better term (philosophers would be furious at the idea that the conglomerate of things with which the viewer is bombarded by a Prince video constitutes a concept—nevertheless, the notion of "high concept," which was in vogue in the '80's, is appropriate here). At that time, he seemed to conceive of each song as it would have to be presented in concert. When Prince performed "I Wish U Heaven" live in Philadelphia in 1988, for example, it seemed as though every one of his gestures, along with the lighting and the development of the song, had been conceived at the same time, as part of a highly artificial, yet "organic" whole. While listening to the song thereafter, I remembered Prince's purple hat, how he wore it tilted to one side in the heavy spotlight, doing a sort of heel-toe movement in time to the opening guitar riffs of the song. All of this rendered the rather banal tune much more intriguing. At first, Prince's message seemed somewhat revolutionary. When he first appeared at the end of the '70's, he was surrounded by an enormous amount of hype. Magazines like *Rolling Stone* said that he could play the guitar like Hendrix, dance like Michael Jackson, sing as soulfully as Marvin Gaye, and so on. Of course, the main issue was his sexuality—was he bi? When he appeared on early album covers half naked or lying in bed with some kind of wool stockings on and his legs in the air, with an unequivocal orgasmic look on his face, people apparently felt intrigued enough to buy his records. Unfortunately, all of this sexual packaging has always enveloped and obscured the immense musical talent of the man from Minneapolis, which is not what interests those who buy his records, after all. I would theorize that, aside from simply liking his songs, which would be the reason that Occam's razor would dictate to us, the people who buy Prince's music are actually buying a little piece of sexual transgression as a commodity, which is extremely ironic. Michel Foucault remarked long ago in his famous history of the subject that sexuality is a focal point at which the disembodied power of the bourgeoisie seeks to control individuals by producing them as sexual subjects who believe, moreover, that their freedom and liberation depend upon their ability to speak openly and endlessly about their sexual lives. Paradoxically, from this perspective, individuals who "confess" about their sexual being (whatever that may be) are being exercised and in fact enslaved by that power. All of my friends and I as we docilely rode a packed subway in 1988 to a massive arena where Prince sang naughty little songs about sex might have served as the poster children for the success of power's hold on us.

The spectators with whom I rode the subway that night seemed intent upon expressing the ambiguity and coolness of their personalities. In general, people who go to pop concerts want to participate in the event that somehow summarizes, uplifts, glorifies, or "iconizes" their own image of what coolness should be, which is why they buy tee-shirts that commemorate the occasion. For almost everyone in the Western world, pop music is intensely personal, even though it necessarily must reach the masses in order to survive, which is why people who write pop songs feel as though they are failures if they are unable to "sell" their work. Everyone who listens to the radio, buys CDs, or downloads MP3s to their I-Pod thinks that he or she has the right and even the obligation to criticize music, and that his or her opinions are perfectly valid and accurate. When it comes to pop music, in other words, everyone is an expert, in the same way that everyone is an expert when it comes to movies, as Walter Benjamin remarked so long ago. The reason for this is that people define themselves today largely by the kinds of products they consume, music being one of the most important in this definition of individual identity, at least for young people. Later in life, this consumption as a factor in one's identity is displaced to the domain of expensive home appliances, decorations, and automobiles. I once had the good fortune to be invited to a sculpture exhibition at the private home of some wealthy collectors near Devon, PA. Everything in the house and on its impressive grounds, from the custom-made cabinetry, to the Sub-Zero appliances, to the art installations in the garden, to the male owner's Andy Warhol haircut, to the female owner's black jumpsuit and Karl Lagerfeld sunglasses, was meant to signify something about the identity of wealth and good taste that they wanted to project. In this sense, even if the people who buy Prince's or Madonna's or Michael Jackson's music don't necessarily want literally to become one of these singers, they still "invest" a part of their identity in the kind of music that they literally own. This means, then, that in our age, in the realm of trash culture, identity is a product that one can buy, try on, wear for a while, and eventually throw away or recycle.

Finally, the Boss, Bruce Springsteen, despite all of his talent, and all of the lovely songs he has written, is the most banal of all of the '80's superstars. Mr. Born in the USA is precisely that, a butter and egg man, the auto mechanic turned teen idol, the high school drop-out who became the hero of the local bar or nightclub, the white guy who wrote (some very good) songs about white guy problems, who was acclaimed by a public of white guys and gals who more than likely knew nothing about Bob Dylan and protest songs and the entire '60's tradition on which Springsteen cut his teeth. The early Springsteen of the rock anthems provided a means for masses of disenfranchised young folks to scream "Tramps like us, baby we were born to run!" along with a really simple guitar lick, much like the "Born to be wild!" or the "We want the world and we want it now!" anthems of the '60's. Springsteen's message was simple, and embodied the despair and the vain pride of millions of working class people in the post-industrial East and Midwest: "we're poor, we don't have nothing, and we have no way of getting out of this hell hole, but we rule anyway." And like the bread and circuses that made the masses of ancient Rome happy, these masses were kept happy as long as they could spare a couple of bucks to buy the latest blue-collar, white-guy, rock anthem record. The pop music industry got rich by glorifying this image of the worker as someone who made the fact that he was trapped in a dead end life the basis of his pride and his identity. Consider, for example, the following verses from Springsteen's "The River": "Then I got Mary pregnant,/ and man that was all she wrote./ And for my nineteenth birthday/ I got a union card and a wedding coat./ We went down to the courthouse,/ and the judge put it all to rest./ No wedding day smiles, no walk down the aisle/ No flowers, no wedding bells." Need I say more?

Postscript from 2005: As I write these lines shortly before the summer solstice, MJ has just been declared innocent of the multiple charges against him, of which he is surely guilty: child molestation, lewd and lascivious behavior, depravity, reckless endangerment, etc. The trial took fourteen weeks, and was covered extensively by the major cable news networks, with pseudo experts examining the minutiae of the case every evening: possible verdicts, possible arguments, inconsistencies in testimony, the significance of the trial's venue, Michael's real or imagined state of health, etc. The talented boy who was deprived of his childhood by a tyrannical and abusive father, and who, by the age of ten, gave us some of the best and purest vocal performances ever heard in pop music (his articulation, rhythm, and pitch on songs like "Never Can Say Goodbye," for example, are nearly perfect), has been completely obliterated by a sickly monster with a pathological penchant for sleeping with children. Like Elvis before him, MJ has been effaced and replaced by a specular, media-generated identity whose multiple facets are continually morphing in unexpected directions. The techniques of visual manipulation that produced his image have completely overwhelmed their material support, i.e., his body, to such an extent that MJ is now a kind of cyborg whose physical being has been replaced by an abstract digital image. Science fiction created this kind of being long ago, but the actual execution of the idea on a real body is much stranger that its fictional model. Darth Vader, whose story in film is on the verge of generating a billion dollars in revenue world wide, was encased in a robot body which, nevertheless, did not impede him from exploiting the mysterious spiritual powers of the "dark side of the Force." As a kind of real life Darth Vader, MJ is kept breathing, moving, and singing by a corporate media machine that is continually adding new "parts" to his abstract and polyhedral body. This spectral body is also now a collective and historical entity, composed essentially of visual and media stories: along with all of the morphing images that stretch from his Motown audition tape to his latest videos, there is the image of him entering and leaving the courtroom with his umbrella and his escort, the parade of body guards and ex-wives arriving to testify, etc. Darth Vader's cybernetic body suit may never be a reality. We are all, however, at least potentially in danger of being superseded and replaced by the images of ourselves that mutate in cyberspace and in the media. "Identity theft" is one of the phantasmal fears on the basis of which cable news proliferates, like the extra-terrestrial entity that fed on human anger in a famous episode of the original *Star Trek* series. As soon as "identity" is construed in terms of credit profiles, transcripts, psychological dossiers, credit card numbers, bank accounts, and the like, its being as an intrinsic, individual essence has already long been superseded by something else. Michael Jackson should serve as the patron saint of what identity and subjectivity may have already become in the age of mutating viruses, both real and virtual, enforced nostalgia, spyware, blogs, sound bites, school shootings, botox, and Manolo Blahnik shoes. By the way, shortly after the end of his trial, MJ moved to Dubai, where he was caught on film (better yet, in binary code) by several paparazzi while he was on a shopping spree disguised as an Arab woman in his/her burkha.

Post-postscript from 2007: at the famous Montreux Jazz Festival in Switzerland in the Summer of this year, Prince, who had been invited by the organizer of the festival, flew in on his private jet and gave a three-hour concert for which the tickets had cost as much as 600 euros. According to the review of the concert that I read in the Spanish newspaper *El Pais*, the kid from Minneapolis blew everyone away with his musicianship. Prince might serve here as a counterexample to poor Michael Jackson: while the latter has been completely overcome by his media identity, the former may finally be freeing himself from his alter ego, which went through some rather bizarre stages that interfered with his genuine musical talents. Could it be that, in the first decade of this new century, pop music has finally come full circle, and musicians can finally be admired and listened to simply because they are good musicians, in the way that Miles Davis and John Coltrane were? One can only hope . . .

Cap'n Crunch: Advertising for Kids

Nothing is more typical of American culture than breakfast cereals. Whether or not the enormous aisles of cereals in our supermarkets are the product of, say, an Irish or English love of oatmeal and porridge, or the Germanic practice of eating muesli in the morning (recently re-imported into the States) is irrelevant—we have developed our own idea of breakfast that has nothing to do with the simple act of pouring oats or wheat into a bowl. The most important part of a breakfast cereal in America is, without a doubt, the package in which it is sold. In one of my earliest memories, I'm sitting at the breakfast table, four or five years old, my legs dangling from the chair, with the top of the table level with the top of my chest. I'm eating a bowl of Cheerios with tons of sugar, but I'm also surrounded by the other boxes of cereal that we have, which are also on the table for some reason. At this point, the memory becomes somewhat fuzzy, since I can't remember if I was reading the things on the backs and sides of the boxes, or if I was just looking at the pictures papering the walls of the little cereal-box house that I had built surrounding my bowl. As we have learned recently, memory is notoriously unreliable, and people can be made to believe that they remember events in which they never took part. Memory tends to compress multiple phenomena into composite images in the same way that dreams do. That's the point of the memory I'm describing—it is an amalgamation of one of the rituals of my childhood, which I'm sure is performed by millions of kids all across the U.S. For the most part, the first thing that enters an American child's mind when he or she wakes up in the morning is the series of messages that Kellogg's, General Mills, Post, Nabisco, and Quaker Oats use to promote and to sell their products. Since childhood is a period when the mind incorporates images and concepts that will leave an indelible mark on the adult who emerges from it, the pictures and drawings that appear on packages of breakfast cereals must have an impact on our collective national psyche that is considerable, if incalculable. The same could be said for the ads on television that are directed exclusively at children.

Advertising for kids has changed drastically in the last thirty years with the advent of video technology, the music video, computer animation, and the internet, which have profoundly changed our conception of the imaginary space in which ads appear. If you don't believe me, watch the commercials some time during the Disney afternoon, or during any after-school cartoon session of this kind. The space that television advertisers imagine for kids is one that is completely strange and alien for adults, who in fact are quite often referred to as aliens in such ads. In a commercial for Kellogg's Frosted Mini-Wheats, for example, a boy tells his neighbor, an elderly woman who believes that he likes the cereal because it is *good* for him (yuck!), that she should "beam back up to the mother ship." In this somewhat fantastical space, gravity and time seem to be out of joint. The normal laws of physics do not apply to kids who bounce off of clouds of cotton candy or eat their way through endless strips of fruit roll-ups that stretch from coast to coast. In order to accomplish this effect, the advertisers use the techniques that were developed in music videos and later in computer animation and video games: incessant editing and cuts, hand-held camera movement, insane angles, swings, and zooms, brightly-colored backgrounds that create their own reality. This essentially new and "virtual" sense of space is reflected on the backs and sides of the cereal boxes that adults buy for their kids these days. In essence, this type of space signifies "childhood," which in the post-Freudian, post-Proustian world is not seen as a mere span of time in a person's life, but more as a separate entity unto itself, to which one can never return, and in which one has more and more special privileges: the right to dream and to space out; the right to be silly and irresponsible; the right to have fun and to play (adult men who obsess about sports are merely trying to prolong this right into their mature years); the right to eat junk food and candy, etc. In a sense, childhood is increasingly bracketed off from the exigencies of adult life, and one assumes that there is a mythical/primitive moment in everyone's existence that constitutes a "right of passage" from the time of irresponsibility to the time of total responsibility. This division becomes extraordinarily dangerous when children are incapable of distinguishing between the adult world and their own: a few years ago, two boys, aged 11 and 13, stole some high-powered rifles from their parents and grandparents, went into the woods outside of their school in Jonesboro, Arkansas, and opened fire on the schoolmates they didn't like. Not long after that, two slightly older students in Colorado killed a dozen of their classmates and teachers before killing themselves, acting out one of the scenarios of the latest video games, in which the player is given an unlimited supply of weapons and ammunition, and is charged with killing everyone in sight, a scene which also famously dominates the first installment of the *Matrix* trilogy. One assumes that in childhood the consequences of one's acts do not take effect immediately, or simply that almost any act may be excused before the non-existent passage into adulthood, or even, in video games, that one's character or "guy" just "dies," and one gets two or three more chances with two or three other guys.

The difference between these two stages of life has its parallel in different kinds of breakfast cereal. I'm thinking of the sales motto of a popular type of cereal: "Silly rabbit, Trix are for kids," meaning that the rabbit who appears on the cereal box, who desires the cereal that he represents, does not have the right to penetrate into the forbidden realm of childhood. The "silly rabbit" of the Trix ad raises an interesting point. The magical breakfast cereal world is populated by anthropomorphic animals, such as Tony the Tiger (who loves Frosted Flakes), the cuckoo bird who is "cuckoo for Cocoa Puffs," etc. Of course, there is nothing new about this phenomenon. The world of the fable and the fairy tale has been full of talking animals at least since the time of Aesop. It wasn't until the late 19th Century, however, after childhood was partitioned off from the rest of life, that this type of story was exiled to the realm of "children's literature." When La Fontaine wrote his elegant and stylized *Fables* in the 17th Century, the audience he had in mind was not at all an infantile one; rather, his alexandrines were destined for the amusement of his fellow members of Louis XIV's court. Similarly, the image of a mother reading fairy tales to her child as he or she falls asleep is one that would undoubtedly be foreign to most of the human beings who lived before the 19th Century. As proof of this assertion, consider the following passage from the memoirs of the Maréchal de Fleuranges, a French nobleman who lived in the 16th Century, and who referred to himself throughout his text as "the Young Adventurer":

> The story goes that the Young Adventurer, when he was eight or nine years old, in the house of M. de Sedan, his father, who had just come back from the war that he had fought against the Duke of Lorraine, this Young Adventurer, seeing himself old enough to ride a little horse, and since he had already read some books about knights errant from the old days, and having heard tell of the adventures that had come to pass, he decided to go out into the world and to go to the court of the King of France, Louis XII, who was the greatest prince in Christendom . . . (*Mémoires* 4, my translation)

Since literacy was extremely limited in European society at this time, it is doubtful that peasant mothers read fairy tales to their children before they fell asleep. The important point here is that childhood as we know it, and as it is represented on cereal boxes, did not exist before Rousseau, Freud, and Proust. In the passage that I have just quoted, it is clear that the Maréchal de Fleuranges is mistaken about the age at which he went off to the court of the King in order to learn the arts of war, which was the standard procedure for noblemen at the time. What is important here is that childhood was formerly a time either of serious preparation for adult life, or of brutal and exploitative labor, as it was until the 20th century in the US, during which individuals were perhaps more responsible for proving their worth than they would be later on. There were no fuzzy animals, no fables with talking rabbits for kids, no recess and nap time, no Cocoa Puffs and Trix. As the Maréchal points out, stories were told to children in order to indoctrinate them into a dominant, belligerent ideology that supported a burgeoning system of nationalism, which would be the plague of Europe until the end of the Second World War, and which dogs it to this day (the recent events in the Balkans and in Kosovo illustrate all too well that nationalism is far from being dead).

One possible conclusion that one might derive from these meditations is that the cereal box version of childhood is also meant to indoctrinate children in the ideology that makes this country run. It is at this point that I run into the theoretical brick wall that the conjunction of the following two images builds in front of me: two boys walking into the Arkansas woods in camouflage, carrying high-powered hunting rifles; "Silly rabbit, Trix are for kids." What could these two incompatible things possibly have in common? As analysts have pointed out on the news, it is clear that *the* rural activity in these United States is hunting, and that the standard image of rural America is a pickup truck with a gun rack and an NRA bumper sticker (late one November, when the brakes locked up on my guests' rental car and we got stuck in the snow on the side of a Vermont country road, a man in a red flannel shirt and a Ford F-150 pickup, with his rifle in the window and his NRA affiliation proudly displayed, stopped to pull us out of the embankment, using a chain that he kept in the back of the truck for just such occasions). It is evident, then, that those two boys from Arkansas entered a conceptual time warp, so to speak, when they opened fire from their position in the woods. They were doing what they saw their parents doing, but they also undoubtedly imagined themselves as the action figures from the Doom video game, or from the countless kill-or-be-killed games for Sega, Nintendo, Play Station, and X-Box. Moreover, they probably were acting in agreement with the basic rule that childhood is a time of infinite possibilities and minimal responsibilities, in which animals talk and fly and eat Fruit Loops, and in which you can kill as many guys as you want because, when you hit the reset button, they'll all come back to life anyway, and so will you. A gigantic issue that I haven't addressed here, because of its potentially generation-shattering implications, is the influence of over-medication on today's children in the United States. The two kids who walked into Columbine High School in Colorado to gun down their classmates had both been taking anti-depression drugs for years. The lethal combination of an ideological suspension of cause, effect, and responsibility in childhood, coupled with young brains distorted and clouded by (perhaps unnecessary) drugs, and easy access to deadly weapons, resulted in a scene of horror that no one should have to witness. Could the special and unprecedented status conferred on childhood in the age of trash culture have something to do with this kind of tragedy? We should perhaps consider this question when we stuff our kids with sugar and images of cereal-eating cartoon animals every morning.

The World Wide Wrestling Federation

Wrestling is one of the most ancient and respectable of sports, especially in the Mediterranean world in which our culture was born. It was one of the original Olympic sports, and if I'm not mistaken, one of the founding fathers of the Western world, Plato himself, was nothing more than a frustrated wrestler or boxer who turned to philosophical contemplation because his body simply was not up to the task of professional competition. Greco-Roman wrestlers are extraordinary athletes who endure a rigorous training routine for very meager rewards, since there are no sport shoe companies offering multi-million dollar contracts even to wrestlers who have won gold medals at the Olympics.

In contrast to this most honorable sport, we in the United States are blessed with the spectacle of what used to be the WWWF (World Wide Wrestling Federation), but is now WWE (World Wrestling Entertainment). There is even something hypnotic about the initials that stand for this most popular and bizarre of spectacles: the two or three W's don't roll off the tongue very easily, and the "double-u double-u double-u" of their pronunciation sounds like a kind of mantra. As for the letters themselves, when you see them written above the ring, the tangle of the W's suggests movement, confusion, even a kind of subliminal message of absolute virility (what is a W but two V's stuck together, V standing for "Virility"?) After all, what is this kind of "wrestlemania" about but virility taken to its ultimate, most vulgar, and most absurd extreme? The striking thing about this display of machismo is that, until ten years ago or so, it was completely devoid of sexual content or connotations (the Glamorous Ladies of Wrestling have changed this state of affairs). Rather, the end of this type of spectacle was to exhibit mutated versions of the characteristics that define male bodies, without necessarily investigating the consequences of this exhibition for breeding; in contrast, we know that in the animal kingdom the goal of these types of display is to ensure that the largest or most powerful male passes on his genes to the next generation. The average wrestler appears to be (and probably is) completely pumped up on steroids, and outweighs an average American man, who is usually on the large side, by at least forty to fifty pounds. He wears absurd tights that accentuate his hypertrophied muscles and the real or fictitious size of his genitals. If the wrestler does not display these characteristics of maleness, he must be physically exceptional in some way: one of the greatest of WWWF wrestlers was a fellow by the name of Andre the Giant, a gentle Frenchman who was seven feet tall and weighed over 350 pounds, even though he was not at all muscular, unlike that phenomenon from another sport who was the same size, Shaquille O'Neal. Another one of my favorite wrestlers when I was a child was an enormous fat man by the name of Haystacks Calhoun, who always brought his 400 pound frame into the ring dressed in overalls and a plaid shirt, as if the local country giant had simply stepped off the street and into the arena to test his luck. These male or mutated qualities are usually accompanied by a great deal of posturing and a certain tone of defiance, which the wrestlers scream at each other with raspy voices that explode from their throats, in which the blood vessels themselves seem about to burst. The idea of this spectacle is, essentially, that so much male energy cannot be contained within the body that serves as the medium of its transmission to a public that is rabidly awaiting its release.

If the wrestler is neither a giant nor a muscle-bound maniac, he must have some kind of story that accompanies his performance in the ring. Another wrestler whom I remember very well was a pseudo-Indian by the name of Chief Jay Strongbow, whom, incidentally, I once saw in civilian clothes, eating a cheesesteak at Pat's Steaks in South Philadelphia. He seemed to be a rather normal-looking man huddled over his steak and his cheese fries. In his heyday, however, the Chief would arrive at the ring dressed in a full Mohawk head-dress, complete with war paint and a skin or leather skirt. This is one of the keys to understanding wrestling, as banal as it is: *anybody* can become a wrestler, body slamming, jumping off the ropes, and applying the choke hold, as long as he or she follows the correct narrative protocols and displays the correct codes. There comes a point in every match when the wrestler identified as the good guy—because there are always good and bad guys in every match, as Barthes remarked so long ago in *Mythologies*—can no longer stand the injustices of the bad guy. You know what I mean by injustices: the choke hold applied when the ref isn't looking, illegal pokes in the eyes, "foreign objects" pulled out of tights and scraped across the face, kicking the guy when he falls out of the ring, the old trick when the manager (or animator, or charlatan, or alter ego) of the bad wrestler breaks a breakable chair over the back of the good wrestler, etc. etc. When Chief Jay Strongbow, who was a good guy (he used to do tag-team matches with Andre the Giant, also a good guy, despite his monstrous appearance), reached his threshold of tolerance for injustice, he would do a war dance around the ring, throwing the crowd into a frenzy, and eliciting looks of dread from the other wrestler. Chief Jay would circle around his evil opponent, or start bouncing off the ropes from side to side of the ring, eventually catching his nemesis with a forearm across the Adam's apple, with a predictable reaction from the crowd. The bad wrestler would start crawling around the ring, gesticulating as if he were choking, and Strongbow would kick him in the chest a few times, body slam him, and cover him, and the ref would slap the canvas three times to signal the Chief's victory. You can rewrite this same scenario a thousand times with different names and characters, and you will have described 99 percent of WWWF, WWE, nWo (New World Order), or WCW (World Championship Wrestling) matches, give or take a few elements that have been added during the last twenty years for the sake of putting on a better show: strobe lights, entry stages, smoke machines, big screen replays, music, costumes, women wrestlers and animators with enormous muscles and breasts, etc.

One of the curious elements of wrestling is its treatment of identity. Even when you can see their faces, wrestlers are usually characters who have pseudo-fictional names, especially the bad guys. For example, I once saw a wrestler named "Saturday Night Fever," who entered the ring wearing white bellbottoms, a black shirt open at the chest, and his black hair blown dry and brushed back, just the way Travolta wore his in the film of the same name. Hulk "Hollywood" Hogan is another case in point, as are Mankind, the Rock, and Stone Cold Steve Austin (named, perhaps, after the protagonist of the '70's series *The Six Million Dollar Man?*), who not too long ago even took to writing books that shot up the *New York Times* Bestseller lists, or to making Hollywood movies aimed at adolescent or pre-adolescent audiences. These cartoon, steroid-fed characters demonstrate a tendency in wrestling to substitute fictional identities for actual ones; perhaps this substitution is a constitutive part of the spectacle. Often, this tendency becomes exaggerated, and the identity of the wrestlers is effaced or erased altogether. There are dozens of masked men in wrestling. Once I saw a wrestler who apparently was very popular, who went by the name of "Vader." He was huge, without being particularly muscular (high-definition musculature is usually reserved for good guys, like Hollywood Hogan or Stone Cold Steve Austin). He had the protruding belly of an adult gorilla, which did not hinder his agility in the ring. The highlight of the match was the moment when Vader jumped from the top rope, slamming his immense chest and belly onto his already prostrate opponent, who had to be carried from the ring back to the locker room. The name Vader, of course, conjures up the image of the famous character from *Star Wars*, Darth Vader, who was the right-hand man of the evil emperor until becoming a saint in the final part of the original trilogy. This name raises an important point. The masked men of wrestling, who are usually on the negative side of the Manichean divide that dominates the spectacle, often are some of the most popular characters with the audience, perhaps simply because these wrestlers incarnate the indiscriminate, unidentified desire to perpetrate evil that Dr. Freud saw lurking in all of us. The act of screaming with delight at the sight of a masked man slamming his 260 pounds into the semi-unconscious body of another man has to provide a release from some kind of repression for those citizens who crowd into Civic Centers several times a week all across the USA to do so.

One of the usual elements of matches in which masked men are involved reinforces this idea. There is always a moment at which the good guy who opposes the masked man has got in a few good kicks and punches, dazing him. Wrestling matches of this kind constantly sway back and forth from the daze of one fighter to the daze of the other. This is the point at which the good guy tries to remove the mask, which always elicits near hysteria from the crowd. I'm convinced that a dual feeling of hope and dread dominates the mind of the spectator at this instant. "Yes! The masked man's identity is finally going to be revealed," he or she thinks at that moment (in passing, the threatened revelation of the super hero's true identity is a constant feature of American comics and cartoons), meaning that the tension of not knowing who this perpetrator of evil is will finally be released. At the same time, he or she thinks, "Oh no, the masked man's identity is going to be revealed," with the consequence that there will no longer be an anonymous perpetrator of evil to hate and unconsciously admire. The tension formed by the couple revelation/secrecy is never resolved in these matches, just as the constant struggle between the basic drives and instincts that oppose the dictates of the super ego is never resolved in the ego, if I may use a Freudian vocabulary to describe a rather banal truth. In other words, every one of us longs at times to be *bad*, and not to be caught at it, that is, to transgress without being recognized, without having our identities revealed to the authorities. Something inside of us—education, training—always stops most of us, by telling us "you'll be caught. You'll be punished." Wrestling embodies, plays out, and "spectacularizes" this eternal dilemma, which is therapeutic for the masses, who engage in an endless repetition compulsion in which the forces of good and evil beat each other back and forth in the finite universe of the ring.

One cannot speak about the WWWF and its analogues without considering the inside and the outside of the ring. The space beyond the ring belongs, of course, to the audience. But this beyond is also the space of preparation for the entrance into the ring. In recent years, wrestling, like it's more serious cousin, boxing, has begun to pay increasing attention to the presentation of the fighters that takes place outside of the ring. Stages are set up at the ends of long aisles. The fighter's name appears in neon or bright lights above the dark space of the curtains. Music begins to play, and often animators issue forth from this space before the wrestler himself does. When he finally does appear, he parades down the aisle toward the ring, mingling with the crowd if he's a good guy, and menacing them if he's a bad guy. In fact, the fighters themselves emanate from the space beyond the ring, that is, from the crowd itself. They are its representatives in the struggle that is played out in the ring. In other words, the fighters arise or emerge from the audience just as the instincts or drives arise from the unconscious to play out their conflicts on the stage of consciousness. The wrestlers are often accompanied in their promenade toward the ring by supposedly voluptuous women, whose exaggerated physical attributes mirror those of the wrestlers: this fact underlines the extent to which this emanation of the wrestlers is akin to the emergence of primary drives from the unconscious. Curiously, however, wrestling displays sexual markers without ever paying any conscious attention to them. The bulging muscles of the fighters and the protruding breasts of the women who often accompany them (and, increasingly, of the "Glamorous Ladies of Wrestling," who themselves take the stage) are empty signs of atrophied sexual drives. From this point of view, then, the audience itself is a kind of living unconscious that repeatedly propels the representatives of its primary instincts toward the ring, which becomes the moment of consciousness. It is for this reason that the notion of identity and the opposition of good and evil are crucial to the sport. It is also for this reason that wrestling as a spectacle is so redundant, since it merely plays out the repetition compulsion that is one of the fundamental movements of human consciousness, if we are to believe Freud.

The outside of the ring is also the space of transgression. In the ring itself, there is at least a token referee, and there are rules that determine what is legal and illegal during the fight, though at times it is hard to imagine what these are. The referee is perhaps the representative of a kind of social authority, but both the combatants and the spectators have an infantile relationship with him: he can be disobeyed when his back is turned, and if he simply becomes too annoying, a chair can always be smashed over his back, or he can be body slammed. There is a distinct relationship of complicity between audience and wrestler when it comes to this charlatan authority figure. Whenever a wrestler is doing something illegal while the ref is distracted elsewhere, he always looks to the audience for encouragement, or in order to demonstrate that he is in fact breaking the rules, which the spectators either approve or disapprove. When they disapprove, the wrestler always pantomimes a kind of "What? I'm not doing anything" attitude, while he continues to choke his opponent, or to gouge his eyes. During the course of any bout, the wrestlers are thrown out of the ring a number of times. While they are on the seemingly hard, concrete floor that surrounds the ring, almost anything can happen to them, or they can perpetrate almost any kind of illegal act against their opponents, while the referee pretends to count to ten, which would mean their disqualification if they did not return to the ring. Those ten seconds are "gang up time," which means that managers and their wrestlers gang up on their opponents, kick them when they're down, hit them with chairs, etc. The implication of this spectacle from a psychic point of view is that one of the drives has been defeated by another within the space of the unconscious itself. Nevertheless, the wrestler who happens to be dazed at the moment is always dragged back into the ring by his hair, and the bout continues until its inevitable surprise ending. For, this is one of the rules of wrestling: the end of the match has to be a surprise of some kind, and in general, the narrative that unfolds in the ring itself follows the strict (or at least regular) rules to which I have already alluded. The narrative of identity, and of good versus evil, is told within the ring itself, and it has a predictable outcome that will be repeated indefinitely, while in the space beyond the ring, the spectators lose themselves in a kind of collective unconscious that generates the spectacle of the ring. The order of the match arises out of the seeming chaos of the audience, which is nonetheless very organized in that it always generates the same kind of spectacle, a literal incarnation of the primary drives that are immanent in the audience. As such, wrestling does not produce its spectators as particular types of subjects; rather, it becomes itself a particular type of psychological subject of which all of the spectators are a part, losing their own identities perhaps momentarily during the course of the show.

Pamela Anderson and *Bay Watch*

Bay Watch was once the most popular program on the planet, which seems impossible to believe when you watch reruns of it on second-rate local television networks. According to the author of the article that communicated this bit of news to me, it was once possible to watch this show almost anywhere on earth where there was a television. This means that CJ and Mitch saved lives and fought bad guys in Cantonese, Serbo-Croatian, Swahili, Finnish, and even Basque just as often as they did in English. The secret of this global success was simple: *Bay Watch* idealized and fantasized (the life of) the body. The character played by Pamela Anderson, CJ, was a fantasy projection of a perfect female body, which was framed in a saturated ideological space that was itself a fantasy version of the American dream. California is often considered the ultimate manifestation of American culture: it's the dream and nightmare factory for the world, as well as the brain center of the US defense industry. It's the source of fads and fashions that are disseminated around the world, like rollerblading, aerobics, low-fat diets, surfing, Tae Bo, personal trainers, etc. The fictional space of *Bay Watch* thus signified this ideological saturation by elevating its depiction of American culture to the nth power. The beaches of the series were the land of milk and honey promised by industrial technology. Mitch and company deployed a collection of industrial objects in order to save lives and combat improbable crimes, including megaphones, cell phones, radars, jeeps, wave runners, speed boats, helicopters, and even submarines. The subliminal message of the show was thus that the machines through which we extend the instrumentality of our bodies almost to the infinite will enable us to conquer the vague dangers that lie in wait for us in the archetypal sea, at the same time that we display our smooth skin, white teeth, and impeccably tanned limbs in their form-fitting bathing suits.

Its most astonishing message, however, was encoded in the body of Pamela Anderson. In this promised land of sun, sand, and machines, technology suggested to the viewer that it might be possible to craft the perfect body, which has always been the dream offered by the cinema: if images of perfect faces and features could be projected onto a giant screen, perhaps they existed somewhere in the world, and could come to "belong" to the viewer. Just as the incidental music videos that appeared in the series signaled the intrusion of a suspended, machine-like temporality into the normal flow of the narrative—why did the camera move continuously in these music videos if not to highlight the fact that their images were recorded with a camera?—so Pamela Anderson's flesh embodied the intrusion of technological perfection into the body itself. The mere presence of her breast implants on screen was one of the driving forces of the series. The image of her running in slow-motion across the beach, with her breasts barely contained in her tight bathing suit, seemed to summarize the gist of the series: technology turns the now-traditional object of desire into a perfect body, the ultimate manifestation of the Western subject racing to conquer the dangers of the sea. In watching *Bay Watch*, spectators wanted not only to *possess* CJ's image, they also wanted to *become* it. The character was a hyperbolic manifestation of everyone's desire in the West to be infinitely desirable, while the notion of desirability itself became increasingly predicated on one's ability to manipulate complex machinery, or to become the protagonist of a narrative, such as the music video, whose very essence was contingent upon the existence of complex machinery.

The frequent puns that people used to make between *Bay Watch* and *Babewatch* revealed well enough the unconscious structure that supported the popularity of the show. The importance of surveillance in modern Western culture can hardly be exaggerated. In *Surveiller et punir* [*Discipline and Punish*], Michel Foucault argued that various categories of subjectivity were virtually generated by the development and refinement of surveillance techniques since the 18th century. For instance, the "career criminal" and the "obsessive compulsive personality disorder" were the products of increasingly sophisticated means of observing prisoners and psychiatric patients, respectively. The idealized bodies of what was once the world's most popular series were in charge of observing and controlling the beach, which converted them into representatives of a certain kind of order. On the other hand, the spectators who watched these people observe their beach eagerly and easily fit the various characters into different categories, separating the career criminals from the representatives of law and order. The series also derived its popularity from that which the pun indicates, i.e., men's desire, which was complemented by a certain kind of women's longing to become ideal objects of desire: *Bay Watch* was a phenomenon of men watching "babes" whom they wanted to possess sexually, and of women watching and desiring to become women of this kind. This identification with bodies that appear on the television screen, as if in an idealizing mirror, is one of the fundamental gestures of identity formation, as Jacques Lacan has demonstrated. Increasingly, the show depicted idealized male bodies beside its female paragons of a certain kind of "techno-body." Increasingly, watching the show for men became what it was for women, i.e., what Foucault would call "a desire in and for one's own body"—the desire to transform one's own body into the ideal model that one sees on the screen, as a means of participating in a given order of power constituted by continual watching and surveillance. It remains to be seen whether this transfer of a traditional male obsession with the visual register as motive of desire to the female domain will become a standard feature of Western culture. For a time in the late '90s, mass media certainly reinforced this saturation of vision with desire: one video by Toni Braxton, in which a group of women were drooling over men with washboard abs (see above), is a case in point. The intrusion of technology into one's conception of and desire for one's own body as a spectator was thus an intrinsic feature of *Bay Watch*.

If life is in fact a beach, as one wants it to be while watching reruns of *Bay Watch*, one might be led to ask what a beach *is*. It's well known that people didn't start going to the beach as a recreational activity until late in the 19th century, and that the idea of lying in the sun in order to get a tan may be a 20th century invention. Everyone can imagine Victorians and Wilsonian Americans at the beach wearing mountains of clothes and sitting under umbrellas. In the film *Death in Venice*, the character played by Dirk Bogarde is often sitting on the beach, under an umbrella, wearing a suit, tie, and hat. This means that during this century, the beach was transformed from a place where one goes wearing clothes that protect the body from the sun, to a place where one goes wearing clothes that expose the body to the sun, and hence to the gaze of the other bathers. While in one sense this spatial metamorphosis accomplished an astonishing liberation of the body, by the end of the century this new freedom to reveal one's flesh in public was co-opted by a new configuration of power. The beach is now a space in which bodies that have been tamed, disciplined, and transformed by a visual regime of power come to exhibit themselves. By displaying their suntans, their chiseled abs, their enhanced breasts and pecs, their cellulite-reduced gluts, their waxed legs and arms, and so on, the perfect bodies and would-be perfect bodies of the beach display the mark of power that has been written upon them. In other words, a suntan displays a bodily submission to a fiat that has been generated by the culture of surveillance, which finds its maximum expression in California. Hollywood is the capital of the visual domain, thus it is also the capital of bodily alteration. Accordingly, there are many actors and actresses who can't appear in public without an appropriate suntan, or seek to obliterate the effects of aging with multiple facelifts, botox injections, body wraps, collagen implants, liposuctions, nose re-structurings, etc. In extreme cases, such as that of Cher, these slaves of the visual can even have body parts removed in order to conform to the phantom archetype that haunts the collective techno-consciousness—in Cher's case, I believe she had her rib cage shortened. There's barely an actor in Hollywood who escapes an hour and a half a day in the gym and a vegetarian diet. This slavery to the gym is another instance of the body's increasing invasion by machines—Sly Stallone, for example, spends two hours a day attached to his Italian "musculation" machines, to use a Latinism. The imaginary world of *Bay Watch* is the Olympus of this visual firmament, which requires that the represented body fulfill a certain number of prerequisites, and in which ideal bodies spend their time surveying the beach, controlling it in their field of vision, and displaying the technical invasions of their flesh. As for the "real" Pamela Anderson, if such a woman can be said to exist, by 2008 she went through a series of painful marriages and divorces, after having had her breast implants removed long ago.

Bigfoot Stole My Wife

As revolutionary as they may have been in the 19th Century, newspapers are a leftover of an almost primitive state of technology at the beginning of the 21st Century. It's hard to imagine the success of the West's three great revolutions (American, French, and Russian) without the mass distribution of information via newspapers and pamphlets. In the age of the internet, Blackberries, cell phones, and reality television, however, newspapers belong to another era in which people actually had time to read and consider texts, instead of merely skimming them and trying to reduce a maximum amount of information into a minimum amount of words or "bullet points" (this is known as "being productive," and is measured somehow by governments as "productivity"). Despite the general outcry during the 19th Century on the part of intellectuals, such as Nietzsche, against newspapers, for precisely the same reasons that I've just mentioned—for them, the newspaper article was too short, too summarized, too frivolous—from our point of view, newspapers still conjure up images of leisurely Sunday mornings that allow for a rather detailed and extensive consideration of current events. The depiction of a state of affairs in a text that is actually printed, and that one holds physically in one's hands, is radically different from the projection of bits of information that have been downloaded from the web onto a screen, with its flickering, flipping, and rotating advertisements. The guiding tool of web surfers is the left mouse button, which causes them to develop a kind of nervous tick in their index fingers: surfing the web compels the viewer continually to move on to the next screen, which means that internauts are conditioned not to *read* and consider carefully anything that flashes momentarily before their hungry eyes. The ideal and perhaps inevitable form of information in the digital age is now seen on web pages and news channels: a steady stream of text scrolling across the bottom of a screen that is crowded with multiple open windows, pop-ups, headings, and talking heads. Increasingly, the readers of the 21st century will have to be like the characters in Sci-Fi movies (such

85

as *Lawnmower Man* and certain episodes of *Star Trek*) who have developed superior mental powers that enable them to read multiple flashing streams of information at ever increasing speeds. At some point in films of this kind, a character of this type inevitably winds up saying, "I have just finished reading everything ever written, Captain."

To return to the slow-paced world of the newspaper, one of the most noteworthy phenomena of trash culture is firmly anchored in this aging technology, which communicates a particularly persistent category of information to a mass public. At the checkout aisle of almost any supermarket in America, and at the entrance of any of the major drugstore franchises that have sprouted like mushrooms all across these United States (CVS, Walgreens, Rite-Aid), you can find *The Globe, The Sun, The National Enquirer,* and *The Star*, those fabulous tabloid newspapers that always have made-up headlines like, "Bigfoot Stole My Wife!" "Woman Gives Birth to UFO Baby!" "Elvis's Ghost Saves Fan From Burning House!" "Psychic Dogs Can Predict Earthquakes!" "Two-Month-Old Baby Weighs Fifty Pounds!" Most of the stories that follow these headlines are accompanied by doctored photographs of babies with alien heads from *The Outer Limits*, ghostly Elvis faces running away from a burning house, a devastated husband pointing to gigantic Bigfoot tracks in the snow, a dog barking at an earthquake-produced crevice in a highway, etc. In the same vein, these periodicals always contain stories about people kidnapped by aliens, psychic predictions of the future by Billy Graham, Nostradamus, the Pope, the Bible, and the famous astrologer of the moment, all kinds of strange births ("Woman Gives Birth to Dog Baby!" "Woman Has Baby That's Forty Years Old!"), statues that bleed and cry, sightings of the Virgin, ghosts, witches, miraculous cures ("Boy Cures Appendicitis—With Bubble Gum!"), visitations by saints and near saints (Mother Theresa, Pope John Paul II), contact with the dead via mediums, etc. In other words, tabloids have become the material support in which an entire "folkloric" realm remains alive in the West. According to Mikhail Bakhtin, in his famous reading of François Rabelais, certain periods and festivals of the year represented a celebration of this realm, which, in the Middle Ages and the Renaissance united the common folk with the nobility and the bourgeoisie. The feast of Carnival, for example, was a time of release from official restrictions, in which some of the more pagan elements that underlay Christian European culture could come to the surface, and be celebrated at least in the disguise of a Christian feast. Carnival is to this day a somewhat pagan feast in New Orleans, Rio, Venice, and the Canary Islands, to name just a few of the more noteworthy sites of its celebration.

While the persistence of mysterious beings, hidden identities, and an uncanny contact with a suddenly ubiquitous spirit world in Carnival is not at all hard to understand—these kinds of feasts are present in virtually all human cultures—what remains unanswered is the question as to why the domain of the occult and the strange has endured and flourished in precisely the form of the tabloid newspaper, in the particular places where they have become fixtures of American culture, particularly in supermarkets and drug stores. A simple answer to this question is that newspapers and specialty magazines were historically sources of information of this type, and the tabloids are merely one branch of this kind of invented "journalism" that has endured and even flourished while all others have declined in the face of radio, television, and the internet (think of the *True Crime*, *Mystery*, and *True Confession* magazines, for example, that were quite common during my childhood, but which have virtually vanished, while the tabloids are still ubiquitous). Surprisingly, while crime and mystery have become the standard fare of television—there's hardly anything else on, if you consider the number of police, hospital, and law dramas on the major networks (see below)—the folkloric domain of the tabloids has remained essentially absent. The abundance of Sci-Fi programs available on television really has nothing to do with the tabloid phenomenon, since serious science fiction can at least have something to do with a conception of the *real*, even if the reality it depicts takes place five centuries in the future. In contrast, the folkloric domain of the tabloids displays a fantasy version of reality in which ghosts walk about, strange creatures walk out of northern woods and swim in the depths of Scottish lakes, people in the here-and-now talk to others in the great beyond, and the multiplicity of human life mutates into new, unseen forms. Similarly, the domain of the occult, including UFO's and strange monsters here on earth, had its moment of success in the TV world, with the popularity of programs such as *The X Files*, which have by now been completely eclipsed by "reality television." Part of the enormous success of this series resided in the public's fascination with the extent to which our own government is beyond our understanding and control (so much for "Government of the people, for the people, and by the people"). In other words, just as television dramas figure a constant interrogation of public institutions (the police, the courts, hospitals), so *The X Files* was at least in part about the monstrosity of the FBI and the CIA, and the theories of multiple conspiracies and cover-ups that hide monstrous state secrets from the American public. Although the entire apparatus surrounding the JFK assassination, for example, frequently appears and reappears in the pages of the tabloids, it is far from being their central issue of investigation. Thus the particular form and content of the tabloids remains unique to them, since the folkloric realm that they depict has not been completely translated to television.

Another, more speculative response to my question here is simply that there is something about the folkloric component of the tabloids that makes it necessary for these stories to be published in a newspaper format. It should be noted, in passing, that the tabloids are at least half concerned with the scandals, trials, tribulations, and successes of actors, actresses, singers, and various royal families and pseudo royal families. This *Paris Match* kind of tabloid has been completely engulfed by television (there are entire cable networks devoted to it), and is thus no longer unique to the American brand of tabloid. While these American versions of the society pages remain obsessed with Oprah Winfrey's weight, Diana's divorce from Charles and the conspiracy theories surrounding her death, Pamela Anderson's tattoos (among other things), Brad Pitt's divorce from Jennifer Aniston, etc., they also devote at least half of their pages to abnormal and paranormal phenomena such as the ones described in the imaginary headlines quoted above. The notion of belief is undoubtedly an important one in exploring this second hypothesis. Do the readers of the *National Enquirer* believe that Bigfoot and the Loch Ness monster exist? Do they believe that Elvis's ghost has been sighted all around the world? Do they believe that Nostradamus predicted the Holocaust? Do they actually believe that certain statues of the Virgin Mary cry real tears on certain key dates of the year, or that some women have had UFO babies, or monkey babies, or even Bigfoot babies? The question of belief in the tabloids is similar to that of wrestling: the spectators are willing to suspend their disbelief, as long as the wrestlers follow an appropriate script, and offer them a good show.

To return to my speculative answer to the question that detains us, there is something about the pseudo-folkloric, pseudo-occult subject matter of the tabloids that requires the format of the modern newspaper as its material support. One of the primary reasons may be that it was, at least until quite recently, easier and cheaper to falsify information in a photographic form than it was in a cinematographic form. The familiar cut-and-paste photographs of *The Star* et. al. serve as documentary proof of claims of the type, "I had Bigfoot's baby," accompanied by a picture of a more or less normal woman holding a furry miniature of Lon Chaney's character from *Frankenstein vs. the Werewolf*. An article with this title simply could not be produced for television within a limited budget, though perhaps the latest techniques of computer super-imposition will someday enable Leeza Gibbons, Geraldo Rivera, or Jerry Springer to interview the mother of the Sasquatch's children on "live" television, holding her potentially giant infant in her arms. Another possibility is that the fantastic stories told by the tabloids need to be *read*, and that there is an intimate relationship between this type of folk culture and a certain kind of reading. It is well known that perhaps one out of every nine or so Americans has difficulty reading, which means that a large portion of our population has an extremely limited experience with narrative in its written form. Could it be that, for this group, reading retains the kind of magical and even diabolical power that it once seemed to possess from the point of view of immense illiterate populations?

I'm thinking of the impulse, for example, that caused the ancient Athenians to execute the diabolical Socrates, who represented a new kind of culture opposed to an older one, i.e., a written culture opposed to an oral one (see the works of Eric Havelock). I'm also thinking of the popular image of the Medieval magician or warlock (Merlin, for example), who guards the secrets of his art or craft in a thick book that only he knows how to read (the *Harry Potter* series exploits this fascination with magical books), or of a certain Medieval saint who was deemed to be possessed by demons simply because he would sit in front of the cathedral reading a book without moving his lips. It could be, then, that reading retains, at least to a certain extent, this magical and somewhat demonic quality for those who do not include it among their habitual and banal activities. Perhaps the tabloids provide access to reading for a large percentage of the population, and confirm the unconscious but historically-rooted perception that reading opens doors to magical worlds.

Finally, we shouldn't forget where these newspapers are sold. The average supermarket reflects rather well the extent to which mechanization saturates the lives of ordinary Americans. Take the example of almost any meat product, say chicken or turkey. The hygienic package that you find in the supermarket, which contains the bloodless, featherless, washed, and eviscerated body of a fowl, wrapped in plastic, or cut into pieces, bears no resemblance whatsoever to the animal itself. In the most radical cases, such as that of the fashionable boneless, skinless, fat-free chicken breasts that are available everywhere, the cubes of protein that we buy are more like tofu than they are like animal flesh. In contrast, in the older markets of our larger cities, as in the large European markets on which they are modeled, it is still possible for one to buy an animal that looks like one, and which was probably running around not too long before it was sold as food. In Paris, in the Fall, one can see the animals themselves (wild boars, piglets, grouse, pigeons, pheasants, sheep heads, etc.) hanging from hooks or sitting on tables outside of butcher shops. In the Italian market in Philadelphia, not too long ago you could hear cows mooing in a garage somewhere near a store called simply, "Sonny's Cut-up Chicken," near another butcher shop that has game birds and whole dead rabbits hanging in the display window. The point of these reflections is the fact that the rather primary and primordial drama of life and death that dominates nature—that is, the enormous amount of energy that the animal world devotes to eating and running away from being eaten by other animals—is completely sanitized beneath layers of mechanization and marketing, often with devastating effects (see the Mad Cow disease afflicting Europe). We no longer acquire, by diligence, violence, or subterfuge, the food that we need to survive; rather, we buy products that are presented to us by an impressive range of companies who concentrate their activity in the supermarket, at least in the United States (as well as in European "hyper-marchés"). We are twice-removed from the imperative to kill and eat, since we have our proteins offered to us as carefully-packaged products. Similarly, the supernatural and primordial realm of magical beings, miraculous births, a future that we can study in the present, and a spirit world populated by the dead is offered to "shoppers" as a rather innocuous little package, with attractive titles that serve as labels to draw the attention of the consumer. This kind of thinking could be extended, of course, to explain why one is always compelled to read about UFO's and Bigfoot upon entering any chain drug store.

Venice, Orlando, Vegas

There are at least four kinds of tourism. The first one is the typical trip that middle-class families take to the beach during their summer vacation, so that they can show off a decent suntan when they go back to the office. The second kind entails visiting the touristic or "historical" sites that are associated with the first kind of tourism, such as the "Sarasota Jungle Gardens," in Sarasota, FL. The third kind of tourism involves taking a trip in order to see one of the contemporary monuments to capitalism, like Disney World, Euro Disney, Las Vegas, Atlantic City, Busch Gardens, Great Adventure, etc. Finally, the fourth kind of tourism is the cultural variety, such as the virtually obligatory trip to Europe for Americans, during which one has to sort of "engulf" the splendid monuments of other countries, with histories that predate our own by hundreds and even thousands of years.

The first type of tourism belongs most obviously within the domain of trash culture. The cult of the "beautiful" body that increasingly imprisons us is accompanied by an astounding array of sub-cultural practices that are peculiar to our time, and which are an inherent part of the basic beach vacation. Consider the seemingly innocent practice of tanning. While we live in one of the most liberal countries on earth as far as dress codes are concerned—I can hear my European friends screaming that "Puritanical" Americans can't stand the idea of a topless public beach—it remains true that there is a considerable pressure for one to conform to a certain beach etiquette and fashion, whatever it may be. Not too long ago, in Wildwood, NJ, it was fashionable for young women to wear men's boxer shorts over their bathing suits, which meant that young women who wanted to be "cool" in that way *had* to wear cool boxer shorts over their bikini bottoms. A few years ago, on a beach in Northern Spain, all young men between the ages of 16 and 25 were virtually forced to wear bathing suits that were mid-calf length. A few summers ago, in Ocean City, NJ, I noticed that an attractive tan was often complemented by tattoos in strategic places: around the ankle or the upper arm; beside a (pierced) navel; low on the abdomen, just above the top of the bathing suit; on the back, beside one shoulder, or just above the backside. While obesity continues to be an endemic problem in the US, and while one can still see dozens of overweight or downright fat people on the beach, it seems to me that the pressure to conform to a certain body type that is appropriate to the beach (P. Anderson and D. Hasselhoff?) is forcing and eventually will compel overweight people to refrain from sea bathing altogether. The paradox of these cultural practices is that the more individual and outrageous ("extreme" is a synonym of "good" these days) one feels as a beach tourist—by enlarging one's breasts or pecs, by getting tattoos and dying one's hair, by starving oneself and wearing a G-string bikini, by getting one's navel pierced, by taking steroids and protein shakes that inflate one's muscles—the more one conforms to a norm that is dictated by the anonymous and unintentional play of forces that drives modern Western culture. In other words, like every other phenomenon of trash culture, this first type of tourism calls us into being as certain kinds of subjects, inscribing its marks upon our bodies. These "wounds" are self-inflicted, however, and power compels us to disfigure ourselves by offering us an unsatisfying but voluptuous pleasure in return: for, what is more pleasurable than lying in the sun, and feeling sexy on the beach?

The second type of tourism is related to the first, and is perhaps more typically American than any other. Consider a peculiar museum in a beach town like Sarasota, FL, called "Cars and Music of Yesteryear." Since genuine historical monuments are lacking in towns such as these—which constitute the majority of US cities—the town fathers and mothers, and any other guy looking to make a buck, try to create "history" where none exists, in museums such as the one I've just named. You could say the same of the Machinists' museum in Windsor VT, or even of the Mummers' museum in Philadelphia. This country was founded at a time when historical consciousness was just beginning to be considered a thing of importance. We know, for example, that some of the great Medieval cathedrals of Europe were virtually abandoned in the 17th century, since their architecture did not conform to the Classical style of the period. Similarly, the great monuments of the roman Empire were pillaged throughout the Middle Ages, when they served as sources of stone or as corrals for animals, as did the Coliseum in Rome. This disregard for history was especially acute in the US until very recently. In 1976, the historical district of Philadelphia virtually had to be reconstructed for the Bicentennial Celebration, since most of the original buildings had been torn down. A historical tour of the "Birthplace of Liberty" consists essentially of visiting a series of plaques that read, "in 17-something-or-other, so-and-so's house used to stand on this spot," after reading which the tourist looks up to see the modern branch of a bank, or a Dunkin' Donuts shop. When Americans wanted to see history, they went to Europe, or attempted to invent their own back home. The sort of miming of history that you see in "Cars and Music of Yesteryear," in which objects that are 50 or 75 years old become historical artifacts, responds to what has become a basic truism of the West. People blindly accept the idea that a knowledge of history will enable them to have a better home and nation. From the point of view of "trash" museums—no disrespect intended—it doesn't matter how banal that history is, or what its object may be, since the idea of history itself sells (witness the existence of the "History Channel" on cable TV—why isn't there a "Philosophy Channel"?).

In opposition to this *idée reçue*, it could be argued that the "history" of popular music and automobile design from the 1900's through the 1920's, which is vaguely represented in "Cars and Music of Yesteryear," or the objects that are in the Ringling museum a little further north on Tamiami Trail, have no effect whatsoever on my subjectivity as an individual. As Nietzsche argued so long ago, history is a conscious and constructive activity that seeks models for our present behavior in the past (see "On the Uses and Disadvantages of History for Life", in his *Untimely Meditations*). He also argued that the past was essentially undiscovered and undiscoverable, which means that the past is essentially what we make of it, while the "truth" of our reconstructions depends largely on the evidence that we choose to accept as real or valid. This fluid and undetermined nature of history is what makes it possible for neo-Fascists to deny the existence of the Holocaust in the face of what is, for the rest of us, overwhelming evidence from living witnesses and documents. On a much smaller and more innocent scale, the visitors to "Cars and Music of Yesteryear" are mining the past in the same way, in search of a certain version of the past that they will ultimately have to invent for themselves. These museums also evince an (unconscious) attempt to glorify the present, or to look for models from the past to imitate in the present. It might be argued, however, that the basic tourist in his pink or orange shorts and his white sun visor who goes into "Cars and Music of Yesteryear" has none of this in mind. I'm willing to bet, however, that he says to himself at some point, "Isn't it amazing that they were able to invent all of these cars?", which is a way of valorizing the present with respect to this primitive past, and of celebrating a culture that was able to conquer its environment and its enemies, for good and for evil, by means of industrial production (the administration of George W. Bush seems to have been the culmination of all of the evils of this kind of thinking). In other words, your basic tourist doesn't look to the past during his vacation in order to revel in the absolute decadence of his own historical moment. At least not always, as we will see in a moment.

The third kind of tourism deserves perhaps a chapter of its own. The fastest-growing metropolis in the United States, Las Vegas, receives about thirty million visitors each year. In comparison, Philadelphia, which is twice the size, and which has some of the most important historical monuments in the country, only receives about three million visitors a year. I'm willing to bet that at least twenty million people visit Orlando every year. This means that these two cities attract more tourists than most countries: the second most visited country in the world, for example, is Spain, which receives sixty million tourists per year. What is behind this mass phenomenon? What is clear from the very nature of these two places is that people want to live in fantasy worlds, like the one offered by Ricardo Montalban in the famous TV series from the early 1980's, *Fantasy Island*, which was shown immediately after an equally famous fantasy series, *The Love Boat*. Eight of the ten largest hotels in the world are in Las Vegas, each of which has between two thousand and five thousand rooms. These aren't just hotels—they're almost the size of ancient cities, which often appear as the theme or motif of the hotel itself. One of the most grandiose, for example, is the Luxor, which contains a replica of an Egyptian pyramid. Another one is the New York, New York, a five-thousand room giant that reproduces the Empire State Building, the Chrysler Building, the Brooklyn Bridge, and the Statue of Liberty at something less than half their original size, right in the middle of the Nevada desert. We could also mention the replicas of Paris and Venice, complete with canals, that have been constructed in recent years. Like the legalized sex for sale that is offered to visitors in this curious town, these enormous copies sanitize their distant originals, so that Ma and Pa America from the Midwest can go to Manhattan without worrying too much about being mugged, or can visit the pyramids without dodging the bombs and bullets of militant Muslim fundamentalists. In a sense, then, these fantasy copies are better than the originals, since they were designed with the comfort of their guests in mind, whereas New York and Egypt were not, as far as I know. Las Vegas also represents the American dream of unleashed capitalism at its most extreme, second, perhaps, only to Wall Street, to which most of us do not have direct access, despite the false advertising of Ameritrade and E-Trade. When you visit Las Vegas, you walk into the dream of easy money, in which everything, including the bodies of the show girls, is for sale. If you bring enough money with you, you can even stay in the fantasy penthouse suites that are on top of every hotel, and which duplicate Medieval châteaux or Venetian palaces, with all of the modern luxuries, and without the inconvenience of European bureaucrats breathing down your neck, looking for increased revenue for the coffers in Brussels.

Since most of the visitors to Las Vegas travel with budgets that are well below these means, however, what is it precisely that attracts so many people to this town? The first obvious answer is the gambling, which has been legalized in virtually every state of the Union (at least on river boats and Indian reservations), and which is successful almost everywhere where it's legal. Las Vegas was the first town in the States to be devoted exclusively to gambling, after the revolution in Cuba that forced the mafia to move its business away from Havana. As such, Vegas had a head start over the rest of the cities where gambling is legal, such as Atlantic City, which is only a distant shadow of its western model, despite the greater population density of the Northeastern megalopolis. Gambling is a sickness or a blessing, depending on your point of view. For those who enjoy it, there is probably no other adrenaline rush that is quite like the possibility of winning or losing large sums of money. This is only part of the reason behind Vegas's appeal. Another part is the climate, which is dry, warm, and sunny when most of the rest of the country is wet, cold, and dark. All of the fastest growing cities in the States are in regions where the climate is enjoyable at least ten months out of the year, such as Florida, Texas, and Arizona (being a part-time resident of northern New England, I can understand this phenomenon better than most). Beyond these two basic necessities—the need and joy of spending money, and the need to live an active life outdoors—the essential and underlying significance of Las Vegas is undoubtedly what draws people to it. This city electrifies the desert, makes lawns and flowers grow out of the sand, makes and breaks fortunes in seconds, and presents the continuous and continuing spectacle of dream landscapes being built, like mirages, out of the ripples of the desert heat. Las Vegas offers its visitors a land of fantasy and impossibility, in which physical, economic, and environmental limits have no meaning. Given the banalities of most of our everyday lives, who wouldn't want to be a part of that? The millions of individuals who visit this town every year seem to be saying, "I, too, want my life to be a fantasy."

As for Orlando and Disney World, the secret of their success is similar to that of Las Vegas. The site of the city is an enigma, even given its wonderful winter climate: Orlando is smack in the middle of an enormous peninsula that still has hundreds of miles of virtually empty coastline, in other words, it is a summer, sunshine resort city that has no sea, which means that they have to provide artificial waves for guests who come to Florida in order to jump in the surf. More important, however, is the subject matter that put Orlando on the map: two generations after the invention of cartoons, 85 percent of the people in this country have been raised with a kind of cartoon mentality. When we go to a place in which talking dogs and mice with enormous heads roam the streets, it seems normal, comfortable, familiar, and even "homey" to us. I remember that when I was a child, I was fascinated by the empty spaces between the houses that appeared in the background when Fred Flintstone would drive down the street in his rock mobile. I wanted to be able to wander around in his neighborhood, and to look through the big cutout windows of those stone houses. For people who grew up watching Disney cartoons, Disney World makes this childhood dream, in which all girls are princesses, and all animals can talk, a reality. Given the popularity of Disney movies, it's likely that this kind of dream will continue to attract millions of people and their exigent children to Orlando for decades to come, especially given the popularity of Disney's next generation of "products," produced by the prodigious Pixart studio.

The fourth type of tourism is at once the easiest and the most difficult to understand. A reasonable admiration for the cultures from which our own was derived makes Europe the number one destination for Americans in search of History with a capital H. In contrast to the popular conception that history should provide us with models for our action in the present, there is virtually no sense in which we can model our own conduct in the present on the monuments of the great European cultures and cities. A large part of the beauty of Europe's cathedrals, castles, and houses derives from the mere passage of time, which conveys an aura of wonder to almost any object: five hundred years from now, a Tupperware container or a Tickle-me Elmo doll will seem interesting and valuable to some future museum-goer. Part of the motivation for going to Europe is the simple pleasure of contemplating buildings and artifacts that are, in some cases, thousands of years old, like the ruins of the Roman Forum. The temporal paradox of looking at destroyed monuments that speak to us with a voice that is, somehow, our own—if we have a Senate, it's because the ancient Romans had one—provides one with an insuperable intellectual pleasure. It's hard to leave the 400-year-old immensity of St. Peter's Cathedral or the 800-year-old complexity of Notre Dame de Paris without feeling somehow renewed and "centered" in oneself as a citizen of the West.

Within the domain of trash culture, however, going to Rome or Paris or London for an American has little to do with these historical conceits. I'll give you an example of what this type of experience is really about for most people. I went to Venice, Italy (not to be confused with Venice, Florida) during the carnival celebrations a few years ago. I was there on a Monday, on Fat Tuesday, and on Ash Wednesday, which means that I saw the best of these days of feasting. The simple act of walking around Venice, across any of its four hundred bridges, and along any of its canals, in gondolas or on the *vaporetti*, is a free lesson in the history of technology. When most of this remarkable island city was built, near the end of the Middle Ages, when Italians were doing more than anyone else to bring a new era of European history into being, the structure of this city was at the cutting edge of mercantile technology. Goods from the farthest ports known to Europeans could be brought directly into the heart of the city via the grand canal, and transported directly to individual houses on smaller boats via the smaller canals. The city was naturally protected on all sides by the fact that it was built upon islands, so that its structure was not determined by the demands of fortifying it against invaders. Venice was perhaps the first city in the world that was built with the notion of commerce foremost in the minds of its creators, as opposed to the idea of protection against warfare: the title of Shakespeare's *Merchant of Venice* is far from gratuitous. Everyone in Europe's educated elite recognized that Venice was the capital of trade with the East, which drove commerce on the Continent for centuries, ultimately resulting in the global colonization of the other continents, and the birth of an essentially new mentality in Europe that came to be known later as the Renaissance. The need for new sources of wealth and to protect the city from outside invaders in an economical fashion resulted in the invention of a new type of city, which was undoubtedly a consequence of revolutionary technological thinking at the time, leaving us with one of the architectural marvels of Western culture.

Wandering through the wonderfully quiet streets of Venice, however, it is evident that this is a city that literally incarnates obsolete technology, and that its physical *raison d'être*—commerce by means of what today would be considered tiny ships—has ceased to exist. One of the guide books that I skimmed during my stay said that Venice was struggling *not* to become a kind of enormous outdoor, living museum. This is quite an apt statement, since the city still exists thanks to the fact that it is a fascinating piece of our technological past, which has seemingly been preserved intact in a block of temporal ice. As almost anyone who has visited the city will tell you, one of the most shocking and gratifying things about it is that there are no cars in its "downtown." While sprawling Western cities such as Los Angeles were built with automobiles in mind, most European cities have to accommodate cars as a bane and a threat to their very existence, since they were constructed (for the most part) with non-polluting, horse-drawn carriages in mind, at least those cities, such as Paris and Barcelona, that received major renovations during the second half of the 19th century. Perhaps the incongruous relationship of the traveler in the present and these anachronistic cities based on obsolete means of transport provides the key to understanding why people feel compelled to visit them, aside from what we view now as their intrinsic beauty (I would be the last to dispute the fact that Venice, Paris, Barcelona, London, Amsterdam, and other major cities are beautiful). When I was in Venice during Carnival Week, I was shocked by the sheer number of cameras that I saw. Everyone had a camera, including the people who were posing for pictures in their costumes. In fact, one extravagant gentleman in a gorgeous Enlightenment costume produced a portable point-and-shoot camera from under his robe, and beckoned to me to take a picture of him, which I did. One of the principal attributes of tourism is this desire on the part of the traveler to transfix himself or herself at a moment in time, in a particular place, especially for the purpose of displaying that frozen moment of space-time in a photo album, which will be inflicted upon an unsuspecting visitor or friend back home at almost any opportunity. The typical snapshots of the Venice Carnival thus encapsulate layer upon layer of suspended animation, in which the stratum of obsolete technology is complemented by a somewhat obsolete set of customs (the abstinence from meat during Lent, which virtually no one practices, is the true meaning of Carnival), costumes that are frozen in time, and by the individual level of the person who wishes to immortalize his or her touristic moment in a photographic, now mostly digital, image.

The most important reason for this desire to suspend oneself in a present that is already the past at the moment that one takes the picture is undoubtedly the desire to tell the story of the trip to those who have not gone to that particular city, or who have not lived through that experience in that place. I'll give you an absurd example of this virtually universal need that we have to transform our touristic experiences into narratives that somehow place us *above* those who listen to our stories. While I was walking through the streets of Venice, insignificant in the midst of the multitudes, I stopped to read the menu of a pizzeria. From behind me, I heard the voice of a Spanish woman who was apparently disappointed by the pizzas that you could see coming out of the oven through the window of the restaurant. She said in colloquial Spanish to one of her companions, more or less something to the effect: "Jeez, that looks lousy. I swear, the best pizza I ever had in my life was at a Pizza Hut in Portugal, it had so much cheese on it . . ." One of the most prevalent forms of trash tourism is, in fact, this desire on the part of Americans and, increasingly, on the part of Europeans, to say that they've been to McDonald's in Budapest, to Dunkin' Donuts in Moscow, or to the Hard Rock Café in Timbuktu. For some people, it's much cooler to say that you ate a piece of pizza walking up and down the Champs Elysées than it is to say that you've been to the Louvre. Perhaps this is to prove that you were so different from the local folks that you couldn't find any familiar food to eat, so you had to eat Big Macs and chocolate glazed donuts, instead of trying lamb cheeks and pig ears and tripe, whereas the more logical adventure would be to say that you ate tripe and loved it at a dirty bar near the Atocha station in Madrid, for example. In short, what really matters in this type of tourism is not the depth of the historical dimension that is typical of the world's great cities, or the breadth of cultural experience that one can acquire by traveling. What really counts to the trash tourist is his or her own personal history as it is immortalized in photographs and in narratives that recount the experience, as banal as it may be. In this sense, eating pizza at a Pizza Hut in St. Petersburg may be more important from a personal point of view than going to the Hermitage museum. After all, all of the great art in the world cannot tell the tourist's own story, whereas the typical tourist photos and stories engrave his or her provenance and identity for all to see. In other words, this last type of tourism calls the individual into being in quite a paradoxical fashion, since he or she goes abroad to discover who he or she already *is*.

Heavy Metal

Many years ago—it must have been in 1978, when I was fifteen years old, after we had just moved to Northeast Philadelphia—the highlight of the summer for me and especially for all of my Beavis and Butthead friends was the spectacular concert at the Spectrum in August for which we had tickets. The headliners were none other than Ozzy Osbourne and Black Sabbath at the height of their marginal popularity, and there was a relatively new band that had just become popular opening for them by the name of Van Halen. What counts as heavy metal today, almost 30 years later, may seem quite different, when groups like Metallica are becoming sort of old hat, and when you can see long-haired and sort of mangy kids in tight pants, biker boots, and chains wearing Sepultura and Megadeath T-shirts almost anywhere in the Western world. I think the essential elements of Heavy Metal were present then, though, in 1978, when August finally arrived, and we went to see Ozzy and company in our raggiest jeans, Black Sabbath T-shirts, dirty white Converse hi-tops, and our paradoxically squeaky-clean hair, blown dry into billowing, voluminous fluffs and puffs.

The most important element of Metal is, of course, the voice of the singer, which can sound one of two ways. Anyone familiar with the Black Sabbath hit "Iron Man," which Beavis and Butthead adopted as their anthem, knows what the first type of voice is—demonic, possessed by the devil, undead, calling out from beyond the grave. When Ozzy said "I am iron man" through some kind of synthesizer, we all cheered our lungs out on that hot summer night of 1978, because that zombie voice embodied something that was important to our way of being out on the streets. It celebrated the "Satanic" undercurrent on which Metal culture floated, but which few people really took seriously. Since we were growing up surrounded by factories that were emptying out, by railroads that soon would no longer carry any freight trains, in neighborhoods that would be abandoned by anybody who could afford to do it, and left to the poorest of the poor, there seemed to be a kind of death everywhere in the air, as if the Catholic underpinnings of the rows and rows of houses had been handed over to Satan. In other words, we were mutants who had been abandoned by God, while Satan kept us in the neighborhood and supplied us with drugs, with Ozzy and company as the high priests of this mock black religion.

The second type of voice is that of David Lee Roth, who was still singing for Van Halen that night—screechy and screamy, straining at the limits of its range, and at times downright ugly, like an animal growling. The lead singer of Metallica is the master of the snarling animal growl, while the singer of AC DC undoubtedly has one of the world's ugliest voices, and sounds something like a donkey being forcibly squeezed by a psychotic maniac into a cage that is too small for it. Axel Rose of Guns 'n Roses is the direct descendant of this tradition, as well as "singers" from bands as diverse as Danzig, Rob Zombie, Limp Bizkit, and Rage Against the Machine. This is exactly the point of this second kind of voice, which is meant to convey tension, suffering, sweat, pain, unbearable heaviness and exertion, while in fact it must be quite easy for these men to yell their heads off. Heavy Metal was, at its inception, a British phenomenon, and from a material perspective, it must have been the result of the decline of the British Empire and the social problems provoked by the petroleum crisis of the early '70's. While disco was the American reaction to these problems—escapism into frivolity and "Good Times," according to the title of the fantastic Chic dance hit ("Good Times/ These are the good times/ Leave your world behind . . .")—the Brits produced a remarkable stream of bands such as Deep Purple, Black Sabbath, and perhaps even Led Zepellin (more of a rock band than a metal band) who embodied the anger and the tensions of urban masses who suddenly found themselves out of work, immersed in drugs, and with nowhere to go and nothing to do. (At around the time when I went to see the concert I mentioned, all of this anger would quickly be diverted into punk rock, a much more serious phenomenon that would require a chapter of its own). The screaming, impotent singers of the metal bands gave voice to this emptiness and mock despair—mock because the kids who identified with this music still had enough money to get high, to buy records, and to go to concerts, while their demonic counterparts brought to life the omnipotence of the devil who seemingly had us all by the balls, so to speak.

The machismo of my last remark is quite appropriate to the world of Heavy Metal, since it was and is a male-dominated phenomenon. The look of Heavy Metal musicians is the second important element in the genre. Even though long hair was obligatory in Metal bands, accompanied by lots of head-banging, hot, loud guitar riffs and solos, and all kinds of squirming and grimacing, this long hair had nothing to do with the femininity of the singers and musicians in these bands. Long hair of a certain type was *the* marker that signified a person's belonging to the social group that identified with Metal bands. I mean the long, curly, stringy, somewhat dirty-looking hair, slightly longer than the shoulder, which rarely goes all the way down the back to the waist. Think of Slash's black locks. A person who had this kind of hair wanted to display definitive proof that he was outside of the social order; today, in contrast, people can die their hair orange and pierce their noses and still work in respectable restaurants and even in banks (recently, in a rather fancy Philadelphia restaurant, La Brasserie Perrier, a bartender with a ring in her nose politely served me a $13 glass of Veuve Clicquot champagne). Most of all, however, a man or boy would grow long hair in the neighborhoods at the time that I'm thinking of for one very important reason: it was supposedly a good way of "scoring with chicks," as Beavis and Butthead would put it, especially with druggy chicks who liked Led Zep and Black Sabbath. In fact, lots of Metal songs, especially in the later, watered-down versions of the '80's, like those of Van Halen at their peak, were about "scoring" with "hot babes." (The descendants of Metal bands, such as Kid Rock, have taken to parading porno movie stars in their videos.) In the '80's, David Lee Roth used to wear sort of cowboy chaps that showed off his crotch, and in fact, Metal is often nothing more than an exaggerated and exuberant means for young men to display their genitals. From this point of view, guitars and basses are merely substitutes or fetishes for the penis (as are so many other things), and the endless guitar solos during which the player invariably looks down at his instrument with an open mouth are nothing more than figurative public masturbation. The originator of this type of solo, Jimi Hendrix, openly "fucked" his guitar on stage before setting it on fire, and Heavy Metal gladly adopted the phallic significance of the guitar, especially since it was apparently an effective means of attracting a certain type of young woman.

At the present time, however, Heavy Metal has become what every other type of popular music is at the end of this century: a product that has been stripped of its social significance so that it can be marketed to a mass public of consumers. A long-haired speed-metal dude today is no more of a rebel and an outcast than a guy in a Brooks Brothers' suit is. He buys a look and an attitude in the same way that a banker buys a Mercedes and a Rolex. We all are constantly called into being as subjects by categories of products that are sold as discreet entities. Heavy Metal bands can quite harmlessly be marketed to kids and sold through I-Tunes to millions of homes in the endlessly sprawling suburbs of this great country. Christ, Ozzy Osborne even had his own relatively successful "reality show" about the boring domesticity of his own suburban life, which was followed, I believe, by a spin-off that followed his wife around during her move to California. The inexorable push of multi-national marketing has the same effect on all of the artifacts of trash culture, however "authentic" they may have been at their origins. I believe that Jim Morrison's long hair, leather hipsters, cowboy boots, and chain belt actually *did* signify a genuine desire on his part to change the society in which he lived. Now this kind of look is an ensemble that you can buy in stores like Urban Outfitters in Boston, at the end of Newbury Street, which is a haven of world capitalism, traversed by Kuwaiti and Chinese students in brand new BMW's and Ferraris, who cruise up and down it in their Armani jeans and their Versace sunglasses. Axel Rose and Kid Rock may not know it, but they're merely dupes who embody the marketing strategies of guys in suits sitting in board meetings in Tokyo, Shanghai, Berlin, New York, and L.A. I suppose they don't care at all, as long as they can cruise for super-model or porn star chicks. The interesting question is, are the guys in suits themselves the dupes of somebody else? Who markets and sells the gray-suit, tasseled-loafer, button-down Oxford look to the man who involuntarily comes to embody this social type? Who tells him to buy a gigantic Mercedes or a yacht so that he can display it in public, in the same way that the Metal guitarist shows off his "instrument" to a crowd of adoring fans? The answer is, quite simply, that all of us in the West have our identities dictated to us by the functioning of what politicians call "the economy," including those dressed-up mannequins who have their lines fed to them straight from consultants and focus groups through tele-prompters, and who run for public offices that eventually someone has to occupy, no matter how incompetent he or she may be.

Cop Shows, Law Series,
Hospital Dramas

I'm a big fan of Lieutenant Columbo, the fictional detective created by Peter Falk back in the '70's. The French, who are no dummies when it comes to culture, recognized that Columbo had contributed something important to contemporary civilization when they made Falk a Knight of the Legion of Honor many years ago. Detective stories are one of the most popular genres in the West, and have been for more than 150 years now, ever since Edgar Allan Poe invented the genre in "The Murders in the Rue Morgue" and "The Purloined Letter," with their brilliant protagonist, Detective Dupin. Ever since structuralism and semiotics started paying attention to detective fiction almost forty years ago, notably in the classic essays by Roland Barthes and Umberto Eco on James Bond, academic critics have written a great deal about the various manifestations of this genre in fiction and film. We all know the various stages in which a detective story unfolds, whether in the Columbo format (actually invented by Dostoevsky in *Crime and Punishment*) of allowing the viewer or reader to see all of the details of the crime being committed, followed by its meticulous reconstruction on the part of the detective, or in the Sherlock Holmes format, with the dead body being discovered at the beginning, and the identity of the killer reserved for the end, or in the Agatha Christy variant, in which all of the suspects are assembled in a room (on a ship, on a train, in a secluded mansion, in a house on an island), where one of them will be proven to be the killer in the end. There is something quintessentially modern about the detective story, in cultures that have become increasingly fascinated by the infractions of rules and regulations that dictate our social roles, and by the logic of stories that apply the identity of "criminal" or "killer" to an individual, or that detail the genealogy of an individual who becomes a killer. The social determinism of this type of fiction confirms our suspicion that the mechanism of the state will get us in the end, and that its various representatives, as quirky and individualistic as they may be (from

Dupin, to Holmes, to Miss Marple, to Hercule Poirot, to Jessica Fletcher, to Columbo himself), will inevitably and efficiently perform their function of putting the criminal behind bars—in fact, their various types of individualism lure the reader into thinking that they are independent, when in fact their quirks are generated by the need to put criminals away. If I were a strict determinist, I might even go so far as to say that the modern psychopathic serial killer, in fiction and in fact, is an inevitable product of our social institutions.

If the detective story is the quintessential modern narrative form, the kinds of series that have dominated the history of television belong to a different paradigm, one in which the logic of the story's unfolding is secondary to something else, perhaps the representation of the mechanisms by which individual identities are both generated and entrapped by the concrete practices of major social institutions. Three types of programs, which I've named in the title of this section, have served as the foundation of dramatic television since its beginnings. This is not at all surprising, given the nature of the institutions depicted in these shows. According to the French philosopher Louis Althusser (a man who himself went temporarily insane, murdered his wife, and spent the rest of his life in a psychiatric institution), hospitals, police forces, and criminal justice systems, along with penitentiaries, schools, and universities, might be described as "ideological apparatuses of the state." These institutions are in charge of forming and maintaining individuals within categories that allow for the continuation and propagation of the state in its current form. They are focal points at which diverse forces interact and conflict with one another, drawing large numbers of people together in presuppositional relationships, constituting entire classes of individuals. For example, policemen are unthinkable without criminals, and vice versa; teachers cannot exist if there are no students, and vice versa; psychiatric "patients" or "cases" have no meaning if there are no psychiatrists; without an enemy, or at least a potential enemy, the military has no *raison d'être*. Within these apparatuses, the relative ideological values that bring them into existence are necessarily posited as absolutes—now that the Cold War is over, Hollywood and the Pentagon still can't get the idea of the Russians as the absolutely evil enemy out of their heads, and spy movies set during the Cold War still appear from time to time. Althusser didn't recognize that television itself and the mass media that dominate our lives are *the* ideological apparatus of what is becoming a multi-national state. You need only read the names of the companies that produce Hollywood films to realize that these multi-billion dollar media conglomerates are no more American than they are European or Asian. The television and cinema industries are thus macro apparatuses of the new, supra-national form of the state that is emerging, and which is linked to the proliferation of global capitalism, in which the ideas of ownership, nationality, and property are beginning to morph into unrecognizable forms.

In my first category, to which I will limit myself for the sake of brevity, I can think of at least a dozen cop shows that I've watched with more or less enthusiasm over the last thirty years, starting with *Highway Patrol, The Untouchables, Adam 12, Dragnet, The FBI, The Mod Squad, MacMillan and Wife, Get Christy Love, Cat and Mouse* (starring a very young and unknown Kim Basinger), *The Streets of San Francisco* (with a young Michael Douglas and Karl Malden), and proceeding through *Police Story, The Rookies, Charlie's Angels, Barretta, Hill Street Blues, Chips, Miami Vice,* and *SWAT,* to *NYPD Blue, Law and Order,* and even absurd things like *Silk Stalkings,* or that show about cops on bikes in Malibu whose name thankfully escapes me, and finally to all of the *Law and Order* spin-offs and all of the *CSI* clones (in Las Vegas, in Miami, etc.). Television critics today are all abuzz about the latest generation of cop shows, including *The Shield* and *The Wire,* which, fortunately for me, appear on HBO, which I don't get. Police shows are and always have been concerned with the exposition of ethical problems. In some cases, as in the earlier ones I've just mentioned, this exposition was close to propagandistic: Sergeant Friday's clean-cut, fresh-pressed suit persona was the virtual embodiment of a square-headed white morality that had to take on the multi-cultural scum of Los Angeles, just as Robert Stack's character in *The Untouchables* stood for the upright members of Prohibition society who were opposed to the evils of alcohol and their Mafia (that is, Italian, non-white) representatives. I won't even mention the propaganda aspects of *The F.B.I,* starring the dashing Efrem Zimbalist Jr., who looked much more like a retired night-club singer of the Rat Pack era than a federal agent. In the early '70's, cop shows tried to co-opt some of the "hip" and "groovy" social changes that had taken place in the '60's. Once the imagery that constitutes a sub-culture and its resistance to power becomes the subject of a syndicated television series, you can rest assured that whatever revolution the members of that sub-culture may have had in mind has failed. This is why VH-1 can now show re-runs of the most radical '60's films and images with impunity, since the external paraphernalia of the hippy generation have become mere fashion items that are being sold to a generation born in the '70's, '80's, and even '90's that has no notion of what the clothes and long hair of the '60's represented for people who lived through the radical movements of the time with passion and commitment. By 1974 or so, when the energy of the '60's was beginning to be defused by the filtering of hippy culture into the mainstream, and by the apathy and impatience of young people, images such as those of *The Mod Squad,* Christy Love, "Cat" of *Cat and Mouse,* and, a little later, *Charlie's Angels*—subject of several recent movies starring banal and boring actresses who look good on screen and can fake doing Kung Fu—became possible. The title of *The Mod Squad* just about says it all: three cops, one a black guy with a huge afro and cool tinted glasses, another a skinny blond chick with long stringy hair in a halter top and platform shoes, and a third white guy with sideburns and curly hair, worked together undercover to fight crime. Christy Love was a hip black chick with the biggest afro, the widest elephant pants, and the coolest VW bug you ever saw, but she was also a cop who could talk the language of the brothers on the street, and deal with her white bosses back at the station downtown. Since she was black, and a woman, Christy approached her police work from a perspective that was much more sensitive to the problems of everyday criminals. Cat was a skinny, sexy cop with long blond hair who had a square guy for a partner, and so they always fought about fundamental decisions of police work. In these series, it didn't matter so much who the criminals were and what they were guilty of; what was important was to see these members of the "counter culture" working as agents for the imposition and maintenance of a given social order. In this way, power inexorably expanded its tentacles to grasp elements (the civil rights movement, the women's movement, the anti-Vietnam movement, the peace and love culture) that had, for a time, seriously threatened the political stability of an America run by white males (like Robert Stack, Broderick Crawford in *Highway Patrol*, Karl Malden in *The Streets of San Francisco*, Efrem Zimbalist Jr., Jack Webb, etc.). From our temporal distance, it may seem as though television executives were trying to do something hip and alternative in their own way by producing shows with black and female representatives of the law, in the same way that today they pull kids off the streets of Baltimore and make them into television stars on *The Wire*. What they really accomplished, however, was to produce the illusion that these elements had been included within the configuration of forces that constituted power at the time. If you look at the statistics of women and minorities who hold political office, you will see that not much progress has been made in the last forty years, even if, as I revise these lines in May of 2008, we have a black man and a white woman as serious contenders for the highest political office in the land. Moreover, these programs included women and African Americans in a configuration of power that remained essentially unchanged, with the forces of order on one side, and those who wanted to undermine it, however minimally, on the other side. By placing members of possible counter-cultures within the state apparatus, power "colonized" subversive movements within the collective imaginary, and eventually assimilated them completely.

By the time *Charlie's Angels* became the number one show on television, whatever "alternative" pretensions the producers of cop shows might have had were completely abandoned. This series was nothing more than an extended advertisement for types of clothing, lines of cosmetics, and what was then the next generation of the Ford Mustang, which these girl cops drove from scene to scene. There was barely a young woman alive in the mid and late '70's who didn't want to look like Farrah Fawcett and Jacqueline Smith, and who didn't dream about having billows and billows of blown-dry hair framing her face with its highlighted cheekbones and glistening lips. The plot of each episode was essentially an excuse for putting these delightful young actresses in different settings in different outfits. In fact, this was one of the uncanny elements of the opening credits of the show, in which we got to see the transformation of the women from uniformed police officers to glamorous undercover agents. Whether they subdued criminals with fake karate chops, or chased down villains in designer jeans and high-heeled "Candies" shoes, the Angels were no more believable as cops than the Dalai Lama would be, which raises an important point: for the most part, dramatic television is absolutely non-realistic and unbelievable, and often verges on fantasy or collective fantasizing, which is, perhaps, exactly as drama has been since Hamlet spoke with his father's ghost or Phaedra suffered the consequences of her mother's bestial passion for a bull. When we watch drama, we don't in fact want to see reality; rather, we want to see what reality would look like if it were put through a series of imaginary and fantastical mutations.

Back in the late '60's and early '70's, a lot of people thought that *The Brady Bunch* was a fairly realistic representation of suburban American life. Watching this show almost forty years later, one can only marvel at how naive and stupid it is, which is precisely the point of the Brady parodies that were produced for the big screen in the '90's. Moreover, *The Brady Bunch* illustrated and instilled what one might call "wholesome white American values" (the sanctity of the large family, the utility of cooperation within it, the valorization of work and industriousness, the hierarchy of male-female in the household, the promotion of "sanitized" sex that is hidden from the children, the perfect harmony of the remarried couple with their brood of children mixed together, etc.) in the viewing public, even if the makers of the show were not conscious of this ultimate effect of their work. Nothing in the show was really problematic, even Jan's congenital jealousy of her older sister Marsha, who was prettier and, consequently, more popular at school than she. As far as I can remember, we were never told what had happened to the biological mother of the boys and the biological father of the girls, other than the fact that "the four men living all together were all alone" before Mike Brady met Carol, "the lovely lady who was bringing up three very lovely girls," as the show's theme song informed us. Did these parents die? Were Mike and Carol divorced? If so, what were the messy details of their divorces? Did the kids ever miss their real parents? Did they have any problems adapting to their step parents? Did they play little mind games to establish their dominance over them? These real-life questions make no sense in the fantasy world of *The Brady Bunch*, because narrative systems of representation such as this one are concerned with presenting idealized versions of reality in order to convey and enforce moral (rather than ethical) messages. Like most narratives, the show served as a support and a point of departure for a given configuration of power, since it is saturated by inequalities or all kinds. For example, Alice the maid has a boyfriend, Sam the Butcher. For some reason, Sam doesn't want to ask Alice to marry him (it's the man's decision, after all), and so Alice keeps living in her little room (which we never get to see) next to the Brady kitchen. We also never get to see where Sam lives, though perhaps we can assume that he lives back in the city, butchers being poorer than architects such as Mike Brady, who has a big house in the suburbs, etc. etc. etc. The show never interrogated these inequalities, since its function was to present them as a given that would be accepted without question by an ideal viewing public, that of the majority of Americans who had begun to flee to the suburbs in the 1950's, most of whom have never looked back (on the other hand, those of us who lived at the time in tiny houses in what is now known as the "inner city" looked at Mike Brady's den and his big back yard with considerable envy).

Similarly, it would be meaningless to apply real-life questions to *Charlie's Angels*. Here are a few sexist ones: did these glamour cops ever have their periods? If so, did they ever feel tired and cranky? Didn't they ever have arguments? Didn't their colleagues at work ever try to harass them sexually? You simply can't ask these questions of an imaginary world in which the cops always catch their man without staining their polyester jumpsuits or messing up their hair. The show portrayed a world in which crime-fighting could be done efficiently, accompanied by the pleasant aromas of perfumes, make-up, and unlimited supplies of hair spray. As a consequence, perhaps the program promulgated a work environment in which women, who were supposedly relatively new to the work force, had to be able to deal with extremely stressful situations without disfiguring themselves as objects of men's desire. From this somewhat unconscious perspective, the women entering the work force of the '70's, that extraordinary decade for feminist thinking, had to be competent, strong, and efficient, like the Angels, but they also had to remain sexy, feminine, pretty, and pleasing to the male "viewers" who worked with them. In other words, the apparently "progressive" premise of the show—that its women (described as "three little girls" in the opening credits) could do police work—disguised the reinforcement of gender stereotypes that made double demands of women who were taking on traditionally male roles. If you don't believe me, consider the fact that viewers have almost never expected male cops to be sexy and pleasant in a kind of Ken doll way, at least until recently (the pseudo lifeguard-cops of *Bay Watch* have to have perfect bodies, hairless pecs, perfect hair, perfect smiles), and with the possible exception of Eric Estrada on *Chips* or Jimmy Smits on *NYPD Blue*.

Speaking of sexy, however, nothing could top that hit cop show of the '80's, *Miami Vice*. Watching reruns of Don Johnson and his partner chasing down criminals with their big guns and their cream-colored suits, it's hard to imagine why this program caused such a stir back in the decade of excess. Nevertheless, the series was innovative in that it was the first to incorporate the techniques of music videos into the development of its plots: hand-held camera movements, staged slow-motion shots in which the cops showed off their suits, their hair, their lips, etc., interruptions in the flow of the narrative in order to present miniature videos that didn't necessarily have anything to do with the story at hand (also the stock in trade of series like *Bay Watch*, which regularly included video swimsuit calendar shots of Pamela Anderson and cheesy videos of singing groups visiting the beach). *Miami Vice* was also revolutionary to the extent that the sex-appeal of its male protagonists was one of its essential features, not in the sense that the actors *happened* to be sexually pleasing to its viewing audience (which may have been the case for series such as *Barretta*, starring Robert Blake, back in the '70's), but in the sense that the actors were specifically chosen for their ability physically to arouse the interest of some of the members of their viewing audience. As fragmentary and rudimentary as the presentation of the male body may have been in this show, it began a procedure that has continued and intensified in subsequent productions. In fact, the plots of the police stories presented in *Miami Vice* played a subordinate role to the exposition of "coolness" that was the show's essence, which, perhaps predictably, has achieved a kind of iconic status: one need only watch the videos of the show that have been posted on YouTube, along with the comments that thousands of viewers have posted about them, to realize that nostalgia often develops in incomprehensible ways. Don Johnson walking along South Beach in his cream-colored suit and his black Raybans evidently has the same effect on people who weren't born when the show was aired as Jim Morrison had on those of us who were in college in the '80's.

But the '80's were also a time of renewed "realism" in the cop show, for lack of a better term. I'm thinking, of course, of *Hill Street Blues*, which made a name for Steven Bochco, and perfected the snappy dialogue and crisp editing that is the norm in the series of the '90's and today, such as *NYPD Blue* and *Law and Order*. The defining characteristic of The Hill was the earnestness of its characters, who confronted moral dilemmas that were almost meant to be worthy of classical tragedy, as in the endless conflicts of interest between Chief Furillo and his love interest, a stunning lawyer who was a DA or defense attorney, if memory serves. The characters of this series spent a good deal of time running through the nitty-gritty streets of their district, while the Chief worked out the higher moral dilemmas back at the precinct. The artificiality of the program was always revealed, however, by a certain tendency on the part of the producers to conclude most of the programs with what I used to think of as "a sexy ending," most of the time with Chief Furillo and his wife or girlfriend, Joyce Davenport (thank you, YouTube) literally in bed together, after having been run through the ringer by yet another conflict of interest. The banality of candlelight and clinking wine glasses in a foaming bubble bath often were integral parts of these sexy endings, which I guess were supposed to be "high-concept," hip, stylish, and '80's versions of the traditional American "Happy Ending." This raises two important points that are characteristic of pop culture at the beginning of the 21st Century: first, it is increasingly concerned with recycling and modifying traditional motifs (such as the happy ending), which are merely disguised beneath variations produced by technical developments (the hand-held camera work of *NYPD Blue*, for example); second, pop culture is more and more concerned with the style or the manner in which a message is communicated, and less and less with the *content* of that message itself. Thus while it may have been striking at the time, the relative realism of *Hill Street Blues* merely presented familiar stories in a package that was appropriate to its decade, and the two ends of the frame in which each story was presented signaled this fact to the viewer, from the slick theme music by Mike Post (which was a hit record in the '80's), to the sexy endings that somehow made the moral dilemmas of Furillo and company more hip and rewarding. Moreover, the ultimate implicit message of this insignia series of the decade of excess was that one deserved a superlative (if hackneyed) orgasmic experience after a traumatic day at work confronting thorny moral problems.

The cop shows of the '90's were all about coolness: cool accents (the New York cop with a Chicago accent on *NYPD Blue*, who also did ads for Cadillac and Pepsi), cool hair (Jimmy Smits, formerly of *LA Law*, who disappeared when alopecia began to plague him), cool camera movements, cool crimes, etc. The stories don't matter so much, as long as they represent coolness in such a way that the viewer feels satisfied that he or she has experienced it or witnessed it. Not only are the cops in these cop shows cool, they're also intelligent, and at times even sensitive. For example, the two detectives on one of my favorite programs, the hybrid *Law & Order*, which is both a cop and a law show, are incredibly efficient and to the point, which is the essence of their coolness. Wherever they go, and in whatever circumstances they find themselves, they are never out of control. They both always wear impeccable suits. One is an older cop with salt and pepper hair and a cigarette voice (though I've never seen him smoking one); the other was a handsome, young Chicano with gelled hair, until he was replaced by a handsome, young black man with a goatee. They ask questions of their imaginary criminals rapid-fire, alternating back and forth, and when they deliver their reports to their superiors, they follow this same scripted pattern. By the looks on their faces, they manifest a detached disgust motivated by the mad crimes committed all around them, which they are in charge of investigating, yet which almost never cause them to lose their control and their cool. This was also a noteworthy characteristic of Captain Furillo, and probably originated with the Joe Friday character of *Dragnet*, who nonetheless often unleashed moralistic diatribes against his adversaries (also well represented on YouTube). In this idealized world, we never see heroic cops who are drug addicts or alcoholics, who beat their wives, who have ulcers, who are on the take, or who are simply unnerved by the difficulties of the job they do, resulting in tragic incidents such as the shooting of unarmed men reaching for their wallets in dark doorways. In my opinion, a truly "realistic" cop would be divorced, troubled, brutal, hostile, touchy, two-faced, and treacherous, or simply over worked, stressed out, or even terminally bored. This does not mean that he or she would not do a good job, and provide a valuable service to the community. One does not have to be morally perfect in order to do the right thing for others. I would love to see a series dedicated to the exploits of a policeman who was loved by his community for his crime-fighting skills, but who was unscrupulous, racist, and brutal in both his public and private lives, verging on being a fascist: such was the case of one of Philadelphia's most famous policemen, who became the city's mayor, Frank Rizzo, for whom a statue was erected on the steps of the Municipal Services Building in my home town.

In the stylized world of '90's television, however, the heroic cops faced few ethical dilemmas. Their righteous indignation translated into the slickness and efficiency of their methods. Perhaps this is the key to understanding what has happened during the last four or five decades in the representation of police work on television. Power in the '90's doesn't bully its objects. It doesn't haggle over details, unleash moral diatribes, mull over problems in its leisure time, and hide the wrongs it does by making sure that its beneficial exploits define its public manifestations. In the guise of its various, imaginary representatives, power merely presents itself as *that which is right*. Like President Clinton, power in the '90's was all surface and representation: it had no underlying principles, no beliefs, no soul. Its definition of right and wrong was in its actions, which were carried out in a certain opaque style, which entailed the right clothes, the right hair, the right tone, the appropriate expression on the face (I can hear the former President saying, "I feel your pain"), and a forcefulness of attitude that seemed to leave no room for the questioning of its motives and ends. After the '90's, power has become so efficient at manipulating images and perceptions that it no longer needs to send out the National Guard to control the population, which believes, for the most part, that it is living through a kind of Golden Age, thanks to the incessant statistics that the media pump at us every day from various government offices. When the government does turn its force against its own population, the damage to its image of coolness can be almost irreparable (Ruby Ridge, Waco, etc.). With the disastrous Iraq invasion still on our hands, this principle has been extended to a global scale: in the age of virtual reality, any actual activity on the part of power is doomed to be overwhelmed by the material facts of the real world. This is why effective government at this stage has to limit itself merely to the manipulation of information, sound bites, images, and perceptions, since governments no longer know how to employ real violence in a world in which subversive power has gone viral, and can strike from any number of locations at any time.

In conclusion, our national obsession with the representation of "ideological state apparatuses" such as police forces, hospitals, courtrooms, prisons, and schools derives from the fact that our very being as individual subjects is in large part generated by the action of these entities. In the examples on which I have focused in this chapter, police dramas are part of an entire spectrum of representations through which, in which, or even *as* which political power disseminates itself. Moreover, as techniques of representation develop locally, such as the camera movements and editing techniques that arose in music videos, they are incorporated into the global depiction of power, transforming its means and its methods, and eventually transforming power itself. The real and actual practices of police work, for example, ultimately mimic the countless representations of it that we see on television and on the big screen. Today's cops are no longer the good-natured Irishmen on the beat who were quick to blow their whistles and swing their billy clubs. Today they're more like Captain Furillo, who undoubtedly would have imposed a course in sensitivity training on his cadets. On every level and in every domain (in the classroom, the courtroom, the precinct, the emergency room—oh, those sexy, sensitive docs of *ER*!), power continually refines its representations of itself, and has its own procedures refined by new technical developments in representation. Within this complex, reciprocal, and pre-suppositional procedure, each individual delineates his or her place in relation to power, at the same time that power generates and restricts each individual's identity. In Nietzschean terms, when I watch these television shows that depict apparatuses of power, these shows are also watching me, and when I go to the movies, the movies also go into me, capture me, and enact imperceptible re-definitions of my very being.

Theme Restaurants

Like most people in my home town, I imagine, I'm quite excited by the idea that a Hard Rock Café has opened on Market Street in Philadelphia. I've even decided that I'm going to buy the typical "Hard Rock Café Philadelphia" tee-shirt in order to demonstrate my pride in my native city, which is silly, I know, but which still means that Philly has finally achieved the status of London, New York, Los Angeles, Beijing, Madrid, Barcelona, Paris, Chicago, Phoenix, Vegas, and Orlando. Why is it that amazingly different people from different countries and cultures are somehow intrigued by the idea of buying a series of tee-shirts from Hard Rock Cafés all around the world? How has this scandalously obvious marketing gimmick managed to convince people to pay the Hard Rock Corporation in order to have the right to wear an advertisement for the restaurant on their chests? The first answer to this question has to do with the desire to project oneself into an adventure narrative. A minimalist example is provided by the following bumper sticker, frequently seen in New Hampshire and northern New England: "This car climbed Mt. Washington." For those of you who don't know it, Mt. Washington is one of the highest peaks on the East Coast (which isn't saying much), and is one of the most inclement places on the planet for most of the year, with temperatures so low in Winter (30-40 degrees below zero) that it is closed to visitors, while in summer it barely remains above freezing. A car that has climbed this icy, muddy, inhospitable mountain has survived some kind of adventure, and its owner is thus inscribed within the micro-narrative that recounts the story of this adventure on his or her back bumper. This is also the case of your typical tourist who buys a "Hard Rock Café Bangkok" tee-shirt. Aside from the fact that the shirt makes money for the multi-national corporation that runs these restaurants (which, in a bizarre twist, was bought by the Seminole nation in 2007), and provides advertising for them, it also allows the consumer who buys the shirt to embark on the adventure narrative of his or her trip to Thailand or China or Spain or Phoenix.

The second answer is that the Hard Rock Café is supposed to be a cool and unique kind of place, which means that the person who is wearing its tee-shirt somehow shares those qualities. The purpose of the shirt is to *display* the coolness of the person who is wearing it, in a culture that is increasingly overdetermined by displays of all kinds. Far from being an abstraction, coolness is produced by conventional material means. The huge Fender Stratocaster that beckons visitors into the Las Vegas Hard Rock Café is the symbol of these methods, which function by accumulation and saturation. There are no empty spaces in the interior of the café. Everywhere the patron looks, he or she must see a photo, an object, a person, or a design that signifies the meaning of the place (pictures of rock stars, framed and mounted musical instruments, outfits worn by famous performers at concerts, waiters in chic, black uniforms, television screens playing music videos), which the patron constitutes in his or her mind simply by absorbing the ambiance of the restaurant. Sometimes, the corporation that runs these restaurants invites rock stars to promote a given franchise; otherwise, the ambiance of the place consists of the *aura* of rock and roll superstardom that the accumulation and saturation of objects and images creates. This aura functions paradoxically by means of presence and absence: the rock stars present in the photos on the walls are necessarily absent, yet they are closer to the clients of the restaurant than they would be otherwise. The clients of the Café have the impression that they are only once-removed from the world of the spectacle that surrounds and even engulfs them. They have been swallowed by the marketing techniques that configure this imaginary world, yet they are the ones who attempt to digest and assimilate the material image of the Café at the same time, and perhaps in the same way, that they ingest hamburgers and French fries. Despite the tenuous existence of "rock and roll coolness" in the Café's images and pseudo-sacred objects, its clients are perhaps unconsciously convinced that they have assimilated its imaginary nutrients. The attitude of the place becomes part of their flesh, which is all the more reason why they should display it on the surface of their bodies, as a kind of branding. Incidentally, in the prestigious business schools into which all universities are investing increasing amounts of money, and where marketing is an academic subject, "branding" has become a sub-discipline of the field (I heard a well-known political party referred to recently as follows: "the Republican brand has become stale"). Its specialists apparently have missed the irony of the fact that the original sense of branding—the marking of an animal's skin with a hot iron in order to mark it as someone's property—is quite appropriate to the ways in which global capitalism "brands" individuals as consuming subjects. Those of us who want to wear the mark of the Hard Rock Café become the "property" of that brand, in some sense.

The encounter with the Hard Rock Café and the other theme restaurants is essentially an out of body experience, which retains remnants of sacred rituals, especially those of the Catholic church (may the practicing members of my culture and religion forgive me for any sacrilege I may commit in these pages). One of the key elements that distinguishes Catholicism from the other major world religions is the representation of the divine in images. Islam and Judaism literally forbid the graphic representation of the deity. One of the major points of contention between Catholics and Protestants in the 16th Century was precisely the representation of Saints and Virgins that vulgarized the sacred in the Catholic Church, and which reached even more exaggerated extremes in the Counter Reformation and its expression in the Baroque, whose principle was excess. In the Catholic Church, in the sacrament of the Eucharist, the Body of Christ *literally* descends into the host, which means that the believer *literally* eats the Body of Christ during this most sacred moment of the Mass. In contrast, for the Protestants, the bread and wine of the Eucharist were merely symbols of the Christian's "ingestion" of Christ's teaching. (Sadly, rivers of literal blood were shed for the sake of these minimal differences in the 16th and 17th Centuries in Europe). In other words, the function of the Catholic Mass is to make the sacred body literally present in the Church, before the body of the faithful. Furthermore, the function of the image in the Church is to embody and, in some cases, virtually to *become* the sacred body that offers itself to the contemplation of the fervent believer. For these believers, the image *is* the thing-in-itself, for example, as in the case of the Virgin Mary who appeared not too long ago in a puddle in a subway station in Mexico City, causing people to line up for hours to catch a glimpse of this rather peculiar Blessed Mother. Or should I say peculiar, but not unusual: manifestations of Virgins are quite common in Catholic countries from Guatemala to Poland, and images of the Virgin paraded about the streets of cities as different from one another as Seville and Boston are the heart and soul of public festivals in both towns in the Spring.

Similarly, the Hard Rock Café projects an ambiance of rock and roll coolness precisely by displaying objects that have a profane yet sacred aura about them, such as Jimi Hendrix's guitar, or Elvis's white cape, or Jim Morrison's leather pants, etc. These objects are almost always encased in glass, with little plaques identifying them, giving the date at which they were used by the "sacred" person to whom they belonged, often with an accompanying photo that shows the object actually in the hands of the (often deceased) person. This kind of display of sacred relics was, of course, one of the basic modalities of Medieval Catholic worship, for example in the most important shrine of Medieval Christendom, the Cathedral of Santiago de Compostela, Spain, in which the bones of St. James the apostle supposedly were (and are) preserved. In the same vein, the supposed bones of Saint Pasiano, the 5th-century bishop of Barcelona, are conserved in a gold-framed glass case built in the 17th Century, beneath an enormous, gilded baroque altar depicting his life and martyrdom, in the church of St. Just in Barcelona. Similarly, in a lovely Benedictine cloister in Toulouse, the bones of St. Thomas Aquinas are preserved in a beautifully decorated wooden chest, that has chairs set up in front of it, so that visitors may sit and meditate on the profound meaning of the Saint's presence there, as I have on many occasions. The Hard Rock Café's displays represent, perhaps, an attempt to restore some of the ancient and traditional uniqueness to objects that was typical of former ages, when objects such as St. Pasiano's altar and display case had to be produced by hand, whereas everyone knows that Hendrix's guitar and Morrison's pants were mass produced (see Walter Benjamin's seminal essay "On the Work of Art in the Age of Mechanical Reproduction"). Or perhaps they are merely atavisms of habits of thinking about objects that are completely foreign to the age of mechanical production. Whatever the case may be, it may be argued that the Hard Rock Cafés of the world are points of pilgrimage in precisely the Medieval Christian sense, and that the Hard Rock tee shirt is an identifying marker of this pilgrimage in the same way that the scallop shell identified persons who were making the pilgrimage to Santiago (to this day, in French, scallops are called "coquilles St. Jacques"—St. James's shells).

While Planet Hollywood shares many of these characteristics, it is different in that the cult of the image characteristic of this type of place is taken to its most extreme. The icons, relics, photos, objects, etc. that adorn the interior of the restaurant are meant to represent, or project, or *imbue* the space with the aura of fictional film characters, who themselves have become the saints of the contemporary world. The display of relics in this case is thus emptied of its primordial significance, in the sense that their contemplation can in no way bring the viewer into contact with a real person who can be located in history, whether it be profane or sacred, allowing for the intervention of the adored personage into the private life of the individual (while many saints may have been legendary figures, they can still be situated in the sacred history that stretches from Eden to the Last Judgment). In the Hard Rock Café, for example, the rock 'n roll figures intervene in the life of the individual often by literally giving him or her an identity and a purpose—how many Americans (and others) base their lives on the fact that they are Elvis fans?—in the same way that the contemplation of the sacred, suffering image of Jesus provided purpose and meaning to the lives of the medieval faithful. Nonetheless, the contemplation of cinematographic images and objects in Planet Hollywood retains one of the visual functions that has been at the heart of Catholicism since its beginnings. By meditating upon these images in an unconscious and "distracted" manner, as Benjamin might have remarked, the viewer or client or diner at Planet Hollywood internalizes, absorbs, consumes, or assimilates the hundreds of stories that are depicted on the walls, thus assimilating an ideology and an order of morality that are propagated by the film industry, whether intentionally or not.

While this process of indoctrination was quite simple and monolithic in Europe—medieval painting depicted mainly Biblical stories and the lives of the saints—the structure and ends of the cinema industry in Hollywood are so complex that one would be hard pressed to discern a single ideology or a single moral code, despite the current European paranoia that their cultures are being invaded by imaginary products from the United States. A brief look at the credits of Hollywood films reveals that most of them are multi-national products, financed with capital that flows through complex circuits linking Tokyo, London, Paris, Berlin, New York, and Los Angeles, directed by Europeans as often as by Americans (Jan de Bont (*Speed, Twister, Speed 2*) and Paul Verhoeven (*Basic Instinct, Showgirls*) are good examples), starring European as well as American actors, and so on. Quite simply, the goal of a basic "Hollywood" film is to make as much money as possible. And while films such as *Independence Day* may embody a distasteful American nationalism, it should not be assumed that they do so in order to propagate this type of ideology. While this slightly nationalistic sci-fi parody of '50's invasion films made American audiences laugh at its mock patriotism—evident in the fact that a black man and a Jew were the heroes who saved the planet from invading aliens—European critics were outraged by what they perceived as the bald-faced apologia of a single American super power. At any rate, it could be that the producers of this and other films included this little dosage of nationalism with these two reactions in mind, given the fact that many knowing Americans like to mock any manifestations of patriotism, while Europeans will bash Americans for their imperialism and cultural ignorance any chance they get. In other words, the ideology that is quite clearly represented in this film was far from the element that sold it to a record number of spectators: what people really wanted to see was cool aliens and the world's most famous monuments (the Eiffel tower, the White House, the Empire State Building, the Taj Mahal) exploding in cool ways. As Jean Baudrillard remarked, this American enthusiasm for on-screen explosions came back to haunt us when the images of the hijacked airplanes crashing into the Twin Towers in New York were repeated countless times on television in the days following September 11, 2001. In contrast, the iconography of medieval painting disseminated and reinforced Catholic ideology and all that it entailed, in a quite conscious and persistent manner during more than a millennium.

The necessity that the Hollywood film industry imposes upon its spectators is much simpler and more insidious than that of the medieval Catholic Church, which at least promised salvation to its members. Films essentially make their viewers want to *see* stories, as opposed to reading them or listening to them. The cinema acts out plots, incarnates them through special effects, and brings the most impossible, otherworldly stories to life on the screen. Contemporary individuals who have grown up with television and the movies need to see their heroes, models, and antipodes represented in flesh and blood by actors who themselves become heroes simply by virtue of the fact that they are able to shed their own identities and assume other ones in the celluloid and increasingly digital world. The need to *see* that the movie industry creates in its clients creates them as *spectators*, beings with a visual or scopic addiction, much in the same way that the tobacco industry created smokers as beings with a nicotine addiction. Thus the images that are displayed in Planet Hollywood have three aspects: first is that which is typical of all images, the fact of representation itself, which embodies three-dimensional beings with flesh and blood in the two dimensional domain, and making present beings who are absent; second is the fact that these images are representations of fictional characters; third is the aspect reserved for the box office stars (Stallone, Schwarzenegger, Bruce Willis, Demi Moore) whose physical being transcends the multiple layers of representation that constitute the ambiance of the restaurant. When a patron of Planet Hollywood sees a poster of Rocky or of the Terminator, he or she also sees the hyper-famous actors Stallone and Schwarzenegger. The kinds of positive reflexes that the satisfaction of this visual addiction generates perhaps explains why this latter figure became governor of California so easily, with no political experience whatsoever.

The visual world that the restaurant puts into play for its clients thus serves as a model for behavior, a vehicle for communicating and perhaps reinforcing ideologies and capitalistic hierarchies, and a source of two types of identity. In my opinion, spectators only vaguely want to be like the characters they see in films, even if the cinema may be the main medium through which fashions and modes of speech are disseminated in the general public. It's one thing to get a haircut like Demi Moore's in *Ghost* or Meg Ryan's in *French Kiss*, it's quite another to quit one's job in order to follow a runaway fiancée to Paris, as Meg Ryan's character does in the latter film. Increasingly, successful films are about people who cannot possibly appear in the average spectator's boring life—Hannibal Lecter, Forrest Gump, the hero of *Sling Blade*, the starship pilots of *Independence Day*, Captain Picard and company, Neo and Trinity in *The Matrix*. Rather, the ultimate model and identity that the movie industry inculcates in all of us who love the movies is that of the flesh and blood figure whom we can glimpse through the layers of representations that constitute the ambiance of the restaurant, and who are among its main stockholders. And what everyone wants in America today, at least until they realize that it's impossible, is to *become* Stallone, Schwarzenegger, Moore, Ryan, or Willis. Everyone wants to live the American dream that leads from waiting tables, driving a taxi, and going to auditions in New York, to a role in a soap opera in L.A., to a break in a major movie or TV series, to a decadent palace in Miami Beach and photo ops in Cannes, to promotional tours in Planet Hollywood restaurants around the world, complete with an attractive stock portfolio. The loop of successive simulacra that the restaurant circulates in its images ends by enfolding its patrons in a phantasmagoric (if banal) ideology of the American dream. In contrast to the Horatio Alger story of rags to riches, the Planet Hollywood version compels individuals into the domain of the simulacrum, and the product that they are called upon to produce as their riches is their own image, and the story of themselves that they apply to that image *as* themselves.

For this reason, individual films have become multi-million-dollar corporations themselves, since so much is invested by our society in the production of each individual's image of him or herself, from health and beauty products, to clothing and shoes, to exercise programs and equipment, to automobiles that reinforce certain self-images, to luxury cruises that provide adventure narratives one can tell one's friends, and so on. Economists have been saying for years that the industries of the future are in entertainment, with industrial giants like Westinghouse buying CBS and General Electric buying NBC, only eventually to be bought out by pure media companies such as Viacom, which owns MTV, VH-1, Blockbuster, and Nickolodeon. While the largest and most profitable companies in the US are still those that manufacture goods for which there is a basic social need—Exxon, General Motors, Ford, General Electric, Dupont, Merck, Philip Morris—the entertainment business manipulates the flow of supply and demand by continually changing the identity types that individuals are compelled to require of themselves. In a sense, then, Planet Hollywood embodies a kind of collective unconscious, which contains thousands of possible identities, all of them empty, serving merely as mannequins onto which new clothes, new cars, new homes, new marital partners are pinned. Actors and actresses are empty beings that may be filled by any combination of attributes. Planet Hollywood is the celebration of the individual as this empty place of desire. In the age of reality television (see below), the emptiness and interchangeability of identity are displayed to the exclusion of everything else on the small screen.

The Spice Girls as Moral Models

I remember perfectly well the first time I saw a Spice Girls video. I was lifting weights in a gym in Barcelona, surrounded by perfect, near-perfect, and wanting-to-be-perfect bodies, both male and female, dedicated to chiseling and maintaining that perceived perfection at the cost of near-starvation and grueling exercise. The context of this first viewing is far from irrelevant. The types of exercise that one performs in a weight room are, of course, gender specific, as are the modes of dress, though this is becoming less and less true as gym culture becomes more and more prevalent in the US. In general, women who work out wear very tight, elastic clothes, which in some cases are meant to highlight the effects of their exercise, especially in their gluteal areas. In my gym in Barcelona, the women were always waiting in line to use machines that worked their hips and thighs, and, to a lesser extent, to use machines that lightly worked their pectoral muscles (they preferred machines to your basic bench press, which is much more strenuous and "masculine"). In contrast, men who work out may wear tight shorts, or even tight short shorts in certain settings and cultures (the French men in a gym I frequent in Paris seem to love them), but in general they tend to wear loose-fitting tee-shirts, even though these barely reveal the desired effects of spending time in the gym for a man, i.e., a bigger chest, more developed shoulders, a wide back, and stronger arms (in every gym, of course, there are always at least a handful of very developed men in either tiny tank tops or tight fitting, sleeveless shirts). Essentially, however, the goal of working out is the same for men and women: to accentuate and shape the parts of the body that signify gender, insofar as this is possible. Women want rounder, firmer butts, while there's virtually nothing that they can do in the gym to enlarge their breasts (on the contrary, it's well known that the size of women's breasts decreases as they become more muscular, and that female body builders often have silicon implants); men want bigger biceps and pecs. Slim and well-developed abdominal muscles have become the bodily signifier of "sexiness" or "sexuality" for both genders, and both men and women in the gym spend a considerable amount of time doing various types of crunches, sit-ups, leg raises, etc. As I sat there distractedly obsessing about the state of my own abs, surrounded by people and apparatuses devoted to the controlled disfiguration of the body, my eye was caught by what was then the number one video on MTV Europe (this must have been in February of 1997), which of course was the constant feature of the various TV screens distributed throughout the weight room.

Imagine the Bonneville Salt Flats, which are a familiar image to American car enthusiasts and speed-trial junkies. Five very young women appear against this dry backdrop, and the music kicks in—a somewhat techno-version of the hip-hop grooves introduced on the West Coast in the '90's, and made popular by Doctor Dre and Snoop Dogg, complete with the whistling synthesizer hook that presents one of the main themes of this song, the Spice Girls' "Be There." Each one of the Girls takes turns singing the lead, and standing in front of the camera, while the other four adopt various poses and dance in the background. The intro is a parody of '70's Kung Fu movies: first there appears a brunette, "Sporty Spice," in imaginary street gear (Adidas running suit pants, tight sports top, retro basketball sneakers, etc.), who is announced in the video as "Melanie C. as Katrina Highkick"; next a two-toned redhead in micro vinyl shorts, "Ginger Spice," announced as "Geri as Trixi Firecracker"; then comes a blonde, very English-looking woman wearing an extremely short black dress, known as "Baby Spice," whom the credits name as "Emma as Kung Fu Candy"; then another brunette, "Posh Spice," wearing a kind of painted-on black jumpsuit, à la the fantastic Emma Peel character of *The Avengers* series of the '60's, named as "Victoria as Midnight Miss Suki"; finally "Scary Spice" appears flying through the air, wearing a very short skirt and a leopard-skin bustier that reveals her perfect abs, with the caption "Melanie B as Blazin' Bad Zula." At times the Girls appear in a retro '70's muscle car that's speeding across the flats. At other times, for instance during the harmonica solo in the middle of the song, they appear individually, assuming various kung-fu and kick boxer poses, and throwing virtual-reality boomerangs at virtual-reality glass bottles that explode atop their pedestals. The look of the video is inspired by *Road Warrior* and *Mad Max*, the implication being that these are post-apocalyptic super chicks who have survived the nuclear holocaust and have become mutant babes who somehow have managed to find brand new clothes. Their fighting skills have been refined to such an extent that they can kill anyone at a distance with what look like titanium boomerangs. They roam the salt plane in their muscle car, perfectly dressed, looking for adversaries, who are men who appear at random in classic cars, only to be tied up and carried away by the girls. These visual semiotics of the video are completely incongruous with the innocuous, even conservative message of the song, perhaps best embodied in the defiantly-pronounced rap in the middle of the song: "I'll give you everything you want, I swear/ just promise you'll always be there." The chorus of the song repeats the same motif: "I'm givin' you everything/ all my joy to bring, this I swear./ All that I want from you/ is a promise you will be there." This is essentially what Donna Reed says to Jimmy Stewart in the middle of *It's a Wonderful Life*. Similarly, the verse of their first big hit, "Wanna Be," could be taken right out of the Mormon Tabernacle Choir Youth Group Indoctrination Manual, which reads something like: "If you wanna be my lover, you gotta get wit' my friends. / Makin' love's too easy, friendship never ends."

This incongruity of song and video highlights one of the essential features of popular music in the era of trash culture, and which reached one of its logical apogees in the '90's, after being born with the figure of Elvis Presley on the Ed Sullivan show. The mass success of any given song depends upon the semiotically-complex image associated with it, rather than being based solely on the quality of the music itself. Granted, "Be There" is a rather clever pop song, written by experienced producers who are evidently well-acquainted with the major musical trends in the West. Nevertheless, it remains a rather simple pastiche of R & B vocals with hip-hop rhythms. What really sold the song were the spectacular images of perfect young bodies that have somehow survived the apocalypse and have become stronger and more desirable ("sexier") because of the experience. Moreover, the implicit message of the song and video taken together is not only that these apparently frighteningly sexy young women have survived the end of the world, they have also done so "intact" in the archaic sense of the term. The phrase, "I'll give you everything, on this I swear/ just promise you'll always be there," appeals to male viewers on two levels: the first is the overt offer of satisfaction from these female figures who present themselves as hyperbolic objects of desire; the second is the conditional demand for a promise of fidelity, which implies marriage as well as *virginity*, as paradoxical as this may seem. In other words, the video and the song combine the fascination of the death instinct, manifested in its post-apocalyptic imagery, with scopic masculine desire (provoked by significant exposed body parts—abs, backsides, muscular legs), and with a desire for the cuddly, innocent, eternally virginal eternal feminine. Judging from the reaction of millions of teenage girls all over the Western world, who apparently used to adopt the identities of each of the Spice Girls (Ginger, Scary, Sporty, Posh, Baby—gender identity now comes in a variety of "flavors," just like any commodity or Barbie doll), especially pre-adolescent young women felt compelled to identify themselves with the complex action figures that the video presented.

Watching the video in my gym, it was evident to me that trash culture continuously develops new variations of the same elements: the distinction of male and female, on which most human cultures and economies are based; the accentuation of this difference within and through social practices; the dissemination of images and narratives that call the individual into being as a subject who reproduces this difference in him or herself, both in the abstract story that defines him or her, and, increasingly, in the flesh that constitutes his or her physical being. The Spice Girls were thus and are still extraordinarily popular because they literally embodied the abstract yet material procedures by which our modern, industrialized economies attempt to bring us into being as subjects within a commodity culture. The collective nature of this and other groups demonstrate that their success depends more upon that which they represent than upon the individuality of its members. As the Latin-American group Menudo showed during the '80's, the members of this type of group are like the components of a machine, and may be changed at will as long as they have the necessary characteristics that allow for the functioning of the group. For the Spice Girls, what counts is their attitude, the way they dress, and the youth of their bodies, which present possible identity suits to avid spectators who apparently are just dying to try them on. To give you an idea of the scale of the enduring interest of the young population in this virtual configuration of gender, the "Wanna Be" video on YouTube has been viewed more than seven million times, whereas a popular song by a singer like Justin Timberlake, "Rock Your Body," was viewed only 131,000 times the last time I looked. Something about the putting on and taking off of external identifications, especially when these acts are performed by women, is extraordinarily compelling to individuals who are "invested" in the functioning of popular culture.

Despite their provocative appearances, which seem rather tame after ten years have gone by, the Spice Girls offered a kind of G-rated, cuddly, moralized, white representation of "feminine" subjectivity that was apt for girls entering their teens (when my nieces were in their late teens in the early '90's, they found the Spice Girls childish and insulting to their intelligence). Their position, at least as it was defined in their songs, was essentially the same as Doris Day's in two of my favorite films, *Lover Come Back* and *Pillow Talk*: a woman can offer herself as the object of a man's desire as long as certain pre-marital and marital conditions are met; a woman's sexuality is limited to her perception of herself as an object of desire, while the purpose of her being as a sexual subject is to accommodate herself to the demands of men's desires (any cover of *Cosmopolitan* essentially repeats this same motif); sex for women is limited to monogamous relationships with men (implicitly stated in the Spice Girls' song "When Two Become One"); sex for women is inextricably linked to the love relationship, and all that it entails (fidelity, friendship, exclusivity, etc.); a woman should always be in control of herself, and should control any situation in which she finds herself with a man by withholding or giving her body as object of desire ("If you wanna be my lover,/ First you gotta be my friend."). In this last instance, even Doris Day enjoyed a kind of freedom that is foreign to the Girls: in *Lover Come Back*, one of the main pillars of the plot is the idea that Doris's character cannot control herself once she gets drunk. One of the most delirious and delicious scenes of the film is one in which Doris sings a song entitled "Surrender," during which she is preparing to serve some cold champagne to Rock Hudson in his bedroom. She is holding two glasses as she goes toward his room, of course, and a beatified look comes across her face as she sings the last three words of the song, "Surrender, surrender, surrender . . ." One of the basic ideas of this film is thus that there was still a part of a woman's sex drive that was absolutely beyond her control, and which could overcome her body at the slightest provocation. We know that Doris will wind up in bed with Rock as soon as she has even one drink, and in fact, after accidentally becoming drunk (it's a long story), the two of them wake up married and hung over in bed in a motel in Maryland (the '50's, East Coast, Catholic precursor of Las Vegas, at least in terms of marriage). Of course, for Doris Day's character in this film, this complete loss of control had to have certain consequences, which are basically those of the Spice Girls: she had to be married after having sex, and her relationship with Rock Hudson had to develop into a loving marriage. (The case of this box-office hero who represented a kind of arche-heterosexual masculinity, while being himself a closeted homosexual in the '50's perhaps merits a chapter of its own.) For the Spice Girls, however, this area beyond the control of the woman as subject does not exist, perhaps for a good reason, with the specter of date rape haunting the consciousness of today's young girls.

For all of these reasons, the millions of middle class parents whose daughters have posters of the Spice Girls in their bedrooms should not be alarmed. Whether they know it or not, these young English girls have become the Third Millennium version of Donna Reed and Doris Day, i.e., they are models for the same kind of bourgeois moral code that limited the scope of female sexuality to its role as object of male desire within marriage. Of course, these middle class parents should not be alarmed if this is indeed what they want for their daughters.

Tractor Pulls, Monster Trucks, Car Shows

The tractor pull is perhaps the postmodern equivalent of the State Fair, from which it derives its origins and its meaning. At the traditional Fair, people from all over the State would come to see the fattest pigs, the biggest bulls and roosters, cows that gave the most milk, hens that laid the most eggs, horses that could pull the largest load, seeds that produced the greatest yields, the largest watermelon or tomato, etc. These agricultural goods are of course still the center of attention at State Fairs that are still held all over the United States, though in States in which agriculture is no longer the main occupation of its inhabitants, the Fair often becomes nothing more than an oversized carnival financed with tax money. For example, I once went to the New Jersey (still known as "The Garden State") State Fair, at which the main attraction was a white jump-suited, overweight, bewigged Chubby Checker, who was still twistin' after all these years, and who undoubtedly is still twistin' in Vegas, Atlantic City, or, if he's been demoted, in Foxwoods or—God forbid—Branson, Missouri. Without a doubt, the moment when tractors were introduced at State Fairs was an important one in American history, whose consequences are still being worked out, including the over-farming and erosion that tractors make possible (the image of the Dust Bowl is a poignant one for Baby-Boomers and their parents). I imagine that at some point, the fascination of ever bigger and more powerful tractors, and the things which they were capable of doing, became so great at the State Fairs that they eclipsed the banality of thousand-pound stud bulls and gigantic zucchinis, and gave birth to a new kind of spectacle. The tractors that are the stars of today's shows in arenas from Philadelphia to Oakland are only remotely related to the McCormack and John Deer machines that are used to plow, seed, and harvest the Bible Belt and beyond. No one would think of cutting hay with the monsters that tear up the turf prepared for them in the heart of America's cities. Imagine a tractor strung out on crack and pumped up

125

on steroids: huge rear wheels attached to a positraction rear that is driven by a top-fuel, nitro-burning dragster engine. In that baby, Uncle Homer could cut a quarter-mile long furrow in his field in under ten seconds if he didn't blow the engine first, though I don't know what good it would do him. The tractor pulls that I've seen on television were essentially simple tests of horsepower; that is, the point of each race was to see who could pull a trailer loaded with junk a certain distance in the shortest time, without flipping over, crashing, blowing the engine, crossing the center line, etc., which seems like a rather easy task until you try to do it, I imagine.

There are four features of tractor pulls which are virtually universal to American motor sports, which are markedly different from their European counterparts. The first is the sheer power of the machines, which enthralls and fascinates racing fans in the States. Fans of drag racing, for example, probably really don't *care* who wins the race or the competition. What they come to see is smoking tires, headers that shoot flames into the air, engines that explode, crashes from which drivers miraculously walk away, and the fiberglass bodies of funny cars flipping into the air because the damn frame of the car was just moving way too fast. In contrast, what people apparently want to see at the Grand Prix of Monte Carlo, for example, is a good race that demonstrates the skill of the drivers maneuvering through treacherous curves in incredibly elegant and refined racers built by Ferrari, BMW, Mercedes, and similar companies. For us Americans, the highlights of your average NASCAR race, stock car race, or drag race are almost always the crashes. The waving of the checkered flag is just a boring afterthought.

Second is the fascination with the mechanics and the pit crew who maintain the vehicle, and with the sponsorship from the various manufacturers who make the construction of the machine possible. Every racing fan has his or her preferences when it comes to car brand names and models, and a fan who is faithful to Mopar parts won't easily switch to Chevy ("Bowtie" to the initiated, due to its logo) or Oldsmobile, or Ford, and vice-versa (this is also true of Formula One racing in Europe—it would be difficult, and, in certain circumstances perhaps even fatal for a Ferrari fan to switch to Williams-Renault, which is not the case for the superstar drivers of these teams). This means that each tractor, like each drag racer, represents an enormous team effort that is admired and respected by the spectator. No televised transmission of a tractor pull would be complete without in-depth explanations of how the machine was put together by a team of experts, especially in the typical situation in which a tractor blows its engine while winning a race, which means that the pit crew has only an hour and a half or so to put the replacement engine into place, or to take apart the original engine and put it back together. In other words, American motor sports are also about sponsorship and teamwork, and the team's race against the clock to keep the machine functioning in adverse circumstances.

Thirdly, tractor pull drivers are overwhelmingly from small, at times microscopic towns, as are truckers and drag racers. Most of the time, you would need a very good map in order to locate most of the towns from which these heroes hail, and this is for a very good reason. As you can imagine, it takes an awful lot of space to build a monster tractor, a monster truck, a funny car, a drag racer, and so on. Anyone who has lived in the *real* American country (and not the phantasmal version conjured up by Martha Stewart and *Country Living* magazine) knows that it is populated by trailer homes and junk cars and trucks beside huge garages, and that the *true* sound of the country is not the whistling of birds or cows mooing, it is the pop of shotguns in the woods, the roar of racing engines being built and tested, and the unbearable screaming of dirt bikes and four wheelers. I know this from personal experience. Until I was in my late twenties, my grandfather owned a small farm in the metropolis of Elmer, NJ, which used to be an important truck stop on route 40 between Atlantic City and Bridgeton. Our daily bread was the sound of the racing engine coughing and exploding to life across the road, and the sound of guns going off in the woods at a rifle range about two miles away. When we finally sold the house, it was bought by the guy across the road, who immediately built a gigantic garage in what used to be a cornfield, in order to house his trucks and the cart racers he built in his spare time. While people trapped in corporate jobs in New York City dream about living in the country in order to get away from noise and machines (which is why parts of the State of Vermont have been constructed as a kind of fantasy countryside by New Yorkers—be sure to visit the picturesque and completely artificial town of Woodstock, VT, which is surrounded by trailer homes, hunters, snowmobilers, and pockets of poverty. This contradiction is best summed up in a popular bumper sticker in the State: "Moonlight in Vermont—or go broke"), people who are actually *from* the country want to stay there because they can let their enthusiasm for machines, guns, and gadgets of all kinds run amuck.

Finally comes the most important and strange feature of all. There is an uncanny correspondence in the male brain of the tractor pull enthusiast between hot engines and certain images of the female body. As my brother-in-law said when we entered the garage of the guy across the road whom I've just mentioned, "no garage would be complete without a girly calendar," and, wouldn't you know it, there it was above the tool box. I'll return to this point in a moment.

Monster truck events are different from tractor pulls in several respects. The most obvious of these is the will to witness destruction that characterizes the spectators of such events. The object of a monster truck race is the same as that of a drag race or a tractor pull: to get from point A to point B in the least amount of time. While drag racing is the most abstract of these, since nothing impedes the dragster from getting from start to finish, the tractor is burdened by the weight that it must pull, and the monster truck by the series of obstacles that it must ride over and crush. In this sense, monster trucks represent American motor sport taken to one of its possible extremes, which I highlighted a moment ago. The pleasure that the viewer derives from seeing the power of the machine destroy itself in drag racing is taken to another level in the monster truck, since the machine in this case becomes an entity that is built entirely for the sake of destroying, at least figuratively, the junk cars that stand in its way. In general machines are constructed in order to do work faster than humans are capable of doing it, and to move loads that are much too heavy for humans or animals to lift. In a sense, then, drag races and tractor pulls are logical tests of the two major qualities of machines, their speed and power. Since James Watt perfected the steam engine in the 18th Century, however, humans have been haunted by the notion that the power they unleashed from nature could somehow turn against them and destroy them. Goethe's *Faust* and Mary Shelley's invention of the myth of Frankenstein were perhaps manifestations of the constitutive paranoia of modernity: that science and its products would turn against humankind and destroy them. During the next one hundred and fifty years, the figure of the Faustian mad scientist, from Dr. Jekyll to the android/scientist of *Alien* (the one who helps the malevolent extraterrestrial kill the other members of the crew, and who is, curiously, both a scientist *and* a machine), became so common in works of fiction and film that we hardly even noticed the strangeness of the suppositions that he represented (rarely is the mad scientist a she), i.e., that the domination of nature caused by scientific and technological innovations were sins that would be punished, and products of acute mental illness. With the invention of nuclear weapons, it certainly seemed as though this modern prophecy had come true.

There is something of this long tradition in the popular postmodern fascination for monster trucks, as their epithet reveals. The dread of the monster that Mary Shelley envisioned became, in the mid 20th Century, the pleasure of seeing Boris Karloff's version of the monster go on a murderous rampage on the silver screen. Similarly, the dread of train wrecks and machinery that maimed and mangled farmers in the 19th Century has become a kind of enthusiasm for the spectacle of destructive power that is evident in the monster truck rallies. Furthermore, in one of the more striking developments in this domain, the trucks themselves have become personified in the latest televised versions of these events. In other words, the talent of the driver, and the teamwork, sponsorship, and brand identification that are the trademarks of racing all over the world have been synthesized and erased into the identity of the monster truck, projected into a combination of cartoon character, super hero, braggart wrestler, and transformer of the Tokyo variety. Actually, this tendency must have started with the famous "Snake" and "Mongoose" duels in drag racing back in the '70's, though it has now become exaggerated to such an extent that instead of seeing Joe-monster-truck-driver from Aura, NJ in his beefed-up Chevy Blazer, now we see "The Masher" or "The Crusher" against "Sledgehammer" or "The Juggernaut." In one telecast of a monster truck rally, the trucks were actually represented by steroid-enhanced former football players dressed in costumes who taunted each other on screen before the beginning of each race (this is almost impossible to describe or to believe if you haven't seen it, though it's almost the same thing as the taunts that precede WWWF matches). In short, at the end of the millennium, in the world of trash culture, our traditional fear of the destruction that we have brought upon ourselves in substitution of nature (politics and wars are bigger threats to us than plagues and famine) has been transformed into enjoyment or pleasure derived from the public removal of the restraints that keep machines from destroying other things. Moreover, the force of this destruction is personified in a manner that is not unlike that of the winds, waves, volcanos and lightning bolts that were given names and personalities by the ancient Greeks. In the world of trash culture, destruction and violence are far from things that cause fear; rather, everything from exploding trains, planes, and automobiles to people being shot and hacked to death is deemed to be "cool" by millions of spectators ("Bombs are cool," I can hear Butthead saying. "Yeah, heh heh, they *rule*" Beavis responds). What this means for the postmodern soul is anyone's guess.

My own hypothesis with respect to this mass hypnotism produced by organized displays of violence and mechanized force is that we have lived for so long in fear of machines that this feeling has become an integral part of our collective personality as an emerging multinational culture. This means that when we see manifestations of the awe and the dread produced by the unleashing of this force, we recognize that which is at once intimately familiar to us and profoundly alien to us as "natural" beings. Thus when we see a truck personified as "The Ripper" on its giant tires crushing a row of ten Dodge Darts, it seems cool to us because it merely confirms our unconscious conviction that machines are inherently destructive. We have lived with this by-product of industrial culture for so long that it has ingrained itself in our very identities: we are beings who are products of machines, and like them, we are liberated when our destructive force is released from its limits. When the spectator sees this liberation in the phantasmal representation of "reality" that is the monster truck show, he has no other choice but to scream his approval, which in itself is a figurative release from restrictions. Why people have this same reaction to the stylized representation of people being killed and tortured on the big screen is a subject unto itself.

Finally, car shows are perhaps the ultimate manifestation of a certain kind of fetishistic masculinity, though I would be the last person to claim that women cannot be car show enthusiasts. I'm not talking about official auto shows of the kind held in Detroit and Berlin every year by manufacturers who want to display their new models and their concept cars. I'm talking about the car show that comes to your local Civic Center, at which you are promised a close-up look at the Batmobile, the Monkee mobile, and the American Motors' Pacer used in the *Wayne's World* movie, and where you may ask for the autographs of *Playboy* Playmates or *Penthouse* Pets. As I said earlier, for the boys and men who buy tickets to car shows, there is a truly bizarre correspondence between the hot engines and shiny chrome wheels of the cars and the enhanced breasts and hairless legs of the girls and women who are paid to sign autographs at these shows. A quick trip to your local convenience store will show you that there are numerous biker and muscle car magazines that have female "centerfolds" in bathing suits, posing beside or on top of different kinds of attractive vehicles. Since the invention of the Hot Rod, the possibility for crude jokes involving semantic shifts from the car to the private parts of the male anatomy has always existed and been exploited. The expression "crotch rocket," which is used to describe powerful Japanese motorcycles, is another example of this phenomenon. As Freud remarked, jokes reveal unconscious truths.

It could be, then, that a certain kind of male fascination for car parts is nothing more than a fascination for the male body's private parts. This fundamental fetishism is evident in the expressions and attitudes associated with certain kinds of cars. Jimmy's or Jack's muscle car is his "baby" or his "honey." "She" has to be waxed and rubbed and stroked every week. For muscle car dudes, a carwash is a sensual experience, especially when done by women, etc. At the risk of being excessive, I would say that the thrill of looking at polished chrome, superchargers, fat tires, and headers for these men is a fetish for the thrill of staring at their own genitals. The inevitable presence of women who have posed naked in magazines at car shows supports this excessive hypothesis. The imperious male need to contemplate stylized versions of the naked female body runs parallel to the stylized versions of automobiles that appear at car shows, often surrounded by mirrors that facilitate the viewing of their hidden parts. Curiously, the objects that are the center of attention at these shows are *inert*, whereas the very essence of an automobile is the fact that it *moves by itself*, as its name indicates. In contrast to races of all kinds, the car's performance is not at all at issue at a car show; rather, it is its appearance, and above all the *potential* for performance that this appearance suggests, that are in play at the show. Similarly, the exhibition of women's bodies in magazines such as *Playboy* and *Penthouse* immobilizes them in order to highlight the potential for sexual performance that their attributes represent. The male interest in these attributes at times reaches a level of *technicity*, evident in the bodily measurements of the models that these magazines often give. In essence, a certain kind of man's need to know the numerical estimation of a woman's hips and breasts is similar to the need to know how much horsepower or torque a car has. Like his emotions and his most primal pleasures and fears, a man's sexuality is invaded by machinery in the domain of trash culture. Needless to say, this masculinist captivation by machinery as fetish mechanizes and alienates women's bodies, which are themselves traversed and captured by countless other phenomena that define them and the subjects who inhabit them.

Talk Shows

There is nothing more ubiquitous in American culture than talk as a media product. It dominates certain hours of radio and television in both its serious and parodic varieties. There are at least two types of talk shows with which everyone is familiar: the afternoon variety, and the late night variety. A sub-category of the second type is the late-late night talk show, which is supposed to be more open-ended, more daring, and far more cool (Tom Snyder started this last trend back in the '70's, and David Lettermann made it more buffoon-like and more accessible to a wider audience, to such an extent that the buffoonish, pseudo-alternative style of Letterman was co-opted into the mere late-night category as the norm, while the supposedly more subversive Conan O'Brien took his place in the later slot). Strictly speaking, the afternoon variety of talk show is more narrowly devoted to the complete exposition of important aspects of trash culture such as divorces, adultery, wife and husband beating, transvestites, forbidden relationships between adults and teenage boys and girls (usually the friends of the former's children), obsessive, *Fatal Attraction* kinds of relationships, kids who save their parents' lives by dialing 911, sexual fantasies and "aberrations", race relations, teenagers who are beyond the control of their parents, beauty make overs and dieting, closet homosexuals of both genders who have secret crushes on their homophobic best friends, etc. Like soap operas, afternoon talk shows are presumably intended for a female audience, or tailored to the tastes of women (or, as one particularly sharp young woman pointed out in one of my classes, it could be that soap operas and afternoon talk shows are merely imposed by the networks on viewers whom they suppose to be women). Whatever the case may be, it is generally assumed that women are more rooted in the life of the family, and as you can see, almost all of the topics I named above are concerned with possible permutations of family life, or with individual identities that are generated by one's belonging to a family. In other words, whether consciously or not, the afternoon talk show contains layer upon layer of identity formations and formulations: kids harassed by their parents, and vice versa; people playing with their gender roles; adults slipping in and out of marriage "slots"; and "women" who are supposedly sucking all of this up as part of their daily routine, between the wash and the ironing.

The late-night varieties of the talk show have been reduced essentially to celebrity interviews, accompanied by various forms of light entertainment: the inevitable monologue produced by the host, which offers timid political and social commentaries in the midst of more or less funny jokes; Lettermann's "Top Ten Lists" or "Stupid Human Tricks," and Jay Leno's skits of various types. The role of the late-night talk show host is, in essence, to be the voice of the average working person who is comfortably falling asleep, and to pronounce the petty complaints that he or she has about a world that is filtered to him or her through television and mass circulation newspapers and magazines. Like the person who is falling asleep, the talk show host is beyond the grasp of the working world. Since he doesn't have a "real" job—and until now, late-night talk show hosts have always been male, as far as I know, and they still are—and since he apparently doesn't have to answer to a real boss for what he says, the host can say anything he wants. I used the adverb "apparently" in the last sentence because Lettermann and Leno evidently couldn't say anything that would be seriously prejudicial to Viacom and General Electric, the proprietors of CBS and NBC, and remain in their jobs for too long (granted, it is hard to imagine anything that they could say that would be seriously prejudicial to these behemoths, one of which, GE, made 7 *billion* dollars in *profits* alone during one year in the late '90's, according to *Fortune* magazine, which is a sum of money that is probably larger than the Gross National Product of such ancient and noble nations as Armenia, Albania, and Macedonia).

In fact, the format of late-night makes it virtually impossible for them to contain any kind of serious political or social criticism of anything that would have any consequences whatsoever, despite the fact that these programs are received and watched in millions of households every evening. As everyone knows, each of these programs begins with the sound of a raucous, rocking band that has been warming up the studio audience for hours, and the kind of "control voice" (as they used to say on the '50's Sci-Fi series, *The Outer Limits*) that introduces the host and helps to whip the audience into a frenzy of applause. Back in the early '90's, when Arsenio Hall was still on the air, this procedure was exaggerated to its utmost limits, with special cameras that were continuously trained on an audience that was standing, howling, dancing, jumping, and laughing along with Arsenio. This same procedure was repeated on the defunct WB's talk show, "The Vibe," which used to be hosted by an African-American comedian, Sinbad, just as the Keenan Ivory Wayans show used to be on Fox or UPN. It's as if the networks want to signify "blackness" or "African-American-ness" by this frenzy of movement and noise in the audience, which must be displayed to the viewer, and which perhaps imitates the spontaneous audience reactions of the "Live at the Apollo" programs that are frequently broadcast on HBO. This wave of overwhelming and unquestioning mass approval for the host leaves little doubt that what he is about to say in his monologue expresses a kind of popular *truth*, which is always underlined with laughter. I would even go so far as to say that there is something *fascistic* about the way in which the host is lifted up upon the enthusiasm of the masses, even if they are artificially selected, magnified, and arranged on a sound stage. If this is the case, however, the "fascism" of Leno and Lettermann is a signifier that has been completely divorced from its signified: at the Nuremberg rallies, the delirium of the masses literally translated into Auschwitz, since Hitler, who was the "host" of these rallies, in a sense, was speaking in order to bring about real and material consequences. In contrast, the late-night host wants to work his audience into a frenzy of laughter as an end in itself, since the content of his messages is irrelevant, as long as he maintains a certain ironic and comic tone about his depiction of events.

Moreover, the laughter that is at the heart of this collective experience acts as a sedative and achieves a kind of catharsis for the television viewer. While he or she may be three thousand miles away from the hall in which Leno and company are the priests who are leading a large group through a profane ritual, the viewer still participates in this collective act. This means that no matter how hard his or her day was at the office or on the job, and no matter how many petty political squabbles he or she may have had to deal with throughout the afternoon, the viewer still ends the day in a comfortable bed, listening to the voice of the masses speak in an ironic tone that seems to say, "yeah, the world sucks, but we're okay, and we can make fun of it anyway." It is at this point that the seemingly innocuous control voice of the host becomes somewhat horrifying, if you think about it. As I have pointed out, Leno and Lettermann are in fact employees of Viacom and General Electric, two of the largest corporations in the world. Could it be that these once and future corporate giants are interested in tranquilizing the spirit of the average worker (who now is typically in an office, not in a coal mine), in order to keep business moving for the sake of their profits? Could it be that these professional clowns merely serve to soothe the unrest of workers who are putting in more hours at the office than ever before, and whose wages are growing at a far slower rate than those of the executives of such companies? Do they provide bread and circuses for the white-collar "working" class that still dominates the beginning of this millennium? I'll leave these pseudo-Marxist ruminations aside, and merely conclude that the late-night talk show host is a paradoxical beast, being at once both completely inside the capital that drives this country, and completely outside of it, since he is a professional buffoon whose job is essentially to do nothing, and to speak from beyond the limits of the usual confines of corporate responsibility.

If the late-night talk show is somehow linked to the repose of the body and its sinking into nightly oblivion, the afternoon talk show is connected to that hour of the day when the kids are in school, and the housewife, or house husband, or dead-beat dad, or high school kid cutting school, or some combination of all of these people are at home attending to some kind of household chores (in my own semi-macho version, I often used to find myself lifting weights in my basement in the afternoon, with the television tuned to the only channel I got down there, the local NBC affiliate, which aired the Leeza Gibbons show, the Montel Williams show, and *Days of Our Lives* in the afternoon, before being taken over by Disney cartoons at around four p.m.). This lull between the bustle of getting the kids off to school and receiving them back home again before soccer or baseball practice is perhaps the ideal time for reflection about the family in general. If late-night talk is inherently comic, afternoon talk is inherently tragic in the sense that it most often details the ways in which the family might come apart at the seams, which is a typical event in families from Peoria to Poland to Perth (Classical Greek tragedy itself is unfailingly about bad blood in the family), while on rare occasions it chooses the care, maintenance, and public presentation of the (female) body as its theme, or the rescue of the family from perilous circumstances. Once again, it seems that gender differentiation drives the production of media which in turn drive gender differentiation.

Race and Ethnicity at the Mall

I recently spent a fair amount of time in two very different malls. The first is the Gallery at Market East in downtown Philadelphia, which was built in the '60's and '70's, and which occupies four city blocks in and among several large buildings that were once occupied by department stores (J.C. Penney and Strawbridge & Clothiers), but which have now been transformed into a Burlington Coat Factory (whatever that is) and a half-empty office building. The Gallery is a paradox of a mall, since it is smack in the center of the city, whereas malls are generally in the midst of suburban sprawl, surrounded by gigantic parking lots. In theory, this mall is a marvel of urban planning, since it sits at the nexus of two kinds of mass transit, the Frankfort Elevated line where it passes underground along Market Street, and the SEPTA Regional Rail lines that stretch from Trenton to Downingtown, Doylestown, Lansdale, and beyond, roughly a radius of forty miles from Center City. Curiously, or perhaps predictably, however, the Gallery is primarily frequented by what they now call "black and brown people," African Americans and Latinos, with recent immigrants from Cambodia, Vietnam, and Laos thrown in, for whatever the reason may be. Here are a few possible ones: the Gallery is relatively close to North Philadelphia, which is populated mainly by black folks, Puerto Ricans, and so on (this is a weak reason, however, since still partly Italian and Irish South Philadelphia is just as close); the Gallery caters to people who have lower incomes (i.e., African Americans and Latinos), which is why Nordstrom's and Niemann Marcus are out in King of Prussia instead of being downtown; Philadelphians in particular, and Americans in general, are unconsciously (and often consciously) racist, which means that white folks won't go to shop where there are a lot of black and brown folks. While the first two reasons probably play a part in the racial mixture of the Gallery, I'm inclined to think that the third reason is the most important one.

You need only go to the Plaza at King of Prussia, PA, twenty-five to thirty miles west of Philly, and a stone's throw from George Washington's camp at Valley

136

Forge, to see a different kind of mall, of the suburban sprawl type. On one hot summer day when I was there (95 in the shade, 90% humidity), The Plaza was packed with healthy-looking white teenagers, mostly girls, shopping with their parents. In the predictably-eclectic California Café, which is a franchise posing as a serious restaurant, where I had lunch, there were also several tables of well-groomed white women nearing middle-age who were treating themselves to gigantic "oriental" noodle salads. Everyone seemed to be in uniform: tee-shirts from the Gap, almost knee-length denim or khaki shorts from Eddie Bauer or Banana Republic, crisp white ankle socks, New Balance trail running shoes, and lots of baseball caps of all kinds, with the appropriate curves and smashed-down tops. What few people were thinking about in this vision of uniformity and whiteness was that something like this type of fashion—excluding the ankle socks, which are a variant—was the norm in part of the black community in the early '80's until it was co-opted by the white community, as is almost always the case. I can remember the poor man's version of this look from when I was growing up in North Philly in the 1970's, worn by a kid who lived next door to my Puerto-Rican girlfriend, and whom everyone not so diplomatically called "Nigger Steve," including my girlfriend's white step brother, who was Steve's best friend: dress pants cut off at the knee, white socks pulled up to the knee, a plain tee-shirt, white Converse hi-tops. A little later, when all of us white and pseudo-white folks were still wearing bell-bottoms and polyester shirts with wild prints on them, like John Travolta in *Saturday Night Fever*, I can remember how strange I thought it was that most of the young black men in my city were wearing baseball caps all the time. The pictures of my family from the summers of the early '80's show quite a different concept of casual summer fashion: polyester short shorts cut off above the middle of the thigh, tight tank tops or halter tops, or tight tee-shirts with stripes on them, big mops of hair, Keds, etc. (By the way, in 2008, this kind of look was fashionable again for certain young hipsters.) White men of my generation wear baseball caps only in imitation of their younger brothers or nieces and nephews, for whom the caps are almost an indispensable fashion item, as they were for black men back in the '80's.

Meanwhile, black folks have continuously transformed their fashion sense, perhaps out of necessity. In contrast to the boring khakis and denims and the marginally more adventurous clothes from stores like Structure, Express, or the Limited in King of Prussia, the people in downtown Philly in the late '90's were wearing big boots from Lugz Sports and Fubu Equipment, or giant yellow and bright blue tee-shirts from Pelle-Melle, in a mix of fashions that to my tired white eyes looked like a cross of construction worker tough with outer space techno (the NASA-like font on the letters of "LUGZ Sports" across the front of an acrylic shirt is what makes this look sort of spacey and techno). As far as I can tell from my comings and goings to the Gallery, black folks are at least three generations beyond the GAP-Banana Republic stage and the next-generation

Old Navy and Abercrombie and Fitch stage at which white folks stagnated in about 1989 (skateboard kids, grunge kids, the ever-present Goths and post punks in their tight black pants with chains hanging from them, techno rave addicts, and '70's punk nostalgia kids excepted). During the Fourth of July celebrations in downtown Philly in 1996, Tommy Hilfiger wear seemed to be the norm for brothers and sisters of color; at around the same time, if I'm not mistaken, the wearing of multi-layered hockey and football jerseys and such, inspired by L.A. gangsters and rappers such as Snoop Dogg and Dr. Dre, first became fashionable. When I went back to the Gallery in 2005, it seemed that a certain Muslim aesthetic was becoming prominent: baggy pants, plain white tee-shirts extending nearly down to the knee (perhaps borrowed from hip hop), and big beards for men; head scarves and long "harem" pants for women. In 2008, sports jerseys, construction boots, giant tee shirts, baseball caps at odd angles, and especially retro sneakers or "kicks" were all the rage. I have a feeling that when the shoppers in King of Prussia finally adopt whatever the latest look is that black people will manage to invent or reinvent, the people in the Gallery will be wearing an unpredictable mix of styles and colors that by then will be well beyond my feeble ability to catalogue them.

All of these ramblings about fashion are merely prolegomena to a more important point: shopping malls are places in which two conceptions of the self as a public, visual projection are brought into conflict. The first is the one that develops within the dialectic opposing one's own body to the continuously renewing stream of merchandise that malls offer for sale. The mall calls upon the individual to "accessorize" constantly, meaning that almost anything can serve as an "accessory" that has a defining function for the projection of one's visual, bodily being, ranging from belts from Old Navy, shoes from Aldo, and handbags from Coach, to plates and place settings from William Sonoma, pine scented candles from Crate and Barrel, Chai Latte Frappuccinos from Starbucks, even Jacuzzis and the latest "special edition" automobiles (the "Eddie Bauer" Ford Explorer comes to mind), to one's very house or "McMansion." From this perspective, one's identity when one lives within this kind of pervasive suburban mall culture is a kind of summation or even sublation of this series of objects, with one's own identity becoming a kind of über-accessory that floats above, or beyond, or even *within* the other accessories. To put this point in theoretical terms, malls of the King of Prussia variety incarnate or allegorize the philosophical mediation of identity (in the Hegelian sense) in and through the production, display, and sale of commodities (in the Marxist sense—we're not talking about petroleum, corn, and pork bellies here).

The second conception of the self is as a member of a community that puts itself on public display in the mall, which is a process that is enforced or encouraged by the conscious character of the stores that rent space within it. This sense of identity as a function of belonging to a community is usually conditioned by race and ethnicity, as it is in my examples: upper middle-class, comfortable whiteness, that problematic ethnic category (when were those sworn enemies, the Irish and the Italians, lumped into the same group?), is as clearly on display in King of Prussia as "blackness" or "brownness" are in the Gallery. Race and (sometimes somewhat imaginary) ethnicities are overriding factors that resist and at times perplex the forces of homogenization at work in the increasingly corporate (i.e., anonymous) structures of the stores in the malls. The rent at most suburban malls (and even some urban ones, like Copley Place in Boston) is simply too expensive for companies that do not have large corporate financing to open for business in them, which means that virtually every mall has the same stores, and that everyone everywhere is increasingly reproducing the visible, external signs of his or her identity on the basis of a global conception of product design, marketing, and "branding." Nevertheless, as the example of the Gallery proves, ethnicity and class are still far more primary elements in the development of personal identity than the forces of global capitalism, at the same time that the expression of ethnicity remains unavoidably mediated by the necessity of doing so in and through the acquisition of commodities, such as clothing. This is where the interplay between personal identity and the late-capitalist commodified production of one's external self becomes most complex, revealing that the persistent self-affirmation of minority ethnicities is perhaps the last line of resistance against the total corporate domination and takeover of constructed space. In more concrete terms, on the ground floor of the Gallery, amid the multinational stores that have remained after the flight of some of the larger anchor stores (Old Navy, Kmart, and Radio Shack are still there, long after J.C. Penney and Strawbridge's closed their doors), and the more successful local stores that cater to the local population (for example, City Blue is a successful Philly franchise that sells the kind of hip-hop clothes mentioned above), there are all kinds of little stands that seem to have popped up on the margins of the thoroughfare (the subterranean, post-modern version of Main Street, USA) that runs from one end of the mall to the other. My favorite one is a stand that sells tee-shirts on which the owners of the business will spray paint a likeness of almost any photograph that one gives to them. An image that they commonly paint on these shirts is that of men who have been killed at a young age on the streets (Tupac Shakur is the almost beatified model for this kind of image), and who are thus memorialized by the people who wear these images. The point of this example is that here at the heart of this capitalist cathedral to conformity, black and brown folks are using this space to express and to depict that which is absolutely local, particular, private, and individual, and to represent the sometimes heart wrenchingly tragic consequences of institutional racism (about which Tupac wrote his poems), which they wear on their bodies as clothing and as signs of their belonging to a very specific community. While their white counterparts out in the suburbs blissfully and unconsciously slip on the accessorized identities that global corporations offer to them, the black and brown folks back in my beloved "inner city" engage in an active resistance to the effacement of particularity that late capitalism would like to achieve. This means, perhaps, that there is still hope for something different, something other, something humane, even if that hope is not far removed from despair.

Harley Davidsons

The *American Heritage Dictionary* that is on my hard drive defines the word "protuberance" as follows: "1. Something, such as a bulge, knob, or swelling, that protrudes. 2. The condition of being protuberant." Harley Davidson culture is all about protuberances. When you see a biker ride down the highway on his hog, everything is sticking out all over the place: arms, legs, gut, hair, beard, tail pipes, saddle bags. Even the biker babe sitting on the back is sort of an appendage sticking out of the biker's back. This last sentence was not at all meant to be sexist, or to imply that women can't ride Harleys, but the fact is that the hog and everything associated with it is the incarnation of a certain kind of maleness. James Cameron realized this when he began *Terminator 2* by having Arnold Schwarzenegger appear naked in a biker bar, where he stole the motorcycle and the clothes of an unsuspecting biker dude. There is something uncannily appropriate about the image of a killer android on a Harley Davidson in this movie (though I have a sneaking suspicion that it's actually a Japanese bike disguised as a Harley). In the figure of the terminator, maleness is raised to the tenth power, so to speak. Schwarzenegger's chiseled body is cold, brutal, relentless, murderous; it will stop at nothing until it discharges its hyperbolic weapons into the bodies of its victims; it melds with the machines it uses to accomplish its purposes. While the Terminator is an asexual being, as far as we know, he represents the ideal fusion of the death instinct with the erotic drive that Freud spoke about so long ago. I've said this before, but I'll say it again: the Harley is a substitute or a magical fetish for the rider's penis, and is meant to embody the phantasmic sexual potency that the rider wants to project. This is why rider paraphernalia merely reproduces the standard signifiers of bondage and S. and M.: black leather, chains, boots, helmets and masks. This is also why biker magazines, such as *Easy Rider*, often feature female models in bathing suits draped across motorcycles on their covers. If I were a psychoanalyst, I would say that, at least from a superficial point of view, bikers are overcompensating for their fear of sexual impotence. But I'm not.

Another obvious element of Harley Davidson culture is its overt display of "American-ness." The mere fact that these motorcycles are designed and built in the United States is a fundamental part of their appeal for riders both in this country and abroad, even after the debacle of the Iraq war. For the American rider, the style of the bike signifies or proclaims the essential attributes of being American. Harleys are big, loud, tough, strong, and devoted to being free and out in the great open spaces, though so many bikers use them merely to roll at fifteen miles per hour down display streets in South Beach and Las Vegas, for example. All of these things are part of a way of life, as the motto inscribed on the engines of these bikes declares: "Live to Ride, Ride to Live." On the other side of the Atlantic, one often sees a very stylized devotion to the cult of the Harley. I've never seen as many Harley hogs as when I was in St. Tropez for an afternoon in the summer of 1993, but there was something shockingly different about them. Their riders had no facial hair, which is virtually obligatory for American bikers; rather, they were sort of extra-clean looking, and tan, and slim, and they had long, glistening, gelled hair, like the guys you see in discos in Rome and Nice. To be honest, I have no idea why these comfortable, obviously bourgeois gentlemen, who were able to pay the exorbitant amounts of money required to buy a Harley in Europe, would choose to ride a bike that, for us, conjures up images of America's underbelly (unless, of course, the kind of fundamental masculinity that these machines project is universally recognized). An American who rides a Harley is far from being bourgeois, and his bike is often a lifetime project, which requires lots of tinkering and rigging out in the garage. Working on the bike is a kind of life-long activity for bikers in the States, and the bike itself is always a work in progress that often escapes the control of its owner. For example, once I was riding my little '78 Honda CB360 (speaking of works in progress) across the South Street Bridge in Philly, when I heard a popping like shotgun blasts pull up beside me. It was a guy in a black pseudo-Nazi helmet on a Harley chopper that had flames shooting out of its extended tailpipes. "You got a sparkplug wrench?" he yelled to me over the racket. "Sorry, I don't," I yelled back, and started up the hill on the other side of the bridge. In the States, there are lots of guys who imagine themselves to be mechanics, and who actually hold on to their old vehicles in order to have the pleasure of working on them, since there is almost always something wrong with these machines after they reach a certain age. There's something of a Henry Ford, Model T mentality ("So simple, you can fix it with a bobby pin") here that has never died, and which is an essential component of the Harley cult. The rider knows his bike so well that he can fix it anywhere, under any circumstances, even when the thing is about to explode while he's riding over a bridge in the middle of big-city traffic.

Another essential attribute of the Harley Davidson is the idea of rebellion that it represents. Two images distill this concept rather well: Nicholson, Fonda, and Hopper riding their choppers across the big screen in the '60's; the Hell's Angels acting as "security guards" at the Rolling Stones' concert in Altamont in the summer of 1968. True bikers are not *above* the law, they're *beyond* it, out of reach of it in some way. Since this was the case, they could be shot at by red necks, as at the end of *Easy Rider*, or they could kill people who confronted their imposition of a kind of alternative order, as at the end of the Stones' concert. The culture of the Harley rider is thus defined by a series of negative propositions: there's no car that I will let contain me; there's no road that is open enough and long enough for me; there's no helmet law or traffic law that will keep me from being free; there's no society that I want to be a part of, except for the one made up of my brother riders; there's no violence that is beyond me, if I need to defend my freedom; there's no party that's too wild for me; there's no dress code that can keep me from wearing my leather and my chains; there's no woman who's going to keep me from riding with my friends. All of these negations are paradoxical, since a Harley Rider who's a purist has to adhere to strict codes of all kinds, which are implicit in these statements themselves: he has to dress a certain way, act a certain way, ride a certain way (we've all seen the beefy stud riding down the highway hanging on with one tattooed arm and with his legs spread wide open), talk a certain way, drink certain drinks, listen to certain kinds of music, etc. You don't see Harley Davidson dudes in their gear at the ballet. All of this merely proves that even the most recalcitrant subcultures are defined by stifling rules and regulations, which produce individuals as limited and predictable subject types. I wouldn't advise you to tell a biker this, however, unless of course you're a killer android from the future.

Amazons, Female Beefcake
Studettes, and Super Cyber Babes

It's well known that the breast is an erotic object mainly in the Western part of the world. The joke from the series *Happy Days* that depicts Ritchie Cunningham, Ralph Malph, and Potsy sneaking down into their basement so that they can look at topless African women in *National Geographic* derives from this opposition between East and West, North and South. Silicone breast implants simply would make no sense in tribal cultures in which the breast is not eroticized, whereas other body parts are often enlarged in extreme ways (from our point of view) for the sake of sexual attraction: lips, noses, ears, foreheads, etc. In Western narratives that exist essentially in electronic media, the importance of the breast as erotic object has assumed Gargantuan proportions. I've already discussed its role in *Bay Watch*. The title of this chapter refers to a trend in trash culture that is having an astounding effect on current representations of the ideal female body, which are quite paradoxical. At the same time that fashion magazines inflict images of "super models" on us who look like emaciated little boys (Kate Moss, the poster child of the "waif" movement in fashion, inspired a whole generation of models), and that Celine Dion is apparently suffering from anorexia as she pounds her chest while singing the ubiquitous theme of the ubiquitous *Titanic* in her continuously running Las Vegas show, there is another series of representations in the media that tends toward the opposite conception of the female body. I'm thinking specifically of three different movements: first, the image of the Amazon, which appeared in the Russ Meyers movies of the '60's (*Faster, Pussycat! Kill! Kill!*—be sure to watch the trailer for this film on YouTube), and which lived on in the popular series *Xena: Warrior Princess*; second, the women who pump iron on exercise programs such as *Body Shaping* on ESPN or who parade around the ring during WWE or WWWF bouts; third, the action figure of Lara Croft, who is the heroine of the *Tomb Raider* computer games. All of these figures have at least one thing in common: they are all extraordinarily, at times grotesquely and even impossibly buxom.

Curiously, the idea of the Amazon has always been associated with that of the breast in Western Culture. The word "Amazon" itself is etymologically related to the notion of mammary ablation, since these female warriors from Greek mythology had to have their right breasts removed in order to shoot arrows from their bows (etymologically speaking, in ancient Greek, "a" = without, "*mazos*" = breast). At the beginning of the 21st Century, when women are literally being decimated by breast cancer, the thought that the ablation of the breast is at the foundation of an ancient and traditional image of female power is frightening and uncanny. The makers of Amazon movies in the last century were apparently unaware of these Classical roots of the female warrior. Far from being breast-less, the powerful women of the Russ Myers movies were beyond buxom—they were simply enormous, like Jane Mansfield and Jane Russell wearing padded Wonder Bras. While the star of *Xena*, who went by the improbable name of Lucy Lawless—did they force her to call herself that for the sake of the role she played?—was much less obvious, I'm convinced that the popularity of this series had nothing to do with the interest of the stories, and everything to do with the visual and iconographic impact of the outfit that she wore, much like the one worn by Lynda Carter in the *Wonder Woman* series of the 1970's. At the end of the '90's, success in the ratings war was guaranteed by the image of breasts criss-crossed and "lifted and separated" (as they used to say in the "Cross-your-heart bra" ads) by leather straps, even if there were no references at all to Xena's torso in any of the episodes. Once upon a time, the ideal figure of the desirable yet still acceptable "sexpot" consisted of a curvaceous and slightly stupid blond woman in a tight sweater (preferably pink, yellow, white, or light blue), wearing a padded cross-your-heart bra, which made her bulky breasts stick straight up in the air. That conventional image of one kind of desirable woman was later transformed into one of a sword-bearing, muscular, tall, tan, athletic, and buxom super-heroin. The means of support have changed, but the object of desire and imitation that is presented to the viewer has remained the same.

Speaking of athletic women, the iron-pumping "babes" on programs such as *Body Shaping*, which used to air on ESPN, offered us daily lessons in impossible anatomies. We live in a time in which corporeal interventions are becoming almost obligatory, at least for those who want to feel as though they are following the coercive code of fashion that shapes our notions of what's beautiful and what's not. The techniques for sculpting muscles that the instructors of this program demonstrate for us are plainly ineffective if they are not accompanied by radical and consistent changes in one's diet. Thus while every exercise program promises that a mere twenty-minute daily "intervention" into one's anatomy will enact its transformation into the ideal figure that flickers on screen, these promises are simply lies. Not only do the trainers of *Body Shaping* kill themselves in the gym every day for at least an hour and a half, they also eliminate carbohydrates from their diets, take protein supplements and fat-burning compounds, wax their entire bodies, and often resort to cosmetic surgery of one kind or another. The most obvious surgical intervention of this kind is displayed on every program, especially during the tiny segments that appear during the introduction of the program and some times just before the commercial breaks. The women trainers appear in "relaxed" mode, wearing bikinis, romping or running in the surf, with ample breasts proudly displayed over washboard abs. Like that of her male counterparts, the torso of this kind of woman balloons out from a wasp waste, and she has impressive back and pectoral muscles to go along with the silicone or saline implants beneath her breasts. For anyone who does not have the time to devote that much energy and money to his or her body, such an anatomical profile is as alien to them as an extraterrestrial body is in a science fiction movie.

Speaking of sci-fi, we arrive at the most flagrant example of all. If Barbie's body was impossible, Lara Croft's is virtual, in the sense that it exists only in a computer-generated environment that is quite *real* for a large and growing part of the population. For those of us who have gone from adolescence to adulthood in the age of computers, video games, and the internet, life without its virtual shadow would merely be a simulacrum of itself. In other words, the internet is actually a *place* that I can go to, and where I *exist* in a certain way in its rooms, and sites, and links, just as I can go to my local café for a latte or a cappuccino, and this despite the flagging interest in virtual worlds in which one creates an "avatar" of oneself. The amount of information about me that is stored on my hard drive is such a fundamental part of my life that I feel genuine withdrawal when I have to be away from my computer and my e-mail for any length of time. Within this world of virtual cities that I construct, and cars that explode at two hundred miles per hour without hurting me, and botched landings on aircraft carriers during which I don't drown or burn to death, there is also the image of an impossibly buxom, wasp-wasted, athletic, killer archaeologist by the name of Lara Croft. Perhaps the most important intermediate stage between Marilyn Monroe in her sweater and Lara Croft with her uzzis and ninja swords was *La Femme Nikita*, the French action film of the '80's which was transformed into a series on the USA network in the '90's. Nikita was a postmodern ideal woman in an ambivalent sense. She represented a certain kind of *coquetterie* that is admired and fostered by a certain segment of the French population, i.e., the one that controls the world's perfume industry (imagine Carole Bouquet or Letitia Casta saying "Chanel Number 5—share the fantasy," while staring into the camera, lying on her belly on a bed in a hotel room at the Place Vendôme, her shoes half off, a strand of her hair falling over her face). On the other hand, Nikita was a trained assassin who could kill a man with her bare hands, or with a single shot from a 9 millimeter at 500 paces. In other words, she was a synthesis of the lion and the lamb, the sex and death drives rolled into one. Lara Croft is the version of Nikita for the next millennium, and she allows the (often adolescent) viewer or player of her video game to enjoy pleasures that were previously reserved for repression in Freud's unconscious, which now can be safely located on the internet and on game consoles. In layman's terms, the adolescent and post-adolescent male viewer or participant experiences the joy of gawking at a pair of impossibly perfect big breasts at the same time that he blows away the mutant monster dude who is chasing him. More importantly, the adolescent boy sitting on his couch with his game paddle in his hands, in the middle of some sprawling suburbs, feels the rush of actually *becoming* the super cyber babe who is a possible version of his ultimate object of desire. I could be wrong, but it seems to me that video games are essentially the domain of boys and young men. Movies that speak of male bonding, such as *Swingers* and *Chasing Amy*, always show their male protagonists playing video games. I have eight nieces and eight nephews, all of whom are adults by now; all of the boys played video games obsessively when they were young, while none of the girls did. The prolonged adolescence that now lasts well into their thirties for young men still includes an avid devotion to video games such as *Grand Theft Auto*, a new "genre" that some critics believe will one day replace feature films.

Nevertheless, if there are young girls out there playing the *Tomb Raider* game, they are receiving the same message that they would get from watching *Xena* or *Body Shaping* or *Bay Watch*, which is: the way to become a desirable woman is to transform your body into the ideal forms that you see on the screen. Ideal women today are not shy, or slightly stupid, or submissive, or overweight; on the contrary, they should be aggressive, and athletic. They should "choose to kick butt," as the British actress who plays la femme Nikita on USA proclaimed on a television commercial that she did for some kind of sports equipment. (As I've already said, the Spice Girls also do some serious butt-kicking on their "Be There" video, in which they are stylized and well-fed take-offs of the characters from *Mad Max*, *Road Warrior*, and Kung Fu movies.) Moreover, an ideal woman has to have a certain kind of body, which requires a certain regimen and discipline. This has always been true for women it seems, at least since the days of whale-bone corsets and 24-hour girdles. The only difference now is that the required changes in the body have become internal and surgical ones, as opposed to prostheses that could be strapped around it.

Fortunately or unfortunately, there is an antidote to the super cyber babe syndrome, and it comes from the world of the ubiquitous and proliferating magazines for women. I would say that, at one time not too long ago, seventy or eighty percent of the young women in their early twenties whom I taught were vegetarians. They always told me that they chose not to eat meat simply because they didn't like it, which is certainly a valid reason, but I suspect that there was something more to it than that. In almost any women's magazine that you might read in the supermarket, or the bookstore, or the convenience store, you will probably find an article about a Hollywood actress, such as Demi Moore, or a singer, such as Fiona Apple, who is a strict vegetarian, not necessarily for ethical or environmental reasons, which also motivate many of them, but simply for the fact that it is almost impossible for a true vegetarian to get fat. One day when the good weather arrived, I saw two of my former young students, both vegans, walk by in shorts. "Emaciated" is the word that comes to mind when I think of their appearance. At this beginning of the century, women's bodies have become places of saturation, and they are "invested" by a plethora of diverging forces. Popular culture teaches girls to starve themselves, to subject themselves to the rigors of physical discipline, and to alter their bodies with surgery, cosmetics, creams, perfumes, conditioners, tattoos, piercings, dyes, and so on. They have to be both vigorous and waifish, buxom and bony, virtual and real at the same time. I once asked a class full of young women whether they felt any pressure to conform to these new bodily stereotypes, and they assured me that they felt none whatsoever, which means, perhaps, that they have assumed the new rigors of being women in our society in the same way that men adopted a certain rite of emasculation, practiced by masochistic priests and made fashionable by Alexander the Great, so long ago, which we perform every morning without thinking about it. I'm talking about shaving, of course. But the rigors to which men's bodies are subjected by the ideological functioning of our society are a joke compared to what women have always had to endure, which it seems to me has been multiplied almost exponentially in the age of trash culture.

Car Magazines, Cars, Sport Utes, and Highways

[Prefatory note from 2008: I wrote this section near the end of the Clinton administration, before the debacle of the 2000 election, the horror of 9/11, the disaster of the Iraq invasion, and the subsequent dramatic rise in gas prices and acceptance that global warming was a reality. It's quite interesting to see how things have changed in such a short time.]

Car magazines are perfect for reading in the bathroom. (Allow me to say in passing that reading in the bathroom is a special kind of trash cultural activity.) Then again, there's something intrinsically male and macho about certain kinds of cars, and about reading about them on the toilet. This is because a certain kind of man *needs* a certain kind of car, especially when he reaches "a certain age," as the French say ("un homme d'un certain âge" is a man who is getting *really* long in the tooth, but you know what I mean), just as he needs to eat and to go to the bathroom. A man who reads car magazines on the toilet has the pleasure of taking care of two primary necessities at the same time. I know this because, as much as I hate to admit it, a large part of my being is occupied by a man's man who loves muscle cars, football games, cheeseburgers, action movies, leather jackets, and fine-tuned Japanese motorcycles (luckily there's another part of me that loves Ronsard, Racine, Botticelli, Van Eyck, and Bartok). When the length of time between the physical prime of a man's life and the current state of his body starts getting close to twenty years, he just needs to sit in the driver's seat of a car that can go from zero to sixty in under six seconds, or at least he needs to imagine himself sitting in the seat of such a car, especially when the seat that is currently under his butt is an oval-shaped piece of plastic that's resting on top of a lot of porcelain.

Every American's second home is his or her car, and it has been this way in the US at least since the 1950's. This is especially true now, when most

Americans live in endless suburbs in which you have to drive a half hour to get anywhere, even if you only want to go out and buy an ice cream cone or a pack of cigarettes (a colleague of mine once proudly proclaimed that she lived "eight miles from milk and cigarettes" in rural Vermont). In contrast, the neighborhood where I grew up in North Philadelphia back in the '60's had three corner stores a block from my house, a bakery at the end of the block, a supermarket two blocks away, a barbershop a block away, a girls' high school three blocks away, a park with a swimming pool four blocks away, and a commercial shopping district six blocks away. Needless to say, we did everything on foot or by bike. The average person in the suburbs puts twenty to twenty-five thousand miles per year on his or her car, which, if you calculate at a generous average speed of forty miles per hour, means that these suburbanites spend 500 hours per year in the car, which is the equivalent of 12.5 weeks of full time work. (Even at a conservative 15,000 miles per year, that's still 9.5 to 10 weeks of full time work in the car per year). It's not surprising, then, that American cars are equipped for the long haul. Your typical mid-sized automobile from Ford, Chrysler, or GM is essentially something like a comfortable living room on wheels, with a big fluffy couch to sit on, cup holders and consoles to hold stuff, a good stereo system, air conditioning, arm rests, etc. etc. I know that my Spanish brother-in-law's top-of-the-line Renault Laguna, which is a typical European mid-sized car, didn't even *have* a cup holder, and that the pathetic little cup holder in my own Canadian-built Honda Civic was made to hold two 12-ounce soda cans (just as its trunk is built precisely to the height of a brown paper shopping bag), which means that Big Gulps, thermoses, travel mugs, jumbo cups of coffee, and even little bottles of Snapple Iced Tea have no place in my car. Even though the Japanese are big commuters, they haven't discovered the joy of commuting with Howard Stern on the radio, 36 ounces of Diet Coke in the center console's gigantic cup holder, and a Big Mac.

In general, we Americans like to think that we have a love affair with our automobiles that is essentially different from that of the Europeans, for example. A Frenchman, German, Italian, or Spaniard who loves cars thinks about a series of mechanical things that are basically irrelevant to most American drivers: horsepower, torque, handling, design, road holding, braking, gas mileage, etc. (of course readers of *Road and Track* and *Car and Driver* are BMW and Mercedes enthusiasts to whom this rule does not apply). Most Americans want to know only a few things about their cars: how big is it? How much stuff can it haul? How much does it cost? What options does it include? This attitude was illustrated to me once by a salesman at a Ford dealer where I test drove a top of the line Contour, now no longer available in the US, but which is still sold in Europe under the name Mondeo. I was interested in this car for all of the European reasons (see above). After telling me the details of the lease, the salesman said something like, "For thirty-five bucks a month more you can get a Taurus. For just a little bit more you get a bigger car," as if the size of the car were the most important thing of all. I rented a Ford Taurus shortly afterward. Indeed, the Taurus was very big, very heavy, and very solid. It was like driving around in a Lazy Boy recliner strapped to a massive steel frame. It took forever to stop the thing, and forever to get it up to 65 mph. In other words, when most Americans drive, they want to feel this way: they want to imagine that they're not on the highway, but that they're in their living room sitting on the couch, and the monotonous landscape passing by is a kind of TV series, punctuated with ads and bathroom breaks.

In fact, the behemoths that are guzzling gas along our highways are like miniature reproductions of the typical family room, sometimes complete with paneling, drop ceilings, and televisions. This is why eating and drinking are such important driving activities. Racking up mileage on the way to Yellowstone or the Grand Canyon in the Suburban with the kids strapped in the back is like racking up hours in front of sitcoms and talk shows: it requires potato chips, nachos, pretzels, Cokes and Pepsis. Sometimes the phenomenon of eating and driving achieves the level of a sport. I remember once driving up the Schuylkill Expressway (I-76) in Philadelphia, eating a cheesesteak from Pat's. It's quite common to see people on the highway eating Whoppers behind the wheel. The size of our country means that anyone who wants to go anywhere beyond their own region needs to consume miles in the same way that a person with an eating disorder consumes calories, and most of us have one kind of eating disorder or another.

In the realm of trash culture, as our bodies have been getting larger and larger with the proliferation of junk food, so have our cars been getting bigger and bigger. The typical car today is no longer a car—it has grown into a Sport Utility Vehicle, with the most popular of these being as large as a full-sized pickup (the Ford Expedition is basically an F-100 pickup with seats in the back and a roof). Beside these monsters, the first car I ever drove, my grandfather's beloved 1964 Ford Galaxie 500 with its small block V8, was like a compact car. The reason these vehicles are popular in the States is primarily economic. The price of gas hasn't risen much since the end of the oil crisis at the end of the 1970's. This means that people can afford to buy gigantic sport utes that get 12 miles to the gallon. [N.B.: in 2008, Ford and GM have lost billions of dollars because they invested most of their production in pickup trucks and sport utility vehicles. With gas nearing four dollars a gallon, instead of costing a dollar and change as it did ten years ago, hybrids are all the rage.] Moreover, the healthy state of the American economy since the end of the Gulf war—essentially, eight years of constant economic expansion—means that people have accumulated lots of stuff that they need to haul around with them. In the most exaggerated of cases, people want to take shrunken versions of their houses with them on vacation, on picnics, to lakes, to the beach, to the local mall, etc. Expeditions,

Explorers, Durangos, Blazers, and Suburbans are large enough to carry dogs, coolers, beach chairs, hibachis and mini grills in the back, not to mention the three kids and grandma in the other seats. In fact, owning a sport ute is a relatively inexpensive way of owning a mobile home, and increasingly America's highways are becoming something like enormous trailer parks.

I once heard a French sociologist, Marc Augé, describe highways, airports, subways, and so on as "non-places," which is the title of one of his books (*Les non-lieux*). What he meant by this was that highways are not really the place of anybody. They have no history, no tradition, no particularities, no character, no culture. I would argue, on the contrary, that highways (and airports and subways) are spaces saturated by capitalism and marketing, and that it is in these spaces that we as members of a global community adopt our most characteristic identities as consumers. In other words, instead of being spaces from which the traditional signifiers of human culture have been extricated, leaving mere emptiness—in passing, Augé's remarks represent a particularly European conception of culture—highways are essentially extended and enormous spaces that are overrun by the objects and commodities that define human social life at the beginning of the 21st Century. Both the asphalt on which we roll and the cars in which we ride are big ticket items that occupy large percentages of the GNP and the Federal Budget. The world economy and its corresponding geo-political order would be unrecognizable without automobiles, petroleum, and highways. While driving along, we are bombarded by ads for services that the highway offers to us, ranging from restaurants, to gasoline, to hotels, to shopping malls, to tourist information. Highways are essentially enormous venues for the sale of goods produced by the disastrous food industry in the United States, such as it has been configured by McDonald's and other large corporations. Except for the once-mighty defense industry, and the pharmaceuticals industry, almost every important element of the industrial base of this country is to be found along our highways. Of course, every rest stop on an important interstate has Tylenol, Advil, Aspirin, etc. for sale, and before long, the drug chains that have come to dominate our big cities (CVS and Rite Aid, for example, have taken over an art-deco movie palace and a former restaurant in downtown Philadelphia) will undoubtedly have everything from Prozac to Viagra for sale at highway rest stops. The traveler heading west on I-76 can make a pit-stop at the King of Prussia mega mall and buy everything from an Armani suit to a black speckled notebook from K-Mart. In fact, for most people living in the USA, doing just about anything is impossible without getting on and off a highway, or in and out of a car. I have to confess that personally, when I have to spend long periods of time away from my car, I feel a kind of pathetic withdrawal and nostalgia for the interstate.

It seems that our material existence as physical and emotional beings at the beginning of yet another chaotic century is both circumscribed and generated by the sheer volume of objects and commodities that are "necessary" to its everyday maintenance. I've placed the word "necessary" in quotes because, quite simply, I don't really need Armani clothes or a BMW to thrive in this world; or, to translate my example to a more reasonable level, I don't need sweaters from Country Road Australia or the latest Honda Civic in order to live and be happy. Nevertheless, there are certain pressures, mainly from advertising, that make me want these things, and that make me feel as though my life is somehow incomplete if I don't have them. Whether the barons of industry want me to feel this way or not, it is clear that the engine of capitalism has produced a situation in which the ideal being of the average American is that of a driver in his or her car, rolling along a highway toward the mall, listening to a radio station that belongs to a giant chain of radio stations, about to pull into a rest stop for a mass-produced burger and fries. In this sense, the identity of a person who lives in a country where trash culture is dominant is that of a consumer, and its optimum manifestation materializes in automobiles. [As we've seen since the beginning of the millennium, the disastrous consequences of these facts for ourselves and our planet are hard to overestimate.]

Postmodern Country Music

Rewind to about 1975: Dolly Parton, all big hair and boobs and bright-colored clothes, with a wicked West Virginia accent, belts out some song about divorce and liquor and cigarettes; on "Hee Haw," Minnie Pearl in her gingham dress with her straw hat on with its dangling price tag introduces Buck Owens, who sings some song about his old dog, accompanied by guys in tight plaid shirts and greasy hair, all named "Bob" or "Billy" or "Jim" or "Charlie." Fast forward to 2000: Shania Twain is on stage in tight black vinyl pants, a midriff shirt that displays her flat stomach, a leopard skin *torera* jacket, and braided Rasta extensions that reach down to her backside. Among her band members are a long-haired Asian man playing an electric violin and a black man wearing ski goggles and black leather pants on the drums. Shania punctuates her lyrics and the guitar breaks with Michael Jackson style "hoots" and "hoos," which Michael himself borrowed from the Godfather of Soul, James Brown, who first started using them, I believe, when his voice began to go on "Get on the Good Foot." Shania is slim and tall and beautiful, and when she speaks, she doesn't even have a Southern accent. She's not even from the South—she's *Canadian*, for Christ's sake. It seems as though the last bastion of good old American obesity and ugliness has been invaded by high fashion. Shania could almost be a fashion model, which was something that was unthinkable for country music even in the early '90's, when the butch and brash K.D. Lang, also Canadian, and now a lesbian icon, was the hottest thing going in crossover country. One of the beauties of more "traditional" country music was that it was often about the quotidian sufferings of poor white folk, which they sometimes examined with ironic detachment and humor. George Strait's "All my ex's live in Texas" comes to mind, with its fabulous punch line, "therefore I abide in Tennessee." Shania Twain doesn't seem to know what irony is. No matter how much VH-1 would have us believe that she is "white trailer trash" who worked hard to become a crossover hit in Nashville, it seems as though the kind of angst produced by difficult circumstances that are beyond one's control is quite foreign to her (far be it from me, however, to belittle anyone else's suffering—I'm sure she's had her share, just like everyone else). Her songs seem as though they were written by a corny 19-year-old who is aware of her considerable personal charms, and who has barely learned to think beyond stock clichés and expressions. Choruses such as "If you're not in it for love/ I'm outta here" or "Man, I feel like a woman" or "That don't impress me much" or "You're still the one I kiss goodnight" come to mind (on a drive I did once from Lexington, KY to Philadelphia via West Virginia, virtually the only thing on the radio was Shania and preachers butchering the Holy Bible, except for a brief hip hop interlude from a Marshall University radio station near Huntingdon, WV).

The concentrated yet detached sarcasm and whimsical bitterness of "All my ex's live in Texas/therefore I abide in Tennessee" is something that is completely foreign to Shania's music, which nevertheless is so appealing to a wide audience that one of her albums made it to the top of the *Billboard* charts. Whereas traditional country music had something authentic about it, since it described ordinary people who were leading lives of passionate yet quiet desperation (think of an absolute gem like Patsy Cline's "Crazy," or Hank Williams's "Cold, Cold Heart"), Shania's music is a slick product that is packaged in such a way that it sells glamour to an audience that has had it with the trailer park, the bowling alley, and the annual rodeo or State Fair. When Loretta Lynn sang about being a coal miner's daughter, she was perhaps reaching out to millions of listeners who lived in mediocre circumstances, and whom the music merely confirmed in their position of poverty. I once had a neighbor from West Virginia who *was* a coal miner's daughter, and who was proud to proclaim it every chance she got. Loretta Lynn gave her and all the other working class people like her a voice that sang for them alone, since no one else who liked pop music ever listened to country music thirty years ago. Today, however, Shania's music has a different message. It says that you, too, can be a fashion model and a diva, even if you're from Podunk or Sticksville, you can be universally liked and desired by men and women of all races, and you can be elevated to the status of a media star (watch the video for "I feel like a woman" on YouTube to get an idea of the kind of "glamorous" image I'm talking about, which parodies the famous Robert Palmer video for "Addicted to Love" from the '80's). Country music used to celebrate a way of life that was rural; now Shania's music is borrowing elements from urban culture, perhaps inciting her fans to abandon their cowboy hats and boots. Her live shows co-opt the mixed styles and samplings that hip hop first made popular; she has become a media product that cannibalizes anything in its path, in the same way that products from the movies to the Gap ads to Mariah Carey and Brian Setzer cannibalized a fantasy version of America's swing era at the beginning of the current decade. What it comes down to is that the authentic voice of the coal miner's daughter simply doesn't sell enough CD's or MP3's, while the media conglomerates are producing consumers who are like ravenous octopuses that want the "art" they buy to be derived from eight different categories at once: Shania as model, as East Village street urchin (leopard-skin jacket, hair extensions, platform black sneakers), as guitar-strumming sylph, as loyal spouse ("You're still the one I run to/ the only one I belong to"), as diva, as post-reservation American Indian squaw, as charitable mother (one of her songs was written for "underprivileged children"), and even as the traditional country barnyard, roll-in-the-hay object of desire (think of the video for the song "Any man of mine/ better walk the line"). In other words, today's media products function in much the same way as complex viruses, such as HIV: there is a "location" on a healthy cell that a virus attacks which has a strange, polymorphous shape to which the virus adapts itself perfectly. As the shape of that location is modified with medicines and drugs, the virus mutates in order to continue its attack. It's appropriate that the disease that is ravaging this new millennium—we've turned a blind eye to the thirty or so million people infected in Africa—should serve as a model for the way in which trash culture now attaches itself to the very being of millions of individuals. But perhaps that's a very large burden for a simple country girl from a trailer park in Calgary to bear.

Look at All This Fabulous Merchandise!

In the film *Rain Man*, the autistic character played by Dustin Hoffmann, Raymond, is obsessed with certain television programs, mainly *Jeopardy* and *The Price is Right*, which he has to watch every day at the same time. This is a problem for his brother, who wants to take him across the country, through different time zones and television schedules. When Raymond finally gets to see these programs, seated in a hotel room somewhere in the Midwest, he repeats the words uttered by the announcer who introduces the program, which have always stayed in my mind: "look at all this fabulous merchandise!" Part of the fascination of watching television is crystallized in this statement. How can there possibly be so many things? More specifically, how can there possibly be so much merchandise, that is, so many manufactured objects that are meant to be sold to so many people? *The Price is Right* allows "contestants" to bid on everything ranging from espresso machines, to living room and bedroom sets from companies with familiar but strange names like "Broyhill," to the latest shiny cars, to boats, to Hawaii vacations, to weekends at Disney World. What this program is really about, then, is the display of this merchandise before a possible buying public. The contortions and general bouncy happiness of the participants as they are overcome with glee upon winning a "showcase" full of stuff are irrelevant to what drives these United States: the manufacture and sale of things, most of which are completely useless, and made in China.

In the realm of useless merchandise, however, *The Price is Right* is downright amateurish compared to that mainstay of airline magazines, the Hammacher Schlemmer section of the *Sky Mall* catalogue. I was completely flummoxed when I passed by an actual building in Manhattan recently that bore the Hammacher Schlemmer name, since I had always assumed that this company existed only in the fantasy land generated by jet lag, bad food, the corporal punishment of anatomically incorrect seats, and thirty-three thousand feet of altitude. The

157

kinds of things that are for sale in the H.S. catalogue cannot possibly exist in any real world. Please allow me to quote and to paraphrase the abridged version of this classic text as it appeared in a *Sky Mall* magazine that I brought home with me from a recent US Airways flight. The first object that caught my eye was the "Solar-Powered Personal Boat." "Safe, clean, quiet, effortless to operate, virtually maintenance free, and requiring minimal nautical knowledge, this is perhaps the world's most perfect boat. Capable of ferrying up to 4 adults, the boat's 700-watt electric motor moves the craft silently at 5 mph. The motor is powered by four deep cycle batteries that are constantly recharged by the sun during daylight hours—even when overcast. Please allow 6-9 weeks for delivery. $9199.95." This description does indeed appear beneath the picture of a woman sitting in a small white boat that has solar panels functioning as a kind of canopy over her head, but the image has the eerie or otherworldly quality of computer-generated graphics. Nevertheless, the delivery time and the exact price lead one to believe that by some miracle of technology and the good graces of indulgent credit card companies, I could visit the Hammacher Schlemmer website and place an order for this thing, and two to three months later, miraculously, a Solar-Powered Personal Boat would actually be delivered on a trailer to my front door.

Facing the Solar Boat is a lovely "Pop-Up Hot Dog Cooker. Operating much like a pop-up toaster, this unique kitchen appliance lets you easily prepare two hot dogs (complete with buns) in minutes. To use, simply drop two hot dog wieners in the center basket, and the buns in the two warming chambers on either side. Its 660-watt electronic heating coil has time settings so that you can heat the wieners and both buns to your taste preference. Crumb basket removes for cleaning." The merchandise associated with food in the realm of trash culture is simply amazing, and what counts as cooking or preparing food is becoming increasingly mechanized, automated, and "microwaveable," to use an adjective that is at the heart of this kind of culture: hot dogs that you pop in the toaster, which themselves are made of "mechanically separated" meat by-products; spaghetti and sauce that come in disposable plastic bowls ready to be heated in the microwave; pizza that cooks in the toaster; pre-cooked cubes of beef and turkey that you throw in that dinosaur of appliances, the oven; instant macaroni and cheese; for health-food enthusiasts, there are tofu nuggets that look like chicken nuggets, seitan burgers that look like hamburgers, soy strips that look like bacon, all of which come in attractive, microwaveable plastic containers. The idea of grabbing a piece of fresh fruit and eating it raw is foreign to trash culture, since food from this point of view has to be something that has been subjected to several stages of industrial manipulation, before it is submitted to the final "cooking" process, i.e., the closing of the microwave door and the pushing of its buttons. Objects like the pop-up hot dog cooker bring this procedure of mechanization into the home, and eliminate the need of watching and timing food that is an essential element of cooking. "I made these hot dogs myself," one can imagine a little boy saying as he brings his plate with its two hot dogs in their warm buns to the couch to watch the Disney channel. Indeed, there is something child-like about this love of automated cooking devices and pre-prepared foods: every time it steams "real," uncooked rice to perfection in twenty minutes, my rice cooker affords me waves of innocent pleasure. I once heard two students behind me in the supermarket saying to one another, "you know, like it always tastes so much better when you make like your own real food." The one speaking was holding a basket that contained a stick of butter, a jar of pre-chopped garlic, a bag of Italian bread, a jar of Ragu spaghetti sauce, a box of spaghetti, and a can of Kraft Parmesan cheese. One day, the Hammacher Schlemmer catalogue will have a pop-up spaghetti cooker, which will have "time settings so that you can heat both the spaghetti and its sauce to your taste preference."

Now we move on to another solar-powered device, "The Place-Anywhere Solar Fountain. Powered by direct sunlight gathered in a solar panel, this highly portable fountain sets up easily wherever desired without the need for an outlet or wiring installation. The solar panel has an extra-long cord that allows it to be placed up to 15 feet from the fountain. A sturdy metal stand deftly holds a terra cotta pitcher, three small bowls, and a larger bowl that gently pours water from one container to the next in a soothing cascade. Easily disassembled for storage or transport to another section of the garden, the bowls simply lift out of the frame. The integral water pump rests unobtrusively in a large bowl, which recycles the water in a constant stream." It's difficult to imagine how one could live without a "soothing cascade" that is "highly portable." There is a vast and unexplored region of trash culture that is occupied by weekend gardeners, their gardens, and especially by the objects with which they decorate their gardens. On his "Prairie Home Companion" radio program, Garrison Keeler has a parodic set of advertisements for the "Power Mower Association," in which the power mower is touted as a cure for all kinds of health problems, such as hypertension and anxiety. The backyard garden in your typical suburban development is supposed to be a place of peace and tranquility, but anyone knows that the babbling of your highly portable soothing cascade is likely to be interrupted on any given day in any section of the garden by the sound of (usually) a man on a power mower obsessing about the height and thickness of his lawn. The assumption of the backyard garden is that the peace and quiet of "nature"—whatever that is—can be brought into being through the usage of gas and electric powered devices, in the midst of pre-fabricated houses made essentially of vinyl siding, plastic, and mechanically separated pieces of wood stamped into the shape of boards, glued together with lots of petroleum by-products. Oh my.

"Not a Girl, Not Yet a Woman": Britney Spears as Phenomenon

This is a subject about which I can't possibly have anything to say. Witnessing the explosive rise and fall and rebirth of Britney Spears during these past nine or ten years, from a comfortable distance, and only paying attention with a very small part of my brain—as Benjamin remarked so long ago, in the realm of media culture, everyone is a kind of distracted expert—I've had the vaguely amused feeling that one gets from watching an animal documentary detailing the rather bizarre habits of a species that one has never seen before: toads that spend most of their lives in suspended animation in Southwestern deserts; fruit bats in the Amazon; giant Komodo dragons with mouths so full of bacteria that one small bite inflicts a fatal infection on their victims; fish that live inside the mouths of other fish. Although we are from the same culture and speak the same language, it seems to me that Britney Spears and I are from different planets. But like the aliens on my beloved *Star Trek*, she has distinctly humanoid features that are essentially the same as my own. And I have to conclude this preface to my following remarks with the disclaimer that I hate everything that she does, says, and represents, except for the music from one of her song hits of 2003 that I've already mentioned, "Toxic," which is a mixture of Moroccan violins, Ennio Morricone soundtracks to spaghetti Westerns, James Bond, and Japanese drum machines. In other words, I shouldn't write anything at all about the media phenomenon of Britney Spears, and allow it to die its natural un-death in the next few years. Nevertheless, I can't resist a critique of such a provocative yet insignificant figure.

In other words, everything that Britney does as a singer and performer has been done already many times, beginning with Elvis in the 1950's, Jim Morrison and Janis Joplin in the 1960's, Madonna and Prince in the 1980's, etc. There is of course an important difference between the legendary figures of Elvis and Morrison and young Britney: the former seemed to be concerned

160

about and conscious of something other than their personae as performers. Jim Morrison, in fact, was a rather intelligent man who read and admired Nietzsche and Rimbaud, and who came to detest and reject the leather-pants wearing, long-haired, hippy poet persona that invaded his life and ultimately killed him. Elvis simply was a somewhat innovative singer (what would he have been without Lieber and Stoller?) whose life was cut short by drugs and the irrational adulation imposed on him by rabid fans. It's remarkable that he lasted so long given the scope and the originality of the situation in which he found himself, for which the experience of the preceding generation, that of Sinatra and company, had not prepared him. In the case of Britney Spears, on the other hand, it seems as though she is nothing more than the persona she is on screen, which has been carefully crafted for her, upon her, and around her since she was a girl by her "handlers," most notably by the producers and directors of children's programming for the Disney channel. Britney "is" a media product made to sell records, videos, DVDs, and—this is really brilliant—toys and dolls to little girls, if this poor child's being can be equated to the series of visual phenomena that have been inflicted on us over the last few years. There is no doubt that some day soon, Britney will star in an action or science fiction film that will allow the producers and marketers of the film to sell Britney action figures, or include them in McDonald's "happy meals." This in itself isn't that troubling, since perfectly normal and intelligent actors and actresses are sold as action figures all the time. The problem is that I'm sure Britney is delighted that little girls will be playing with sexy little dolls, with bare midriffs, who represent the kind of problematic, mutated-Lolita sexuality that Britney herself is meant to project. As for the mysterious Drs. Frankenstein—and it seems to me that all of them have to be males—who have created our little monster, they must not have given much thought to the consequences of creating the figure of a little girl overrun and saturated by sex who is exposed to concupiscent viewing eyes (see the YouTube video of "Hit me baby one more time" on this).

Far be it from me to bemoan the presence of "sexual," "sexy," "erotic," or "provocative" images on television and in the movies. We live in a country that is a curious mixture of absolute "Puritanism"—as our European friends love to remind us all the time, with evident satisfaction—and absolute depravity. In any gasoline station near an Interstate, or in any country store in the most buttoned-down and uptight of New England towns, one can still find the hardest core pornographic magazines and videos for sale, right next to the maple candy and the red and black flannel jackets for hunters. Sex is an inevitable part of life, and, if we are to judge from the animal documentaries mentioned earlier, it is the most important part of life, along with eating. The sale of sex has been part of human culture from the beginnings of civilization, which may evoke two kinds of reactions: the first being the moralistic one, which abhors the virtual enslavement of mainly women who are forced to sell their bodies in order to survive, the second being the cynical, smug one, which states that sex always has and always will be for sale, no matter how one tries to legislate it. The first of these is often hypocritical and downright insane, as a recent dean of the Harvard Divinity School taught us when he demanded that the University's technicians download all of his child pornography on to his new computer, which had a larger hard drive, and hence a greater capacity to store images of children engaged in sexual acts. The second of these is simply that of the dirty book store owner and the pimp, both of whom profit from our unwillingness to outlaw the sale of images of sex. In the United States, because of our archaic Constitution, we are loath to outlaw anything that could remotely be considered to be speech, such as exorbitant campaign contributions, or images of virtual children having virtual sex that are circulated on the internet, as was evident from a Supreme Court ruling that overturned a law interdicting even the imaginary representation of sexual acts performed by minors, in media such as comic strips, cartoons, and films using adult actors who look like children. Images of sex can perhaps be healthy tools for consenting adults who wish to use them to "add sizzle to their sex life," as some pseudo-porn ad might say. I certainly have nothing against the use and circulation of sexual images for the sake of enhancing anyone's pleasure, as long as those images are produced without violence, rape, exploitation, enforced drug addiction, kidnapping, etc.

Britney Spears, on the other hand, presents a much more problematic case of the image of sex as commodity. First of all, when she appears on award shows to accept whatever prizes her public and sponsors may deem her worthy of, such as she did at one or another of the MTV music awards, wearing a dress that revealed seemingly impossible cleavage, Britney first of all thanks Jesus Christ her Lord and Savior for giving her so much talent, or so much luck, or so much money, or a body that she can partially expose to a salivating public that will pay her for doing so. This revelation that Britney is a "born-again" Christian adds quite a bit of interest to my conception of her. If I'm not mistaken, fundamentalists of this type read the Bible as the literal word of God, in which, among other things, St. Paul tells us that a woman's hair is the glory of her body, and as such should always remain covered (see, for example, 1 Cor. 11:6: "If a woman will not wear a veil, let her also cut off her hair. But since it is a dishonor to a woman to have her hair cut off or her head shaved, let her wear a veil."). We'll stick to this one fact, and leave aside for the moment the Bible's condemnation and restriction of sex in almost all of its forms, ranging from simple masturbation (poor Onan!), to garden variety adultery and fornication, to the more exotic bestiality and the "sin against nature" of sodomy, for which entire cities were destroyed by fire and brimstone, whatever that was. Unless Britney is some kind of new-age, postmodern born-again Christian, of the variety I saw not too long ago in a film entitled *Relax, It's Just Sex*, in which two gay Christians thanked Jesus for their orgasms while engaged in the act itself, she must find herself in one of the three following situations: 1) she has sex with her boyfriend Justin Timberlake of 'N

Sync fame, and is wracked with anguish and guilt by her sins, which she has to discuss in her Bible study group; 2) she is a virgin who refuses to have sex with Justin until they are married; 3) she has sex with Justin and doesn't think much about it, and pays lip service to Jesus only at awards ceremonies. Not that it's any of my business, but I hope for her sake that number three is the case. [The preceding notes were written, of course, before the famous breakup of these two stars, and well before Britney's chaste marriage, highly-publicized and photographed pregnancies, and her equally publicized divorce and pseudo nervous breakdown from which she is still recovering in 2008. Along the way, Britney shaved her head, as St. Paul advised.]

You might object that I'm being extremely old fashioned with this critique, and that Britney's intentions, conscience, and subjectivity are completely irrelevant to the performance of her persona as a media image. As they say so eloquently in French, *soit*. We are very far removed indeed from a point of view in which we require the coherence and consistency of one's acts with one's conscience. Otherwise, we wouldn't have elected to a second term one president, Bill Clinton, who seemingly had no conscience, and who could successfully and happily divorce his private life from his public persona for the good of the general commonwealth, while electing a second president to a second term, George W. Bush, who lacks not only a conscience, but a brain as well. In the final analysis, one cannot possibly blame Britney Spears for being inconsistent when we know that the only education she received as a child was on the set of a Disney variety show, especially when we have a president who graduated from Yale University (the shame! the shame!) without learning how to pronounce the word "nuclear," or how to form a grammatically correct sentence in simple spoken English. Nevertheless, in the name of all the devout Christians in history whom I honor and respect, ranging from Erasmus, to Bach, to Martin Luther King, I find it extraordinarily troubling that Britney should thank Jesus for the fact that her bare belly button and her almost bare breasts make little girls buy her CDs and vote for her via the internet in popularity contests that are called award shows.

This is at once the most disturbing and the most encouraging aspect of Britney as media phenomenon. One would think that a person who exploits her supposed sexual charms, and who is "not a girl, but not yet a woman," as one of her songs proclaims, would somehow be marketable to men. Nothing could be further from the truth, however: men and even boys are not even the slightest bit interested in Britney, and a glance at any of her lip-syncing concert films, with their armies of little girls with their mothers in row after row of large stadiums and sports arenas—the same ones that female evangelists fill with Bible-toting mothers and daughters in America's heartland—will confirm that Britney is an image of a certain kind of girl that appeals almost exclusively to girls within a very narrow age range. Girls who have reached the ripe old age of thirteen are probably already too old and cynical for Britney.

In the Future, Everyone Will Always Already Be on the Phone

Not too long ago I experienced a quite gratifying kind of time warp. I was sitting in a shiny new Acela express train, traveling from New Haven to Philadelphia, with two computer wonks sitting across from me, discussing million-dollar internet servers in quite technical terms. Finally, when there was a lull in the conversation, one of these men (in passing, it's perhaps hard to imagine women getting that enthusiastic about servers, SCSI interfaces, fiber optic cables, buffers and caches, perhaps due to generations of enforced gender inequalities) returned to his laptop, which had five different windows open at once, while the other turned to his cell phone, and slipped into the familiar position that all of us have seen all too often recently: head slightly tilted, looking down at the tiny screen on his phone, both of his thumbs engaged on its number pad, "texting" a message or playing a game. We were somewhere between Stamford and New Rochelle, rolling on ancient tracks that crossed iron bridges in the middle of some picturesque town that unfolded before us quite slowly since, in this marvel of modern technology, we were comfortably tooling along at about thirty-five to forty miles per hour, which is a speed that frightened Henry David Thoreau, but not those of us who were on that train. "We might as well be on a steam locomotive," I thought. This was during the darkest days of a bear market, so long after the internet bubble had burst that "dot com" millionaires might as well have been dinosaurs, while senators in Congress were grandstanding about the constitutionality of a resolution to drop even more "smart bombs" on Iraq. In other words, these were hard times for technology in general, since so much of it had proven to be utterly disappointing and pointless, while the seemingly infinite promise of the internet had turned out to be nothing more than a convenient way to buy tickets, to steal music and movies, to have endless, meaningless chats with total strangers, to plagiarize bad articles on great literature and works

164

of art, and, above all, to download pornography to the now gleaming privacy of one's own home or office.

I'm almost sure that the wonk across from me was playing a game on his phone, which brings me to my point. All of the vaunted technology that surrounds us during this first decade of the century serves only to provide one with amusement during the seemingly limitless "boredom situations" in which we find ourselves while traveling. (As I wrote the last sentence, another man seated near me paused *Monsters, Inc.* on his mini-DVD player in order to answer his cell phone.) These amusements usually take the form of games in which one tries to kill spiders before being devoured by them, or to blow up gun ships and attacking helicopters before being shot down in one's own helicopter, etc. And your standard cell phone conversation usually takes the following form: "Hello? Yeah, hi! How are you? I'm on the train just outside of New York. No, I'm just coming back from New Haven. It was boring as hell up there. What are you doing tonight? Where's that? Who's going to be there? Should I bring anything? You sure? Okay, what time? I said what time? Hold it, we're going into a tunnel so I might start breaking up. Wait. Wait. Call me back in a few minutes," etc. Whatever happened to people encountering mysterious strangers on trains, or plotting future murders, or trying to hide from assassins who were chasing them, or falling in love with women with elegant accents, perfectly smooth blonde hair, and luxurious cigarettes with matching boxes of matches in their tiny handbags? Obviously, I'm thinking of Agatha Christie's or Alfred Hitchcock's version of train travel, which is a fantasy that's as potent as any other, but it seems to me that technology such as that of cell phones has served only to invade spaces, like train interiors, which used to be characterized by silence, meditation, the contemplation of the landscape, etc., with a wide range of banal information that is perfectly useless. What did we do on trains before we were able to tell all of our friends, one by one, that we were in the process of traveling on a train? Was it really better back in the days when we were forced to read a newspaper or a novel, or to strike up a conversation with somebody we didn't know, or to eavesdrop on the conversation going on next to us, or simply to stare out the window, without DVDs, CDs, video pinball, and instant messaging? During one particularly memorable twelve-hour train trip from Gijón to Barcelona, I listened to a conversation about daughters who never visit and different types of sausages that seemed to go on for an eternity, as I stared out at the fabulous Spanish landscape. In contrast, I once dragged a group of American teenagers from Gijón to Madrid on a train, through some very beautiful landscapes which none of them saw, because they all had their heads buried in magazines, with their headphones on and their CD players spinning away (obviously, this was before the invention of the ubiquitous I-Pod). Luckily, at that time, the disposable cell phones that all American travelers in Europe seem to have now were not yet available, so at least I got to enjoy the mountains and the great Castilian plain, with its herds of sheep and small towns with their stone churches, in silence.

I don't know what kinds of conversations people who are cell phone addicts have, but it seems to me that they need the sound of digital static in their ears, and the feeling of plastic pressed up against their temples in order to speak to anyone. This is another of the typical cell phone scenes that one sees constantly these days: two people walking together along a city street, with one or both of them talking on the phone. Why aren't they speaking to each other? When they finally meet the person with whom they're speaking on the phone, will they speak to that person directly, or will they call someone else? It seems that every group or couple of people is always supplemented by other people who could potentially be reached on their cell phones at that moment, so that one is not only with those who are present, one is also with everyone else who belongs to one's circle of friends. And when you're with "people of the cell," if I may use a science fiction turn of phrase, you always have the feeling that they're not really with you, they're always itching to exercise their thumbs on the cell phone number pad, to see who may have called, what calls they may have missed, what messages they may have, and so on. This tendency is especially pronounced in teens who have been weaned on cell phones. My wife and I witnessed the following incredible scene while we were in a megaplex cinema in South Philadelphia as the previews came to an end and the first installment of *The Lord of the Rings* began: two adolescent Asian kids—a significant fact, since cell phones are particularly prevalent in countries like Japan, Taiwan, and even my grandfather's native country, the Philippines—were sitting next to us, each of them with their individual cell phones gleaming bright blue in the darkness of the theater. They weren't speaking to each other, of course, as they "messaged" their friends, but as the film finally began, the boy actually asked his girlfriend the following question as she turned off her phone: "What, do you want to watch the movie?" "I don't know," she responded, at which the young man turned off his phone and put his head on her shoulder as if to fall asleep. We were astonished that such a question could be asked in a movie theater, and that these kids had a relationship that seemingly involved no communication whatsoever. (When I recounted this anecdote to a group of students, they immediately thought of the possibility that the question was meant to ask whether or not they were going to make out, which gives a charming, 1950's spin to the story.) We're reaching a point at which the kind of distracted attention that Benjamin remarked regarding the public interest in the cinema has reached exponential proportions, so much so that one's attention seemingly cannot be focused on the present, and constantly requires a kind of digital or electronic interface, crackling with micro amplifier noise and satellite signal breaks. My Asian kids apparently had a relationship in which they spent time together having cyber conversations with other kids who, logically, were probably sitting in other movie theaters not watching the movie that was flashing on the screen in front of them. In the age of the cell phone, trash culture is sublimated into the white noise of the earpiece, to such an extent that one requires this sound in order to feel comfortable with oneself and with others, and even in order to follow and understand spoken language. Or, it could be that people habituated to this mode of communication can have a conversation with someone only when they are already having a conversation with someone else on the phone, while there is also a second position that is required for almost any cell phone call: there apparently must always be a third person—the one walking beside the person on the street who is on the phone—who is listening to the phone conversation, reacting to it, and attempting to add something as the discussion is going on and the street is moving by.

In the future, then, everyone will "always already" be on the phone, as dear Derrida might have said if he were still with us (*toujours déjà* sounds even better in French, with its internal "zh's" grinding against the palate), since handsets and headsets will be replaced by implanted microchips that will allow one to maintain constant and multiple phone conversations all the time, while surfing the next mutated generation of the web (ten windows open at once, pop up ads coming and going, music playing off screen and on, a chat room on the left margin, the latest headlines up top, weather and sports scores on the bottom, a live blog somewhere else), and playing a video game at the same time. Then one will be able to tell everyone else exactly where one is, what one is doing, and where one is going at all times. And, if I may venture into the realm of science fiction once again, the sound of speech will no longer be heard, as the constant transmission of these coordinates will be reduced to cell phone code speak, and there will only be the sound of a high pitched buzzing, like that of mosquito wings, as in that old episode of *Star Trek* in which Spock was accelerated into an alternate time dimension, and was making repairs to the Enterprise at such an incredible speed that his movements sounded to Kirk and company like the buzzing of tiny insects. Imagine cities full of people, walking in pairs or trios on the sidewalks, not speaking to each other, looking at the invisible screens that flash before their eyes because of the implants in their optic nerves, murmuring and making strange guttural sounds of pleasure as they scroll through infinite links and windows in their minds. This nightmare scenario is the apotheosis of trash culture raised to the nth power, when individuals are interpellated as subjects who require more and more absent information, while they are unable to see the person standing next to them, or the street on which they are walking. In its current state, this kind of information—headlines scrolled across the bottom of the television screen, advertisements that pop up on internet websites, endless windows that open of their own volition—is immediately consumed in the most distracted state possible, and immediately consigned to the landfill of oblivion in our overloaded brains.

If you find yourself in this situation, and you want an antidote, I suggest that you read chapter fifty of the first volume of Montaigne's *Essays*, "On Democritus and Heraclitus," which is two and a half pages long, over and over again, until you think that you understand something. That will be the beginning of your rehab from your information addiction.

Going to the Gym

I was sitting on the quadriceps machine the other day, in between my second and third sets of ten, when I had one of those moments that occur often in the gym: I had no idea where I was, why I was there, and what I was doing. I hope that this happens to everyone who goes to one of these modern health clubs, where the abdominal obsession phenomenon has reached vertiginous levels. I felt as if I were in one of those dream sequences in science fiction films, when a character, through some time warp or rift in the fabric of space, is suddenly offered a glimpse of an alternate reality. I also simultaneously imagined Benjamin Franklin, who started the first fire insurance company in America about four hundred yards from the machine on which I was seated, suddenly transported to the machine next to me. What would he, who loved gadgets and inventions of all kinds, think about the scene I was witnessing? Three rows of twelve machines of many different kinds: Stairmasters, elliptical trainers, treadmills, stationary bicycles, rowing machines, climbing machines, skating machines, etc. Machines to tone your butt, your thighs, your calves, your upper arms, and your entire body. People moving brightly-colored plastic balls of various sizes, ranging from small medicine balls to giant yellow, blue, and red bouncy balls, in a variety of complex ways: with their feet suspended in the air, twisting their torsos from side to side; lying on their backs, and raising a giant ball with their feet, transferring the ball to their arms, which they raise over their heads, then transferring the ball back to their feet; lying with their backs on the giant yellow balls, and twisting their torsos in every direction, or lying on their stomachs with the ball overhead, etc.

Going to the gym is like submitting oneself to a surgical procedure: one is often literally strapped to a machine and practically penetrated by it, required to perform "unnatural" maneuvers that are literally intended to change the morphology of one's body. Of course, when working out doesn't have the desired effect, increasing numbers of people submit themselves to actual operations to increase or decrease or transform the size and shape of their noses, chests, lips, eyelids, chins, backsides, etc. Of these, it seems to me that the gluteal implant, inspired by the full rumps of J. Lo. and Beyoncé, wins the prize as the most unimaginable operation to be invented by "cosmetic" surgery. As that now classic rap song, "Baby Got Back," says, "I like big butts" as much as the next guy who grew up drooling over black-and-white images of Marilyn Monroe, Jane Russell, and the divine Sophia Loren. But the thought of your average, slim-hipped, blonde, Anglo Midwestern transplant to Vegas or Hollywood, with her buns, lips, and breasts full of silicone or whatever has taken its place, seems extraordinarily strange to me.

The sad truth is that, in this business of enforced body alteration that has apparently taken control of everyone in this culture and in many others, both men and women are still attracted to all sorts of body types and styles. This means that the men in the weight room at my gym, who are dropping sixty-pound dumbbells on to the rubber floor above the heads of the women in the yoga class below them (in which I often find myself struggling to do the downward-facing-dog), don't realize that women are not necessarily attracted to biceps that are the size of a "normal" man's quadriceps in some cases. Let's face it: men who have enormous muscles are simply ugly, and those who compete in body-building competitions look, well, fat when they are dressed in regular suits and pants which were designed by people who never could have imagined that men could have bodies of that kind (look at the latest cover of *Muscle and Fitness* magazine if you want to know what I mean). Similarly, the women whom one often sees in the gym, who spend an hour and a half on the treadmill or the ellipse taking thousands of tiny steps, and then spend an hour lifting small weights that make their already stringy muscles even more defined, look absolutely absurd when they dress up for the evening in a gown that has spaghetti straps that reveal their ribs and the taut sinews of their muscular arms. In the era of trash culture, we are not satisfied with the bodies we have, for one reason or another. Do men who bulk up like Governor Arnold Schwarzenegger or his spiritual cousin Sylvester Stallone actually think that their bodies are attractive to women or to other men? Do women who are all sinews and tight muscle think that they are attractive to men or other women?

Fifty years ago, the models for female and male beauty and desirability were quite different in these United States. Marilyn Monroe, who was at the peak of her fame in the 1950's, never worked out, as far as I know. Her body seemed to be made completely of soft flesh. In fact, what was appealing about her buxom, full-hipped form was precisely that it had *so much* flesh, and that some of it seemed to be bursting beyond the bounds of her clothing, but not in the way that it does now when one sees the body of surgically-enhanced women whose overly-round breasts seem as if they are about to bounce like beach balls out of their dresses or bathing suits. Marilyn was all about flow: her mellifluous voice seemed to float out of her mouth as her lips caressed it; her torso flowed out of her waist that seemed to be squeezed into an impossibly small space above her ample hips; her breasts didn't explode out of the top of her dress, they simply offered themselves to avid male viewers. On the other side of the gender divide, Rock Hudson, good old gay Rock Hudson, always wore his pants too high above his waist, perhaps to cover his slightly bulging gut, as did an aging yet eternally tan and silver Cary Grant. Both Rock and Cary essentially hid their bodies in well-tailored suits, beneath ties, button down shirts, and cufflinks. Rock Hudson in a bathing suit is utterly ridiculous, as he appears in the extraordinary film, *Lover Come Back*, with Doris Day at her prudish singing best (both of them serving as models for Almodovar's characters in *Mujeres al borde de un ataque de nervios*), and Rock sporting his flab on the beach in a particularly memorable scene when Doris discovers that he has been deceiving her by impersonating a cowboy from Texas. In short, fifty years ago, even bodies to which one paid a kind of hyperbolic attention because they appeared in popular films were simply bodies that had to be dressed in a certain way in order to be judged as desirable by spectators. Today, body alteration is the mark of desire. Nearly all the actors in Hollywood have personal trainers. There are entire programs on the "E" network devoted to the workouts and diets of our favorite stars. How does Janet Jackson maintain those abs? And what is Madonna doing these days, besides her hour and a half cardio workout and the "fun Kabbala things" she does with Gwyneth Paltrow and Demi Moore? We're all stuck in the goddamn gym because movie executives in Hollywood don't think that a woman with Marilyn Monroe's body or a man with Rock Hudson's gut should appear on the screen. Like athletes, actors and actresses have incentives in their contracts, but not for touchdowns or assist-to-turnover ratios, but rather for "achieving weight loss and personal training goals." When the immortal film *The Invasion of the Body Snatchers* scared the living bejeezus out of moviegoers in the 1960's, they had no idea that Hollywood and the entire United States would, one day, be invaded by hordes of experts who have stolen our normal bodies from us, and replaced them with tattooed, pierced, branded, buffed, and surgically modified corpses that we merely inhabit, but which, hopefully, have nothing to do with our "genuine" selves, whatever they may be.

Reality invades Television

Without getting into specifics, let's examine the "plot" variations of a diverse set of shows that have dominated American television, but also to a certain extent European television, for the last few years. The most popular of these, called *American Idol* in the States, *Star Academy* in France, and *Operación Triunfo* in Spain, is quite simple: a jury of experts goes around the country, auditioning young singers—who have to be below a certain age, let's say twenty-five—to see who will be offered a record contract after the end of a year-long contest in which the public votes which one of the singers will not be asked to return for the following week's show. Various alumni of this program, both winners and losers, became pop stars for brief periods of time, and then faded away into oblivion, as most pop stars do. On *Survivor*, a dozen contestants are sort of stranded with a film crew on a remote, picturesque tropical island, given various tasks to accomplish in teams, and then they are forced to vote one of their own "off of the island." At the end of each program, with a flourish, the host extinguishes the inevitable torches that light the darkness under the palm trees, and says "the tribe has spoken: you, X, have been voted off the island." In *Dancing with the Stars*, semi-celebrities such as former Olympic athletes, ice skaters, aging actors, has been singers, and so on learn how to dance with professional dancers, are judged by a jury of experts, and are voted on and off the show by the viewing public. There are programs in which the contest is to see who loses the most weight (*The Biggest Loser*), who can live with a group of people in a given house (*Big Brother*, and, the father of all reality television, MTV's *The Real World,*), who can win a race around the world (*The Greatest Race*), which of a large group of single women can convince a millionaire to marry her (*The Bachelor*), who gets to run a company owned by Donald Trump (*The Apprentice*), who gets to have his or her rather run down house completely renovated by a team of architects and builders, and so on, perhaps *ad infinitum*. There are programs in which people learn how to cook, to decorate, and even how to ice skate. I won't even mention all of the variations on dating programs, one of which, in 2007, was a show called *Gay, Straight, or Taken?*, in which a woman had to decide which of three men was available to her to go on a date depending upon the three categories listed above. The results of this program were, perhaps, a bit predictable ("Oh my God, you're gay! I can't believe it!" etc.).

Several questions would have to be asked of the explosion of these programs. It should be remarked first that the increased demand for programming with the sudden rise in the number of television channels perhaps generated the proliferation of these low-cost shows. When *Friends* went off the air in 2005 or so, each of its six cast members was being paid a million dollars per episode, which means that just their salaries cost six million dollars per show. In contrast, reality shows must cost a mere fraction of what was paid to one of these actors. While walking through my neighborhood once in Philadelphia, I came across the usual array of catering trucks, trailers, equipment vans, film crews, and hired workers that accompanies the filming of anything. There were literally dozens of people sitting around on doorsteps and even on the sidewalk eating their lunches. When I asked what they were filming, a kind neighbor whose street was invaded by all of this stuff told me that it was a show about obese people who were walking from Boston to Washington, with of course the implication being that the person who lost the most weight would "win" the program. Even paying and moving all of this material and people surely couldn't cost more than a few hundred thousand dollars a month, mere pennies when compared to what David Schwimmer or Courtney Cox made every week on *Friends*.

What is really interesting about reality TV, however, is precisely the notion of "reality" that it presents. What is there in these shows that is "real"? The answer that immediately would come to a "normal" person's mouth would be, "the stars of the show are real people," as if actors acting in fictitious roles weren't real people. Secondly, how long do these "real people" remain "real" when their lives are invaded by the gigantic apparatus of television? Even if we assume, for example, that Kelly Clarkson, the singer who won the first edition of *American Idol*, was really an everyday girl from Topeka or Peoria or wherever she was from (the *Wikipedia* tells me that she was from Burleson, TX, a suburb of Fort Worth, which is, as I understand it, itself a suburb of Dallas), did the series of tests she had to go through in order to be voted the winner of the show have anything whatsoever to do with "reality"? Wasn't it rather one of the most artificial, staged, and superficial kinds of spectacles one could imagine, which arrived in the homes of America's consumers and spectators only after extensive editing? Like almost everything else in our culture, the reality we are offered on television is a packaged one, just like the de-boned, skinned, supposedly sanitized, and chopped varieties of meat that we buy wrapped in cellophane and styrofoam in our local supermarkets. This analogy allows for the following reflection: just as ground meat that is sold in the US, the industry of which has had disastrous consequences for the environment and for labor practices in this country, often contains invisible bacteria that are deadly if it is not cooked properly, could it be that the packaged realities we consume on our super television sets contain invisible and noxious "substances" that we should "cook" properly before consuming them? My proposition as to what these media bacteria are would be this: in George W. Bush's America, in which millions of people have slipped into poverty, in which fifty or sixty million people do not have health insurance, and in which an entire class of people, known as "the working poor," work two and even three jobs just to be able to scrape by at the end of the month, reality television simply retells the good old Horatio Alger kind of story in which a poor boy or girl from a trailer park can become a wealthy celebrity for a few months, which is what this type of story has become in the new millennium. People no longer dream of going from real poverty to real wealth; they prefer to live a kind of spurious wealthy "lifestyle" that is made possible by credit cards that have $30,000 credit limits even if the holder of the card is working for minimum wage. Better yet, most people dream simply of being able to live like Paris Hilton or P Diddy for a weekend or a month, driving around in Bentleys, sipping Cristal Champagne, and trashing hotel rooms after wild parties, only to fall back into a full time job with no benefits at Walmart or McDonald's. The infection that reality television transmits to us is, then, the idea that the American dream is still a possibility, but this dream has been transposed to the nightmarish, hyper capitalist terms of an all-expense paid weekend fantasy vacation to Las Vegas or Miami Beach. The house with the white picket fence in a small town is simply too boring for a generation raised on the internet, I-Pods, Playstation, Myspace, YouTube, Google, Blogs, and that good old work horse of trash culture, the *Star* magazine.

Conclusion: The Problem of Contemporary Criticism

"A kindred problem arose with the advent of new velocities, which gave life an altered rhythm. This latter, too, was first tried out, as it were, in a spirit of play. The loop-the-loop came on the scene, and Parisians seized on this entertainment with a frenzy. A chronicler notes around 1810 that a lady squandered 75 francs in one evening at the Parc de Montsouris, where at that time you could ride those looping cars. The new tempo of life is often announced in the most unforeseen ways. For example, in posters." (Benjamin, *The Arcades Project*, 65)

Near the beginnings of a certain kind of critique of modern culture, which in Benjamin's case grew out of a Marxist critique of capital, and hence of the increasingly diverse products of a capitalist culture, the mere fact that one could speak about loop-the-loop cars, bicycles, and advertising posters must have seemed extraordinarily exciting for scholars constrained within the strict limits of scholarship about the sublime products of ancient Greece and Rome. If we were to see the loop-the-loop cars that Benjamin mentions, we would undoubtedly find them quaint and charming relics of an age when simply riding in a circle in a motorized vehicle must have seemed new and remarkably fast, whereas now even eight-year-olds wouldn't get on such contraptions, considering them beneath their dignity in an age when roller coasters at amusement parks go a hundred miles per hour, while other machines drop people from five stories up and allow them to free fall for two seconds. A visit even to amusement parks that were built not long after Benjamin's tragic suicide in Port Bou, such as the one at El Tibidabo in Barcelona, or certain piers in Wildwood, NJ, engenders a wave of nostalgia in the visitor for a time—the 1950's—when clunky rides made of wood and steel and rolling along at fifteen miles per hour tried to look like space ships traveling at ten times the speed of sound. Every critic, Marxist or not, looking at the current state of capital and its products has been struck by phenomena of acceleration, to such an extent that certain thinkers, such as Paul Virilio, have made the notions of speed and "escape velocity" the bases of their entire view of the cultural world and its apparently imminent demise. The problem of criticism in the present is now the same as it has always been since the beginnings of high modern philosophy in Hegel: how do we grasp this moment of time that is running away from us? What do we consider its essential manifestations? To what extent are our conceptions of acceleration and change over-determined by misconceptions of the past?

In other words, what should we examine as our objects of study on, to take an arbitrary date, May 21, 2008? At this apparently crucial time—and all times are crucial for the people who write at the crest of the wave that is the movement of time into the future—there are two obvious objects of study that have to be explained. The first is the set of phenomena surrounding the reporting of the U.S. military operation in Iraq. I'm not talking about military strategies, troop movements, victories, and terrorist attacks; I'm talking about the reporting of the invasion with "embedded" reporters, the military briefings that the Pentagon would like to control as they did those of the first Gulf War, and especially the diffusion, via the internet, of "unauthorized" images of torture and death taken with digital cameras belonging to soldiers, some of whom were actually guilty of these atrocities. Since 9/11/2001, these kinds of phenomena have been beaten to death, so to speak, on talk shows, in films, and in books, most notably by some of the most famous critics in the West—Baudrillard, Derrida, Habermas, etc. In the face of such enormously depressing tragedies, which have caused the deaths and suffering of thousands upon thousands of innocent people, I believe that the best strategy is an ancient one that was recalled by Montaigne four hundred and fifty years ago: the enormity of the grief that they cause simply cannot be represented, which means that a critique of these phenomena is, to a certain extent, irreverent and perhaps even irrelevant. I also believe that it is the duty of a responsible intellectual community to express its most energetic opposition to the policies of politicians such as George W. Bush and his coterie, who place profits and petroleum supplies at the center of "American interests" that they judge to be above international law, the Geneva convention, and the universal declaration of human rights. This opposition should not, however, allow famous writers and thinkers to publish yet more books on topics that are perhaps beyond our ken due to their sheer magnitude.

The second obvious object of study would have to be the internet, which is one of those unprecedented and unexpected developments in the history of the human race that is on a par with the invention of the printing press, the impact of which will perhaps never be equaled. From the point of view of trash culture, the internet is beyond a garbage dump: it is an international land fill of unlimited proportions, which can continue to grow in all directions and languages at once, as server capacities increase around the world. Moreover, to continue with this metaphor, the net as landfill contains everything that a similar object on, say, Staten Island would contain: the still-to-be-sifted remains of the World Trade Center, among which the mafia managed to pilfer tons of re-usable steel (the rest of which wound up somewhere in India); scores of dead bodies and body parts in contractor cleanup bags; tons of batteries dripping their toxic contents into polluted aquifers; layer upon layer of organic waste from the decades it took to fill the landfill; birds, rats, raccoons, perhaps even bears scavenging for food; tons of glass and plastic in all colors; billions of insects and worms; enough bacteria to populate a small planet. The internet is perhaps the first written or representational object in history for which an index cannot be written, since it potentially can contain at least references to everything that has ever been documented, which is why it requires "search engines" such as those of Google and Yahoo (whose interesting names undoubtedly contribute to their popularity). The web can neither be indexed nor mapped; it can only be searched, combed over, and referenced, since it is growing and morphing out of control at every moment, being filled by millions of people with the absolute best and the absolute worst of human culture: you can just as easily find nearly all of the editions of Andrea Alciato's *Liber emblemata*, or the *Roman de la Rose*'s manuscripts as you can the most vicious and predatory child pornography or recreational sado-masochism websites. Moreover, if the wireless web keeps expanding the way that it has been in recent years, you will be able to do this from a hunter's deer stand in the middle of the woods in the Green Mountains of Vermont, for example, if the companies who run the wireless web manage to hide a tower, disguised as a pine, on an Interstate that will inevitably be within a few miles of that deer stand. Hell, they don't even need to install cell phone towers in central Vermont: soon enough, all of our wireless and cell transmissions will be done via satellite, just like Elvis's legendary *Aloha from Hawaii* performance was thirty-five years ago.

So what does this mean for us and for our being at this crucial moment of our collective existence? Our contemporary notion of subjectivity is contingent upon a mode of cultural production that is linked to the internet, to giant media corporations, and to multinational companies that dictate fashion and shopping trends. To be is to shop, as so many consumers know as they guzzle down their 32-ounce sodas while walking across the parking lot from their sport utility vehicle to the local mall. If the subject was already hopelessly decentered with the advent of postmodernism (see Jameson's famous essay on the Bonaventure Hotel in Los Angeles on this point), one might conclude, from the series of analyses that I have undertaken here, that the subject is now a vanishing point or a black hole into which material is constantly being poured, in the hope that it will congeal or solidify into something, but which never assumes a stable form that can be recognized as a "real" or an "actual" identity. All subjects, all beings, all identities are now only virtual; they are composed of "links" to other identities and modes of being, which are continuously recycled, cannibalized, reified, and reactivated by the imperious needs of market production and consumption, especially in post-industrial societies such as ours in which the only things that our "economy" produces are sound bites, debt packages, and marketing concepts (a pop song, like a dress or a pair of shoes, for example, is today nothing more than a marketing concept), at least on the public and visible media surface beneath which the sinister sound of US manufactured bombs dropping on civilian cities (like Fallujah) may constantly be heard. In our society, in which use-value seems to be increasingly eclipsed, exchange value has been replaced by pure fetishism that represents only the relation of individuals to concepts, and no longer the relationship of individuals to each other and to the tasks that they perform as part of their everyday lives. These concepts, however, are far-removed from their philosophical ancestors. Plato's abstract and universal ideas or forms, which he illustrated using everyday examples such as shoes, tables, and chairs, are now no longer accessible to school children (as they were to the slave boy Meno in the famous dialogue of the same name) who have been raised on Ritalin, Prosac, Lithium, I-Pods, Game Boy, Wii, X-Box, cell phones, reality television, and computer games. Concepts now have to assume iconographic forms upon which our collective minds can click in order to make them open, in the same way that computer icons allow one to open ever new windows, screens, pop-up ads, advertising banners, chat rooms, message boards, blogs, etc. I'm willing to bet that when an average person thinks today, he or she does so not in words, but in images that materialize the concepts upon which his or her identity is based. Better yet, to use Peirce's terminology, one's identity and subjectivity are now indices that merely point others as viewers toward these icons. On the whole, our mode of being has returned to a kind of medieval obsession with images. Medieval and Renaissance churches were full of remarkable images of saints and their suffering; people of faith were supposed to "read" these images and to "apply" their lessons, which required very complex and codified interpretations, to their everyday lives. Today we do the same thing with the products of trash culture, only now we have the capacity to contemplate hundreds and perhaps even thousands of images simultaneously, which is why "fashionably dressed" people today are beginning to look like the characters in the *Mad Max* films: that is, each part of their outfit has to be referred back to a different source, or to serve as a link to a separate trend. The idea of the "I" as an essence that precedes the contemplation of these images disappeared long ago. Today, the "I" is the point at which thousands of images as concepts converge and vanish. As our beloved and recently-departed Derrida remarked prophetically so long ago, our being now has reached a pure level of deferral, detour, *différance*. Never has this been truer than in the realm of today's trash culture.

If this description of identity in a time of trash culture is correct, does this mean that withdrawal from the world of images and objects that surrounds us is a viable means of returning to a notion of the self as essence? The complex cultural objects that constitute our conceptual world offer us a choice: we can either play with them and the multiple and shifting identities that they make available to us, or we can withdraw from participation in these procedures, either through a reactionary reaffirmation of the "grand narratives" that constituted modernism (the transcendence of the subject, the faith in progress, the belief in history as a causal procedure, the belief in ever more fundamentalist modes of religion, etc.), or a simple refusal to be identified by a dialectical relation with any of the artifacts that trash culture displays and uses to interpellate us. A critical analysis of these objects perhaps makes this latter option a possibility.

Does this mean, then, that one would have to agree with the right-wing politicians and their constituents, who dominate politics in the USA at the beginning of this millennium? Do we desperately need to reaffirm our being and our identity as essences, as *souls* that precede our existence in what this particular world has become? Nietzsche's solution to this aporia, which was also Montaigne's, is a much more satisfying one: I am this body, with its own peculiar chemical reactions, pumping this blood, breathing this air, in this space, at this time in history. My being in this body is an accident, but so be it, and if I had to repeat every moment of my life, every commercial I've seen, every bad movie I've watched, every terrible meal I've ingested, every useless argument I've had, I'd say "amen" to the whole of it, because it could not have been otherwise, if it is so now. Foucault also proposes something similar at the end of his first volume of *The History of Sexuality*, where he proclaimed the necessity of simply living one's body and one's pleasures, instead of constantly speaking about, displaying, and acting out one's "sexuality." So as an antidote to trash culture's capture of our existence, one could simply refuse the processes of identification and subjectivation that are constitutive of this dominant cultural mode. This refusal might take the form of a defiant statement: I will not be identified by or project my identity through the clothes I wear, the restaurants I frequent, my pec or glut implants, the gym of which I am a member (and whose tee-shirt I wear), the BMW I drive, the pop music I download, or the Pussycat Dolls posters on my bedroom wall. On the other hand, this is not to say that I can't play with these modes of identification from time to time, as Judith Butler recommended. If one's being is either trash or its negation, since our historical context is increasingly dominated by the production of disposable commodities of all kinds, both abstract and concrete, play is the only possibility for pleasure within the current configuration of objects that constitutes our world. Like the body, the self is a container that can be filled with things of one's choosing, which means that its existence is dependent upon what it ingests from the world that surrounds it. Multiple ingestion and digestion in the form of play might be conceived of as an affirmative and active means of creating one's being in the present, and in a dialectical relation with the material conditions of the present. Unfortunately, just as our bodies may become monstrous if we indulge their appetites too freely, our spiritual and intellectual selves may morph into unexpected and frightening forms through the indiscriminate assimilation of the ever-changing products and "by-products" of the social, political, and material world in which we live, breathe, and think.

To use a completely different analogy, living today is like surfing on an ocean of trash cultural objects (as I write these lines, the water of the literal ocean is being increasingly contaminated by tiny particles of plastic that become ever smaller without breaking down). Like most activities, surfing requires a well-developed technique in order to be pleasurable and good, which means that a surfer needs to learn how to move his/her body and board with the waves and the tides in order to have a good time. Or, one can forego the board altogether and simply go body surfing. The moment when one catches a good wave on a sunny day, and allows one's body and being to dissolve in the breaking foam as it moves toward the shore, is close to being mystical ("Be the wave, man!"). If we only could do that as we float in the ocean of commodities that surrounds and continuously threatens to engulf us.

References

Althusser, Louis. "Idéologie et appareils idéologiques d'état," in *Positions*. Paris: Éditions Sociales, 1976, 67-125.

Augé, Marc. *Non-places: Introduction to an Anthropology of Supermodernity*. Tr. John Howe. London; New York: Verso, 1995.

Bakhtin, Mikhail. *Rabelais and His World*. Tr. Hélène Iswolsky. Bloomington: Indiana University Press, 1984.

Barthes, Roland. *Mythologies*. Paris: Éditions du Seuil, 1954.

Benjamin, Walter. "The Work of Art in the Age of its Mechanical Reproduction," in *Illuminations*, Ed. Hannah Arendt, tr. Harry Zohn. New York: Schecken Books, 1968.

—, *The Arcades Project*. Tr. Howard Eiland and Kevin McLaughlin. Cambridge, MA: Belknap Press of Harvard University Press, 1999.

Butler, Judith. *Gender Trouble: Feminism and the Subversion of Identity*. New York: Routledge, 1990.

Derrida, Jacques. *Marges de la philosophie*. Paris: Éditions de Minuit, 1972.

Eco, Umberto. "James Bond: une combinatoire narrative." in *L'Analyse structurale du récit*, *Communications* no. 8 (1966), 77-93.

Fleuranges, Robert III de la Marck., seigneur de. *Mémoires du Maréchal de Florange, dit le Jeune Adventureux*, eds. Robert Goubaud and Pierre-André Lemoisne. 3 Volumes. Paris: Renouard, H. Laurens, 1913-1924.

Foucault, Michel. *Histoire de la sexualité I: la volonté de savoir*. Paris: Gallimard, 1976.

—. *Surveiller et punir: naissance de la prison*. Paris: Gallimard, 1975.

Freud, Sigmund. *Beyond the Pleasure Principle*. Tr. James Strachey. New York: Norton, 1989.

—. *Three Essays on the Theory of Sexuality*. Tr. James Strachey. New York: Basic Books, 1962.

Havelock, Eric. *The Literate Revolution in Greece and its Cultural Consequences*. Princeton: Princeton University Press, 1982.

Hegel, Georg Wilhelm Friedrich. *The Phenomenology of Spirit.* Tr. A. V. Miller. Oxford: Oxford University Press, 1977.

Jameson, Fredric. *Postmodernism, or, the Cultural Logic of Late Capitalism.* Durham, NC: Duke University Press, 1991.

Jacques Lacan, *Écrits.* Paris: Éditions du Seuil, 1966.

La Fontaine, Jean de. *Fables.* Ed. Jean-Pierre Collinet. Paris: Gallimard, 1991.

Lyotard, Jean-François. *L'inhumain: causeries sur le temps.* Paris: Galilée, 1988.

Marx, Karl. *Capital: a Critique of Political Economy.* Tr. Eden and Cedar Paul. London: Allen, 1978.

Montaigne, Michel de. *Oeuvres complètes.* Eds. Albert Thibaudet and Maurice Rat. Paris: Gallimard, 1962.

Nietzsche, Friedrich. *The Portable Nietzsche.* Ed. and tr. Walter Kauffmann. New York: Viking Press, 1973.

—. *Beyond Good and Evil: Prelude to a Philosophy of the Future.* Tr. R.J. Hollingdale. Harmondsworth, UK: Penguin, 1973.

—. *Untimely Meditations.* Tr. R. J. Hollingdale. Cambridge: Cambridge University Press, 1983.

Paglia, Camille. *Sexual Personae: Art and Decadence from Nefertiti to Emily Dickinson.* New Haven: Yale University Press, 1990.

Peirce, Charles Sanders. *Peirce on Signs: Writings on Semiotics.* Ed. James Hoopes. Chapel Hill, NC: University of North Carolina Press, 1991.

Plato. *Dialogues of Plato.* Tr. Benjamin Jowett. Chicago: Encyclopedia Britannica, 1952.

Rabelais, François. *Œuvres complètes,* ed. Mireille Huchon. Paris: Gallimard, 1994.

Virilio, Paul. *Open Sky.* Tr. Julie Rose. London ; New York: Verso, 1997. [translation of *Vitesse de libération,* "Escape Velocity."]

CPSIA information can be obtained
at www.ICGtesting.com
Printed in the USA
BVHW072153281118
534272BV00002B/99/P